CONTENTS

SECTION 3: CHILDREN'S LITERATURE

SECTION 4: EARLY LITERACY AND FAMILY LITERACY

Foreword by the President of the Reading Association of Ireland

It gives me great pleasure to write a brief introduction to this, the proceedings of the 12th European Conference on Reading, hosted by the Reading Association of Ireland at Dublin City University in July of 2001.

The conference was a wonderful event, bringing together as it did, educators and reading specialists from the far-flung corners of the globe. It was also a truly international event. We celebrated our diversity from our common interest in literacy and in the written and spoken word. It was a very gentle and gracious event, marked with good humour and tolerance for our many differences. And all of this was made possible by the hard work of a truly remarkable group of people on the organising committee! We owe each of them a debt of gratitude, especially those who may not have found themselves in the limelight during the week, but who quietly went about the work of making sure that each and every delegate was looked after, and made welcome. And on your behalves, I would like to acknowledge the work of the organising committee and to thank them.

This book is an 'éacht oibre' – a great work. It brings together a selection of papers on a range of topics on the teaching of reading. Each paper adds to our collective understanding of the efforts we are engaged in to bring reading education into focus at the centre of the wider education debate. We thank each one of you who submitted papers and hope that you find as much to think about in the other papers here as their authors will in yours!

Le Gach Dea Ghuí,

FINIAN O'SHEA
(President, RAI, 1999-2002)
Learning Support Department
Church of Ireland College of Education
Dublin
June 2003

Foreword by the President of the International Development in Europe Committee of the International Reading Association (IDEC)

It was a great pleasure and honour to preside at the 12th European Conference on Reading in Dublin, in Ireland, my mother's native land. As Declan Kiberd powerfully argued in his opening keynote address, there is every reason to resist being forced into false dichotomies – and I am proud to be both English by birth and (half) Irish by ancestry. It gave me great pleasure to hear so many excellent presentations and see the interest and friendship that grew from this truly international occasion, for which we thank the host organisation, the Reading Association of Ireland (RAI), most warmly.

These volumes of Proceedings from the conference contain almost 70 papers from 19 countries. Forty-two papers come from Europe and 28 from elsewhere. Within those from Europe, the host country features strongly (15), and 14 other countries are represented.

Having given some idea of the quantity, let me give you some feeling for the quality. In the three keynote addresses, Declan Kiberd ranges over Irish literature in Irish and English and the complexities and ambiguities of identity involved; Bente Hagtvet reports on research tackling the pressing problem of poor reading through prevention rather than remediation; and Vincent Greaney, former President of RAI and now working for the World Bank in Washington, DC, writes movingly of the problems of literacy in developing countries.

In addition, the Contents pages show that the papers cover the full gamut of literacy processes and topics (except that information and communications technology is curiously absent), and that every topic is shared across countries (except that all the papers on teacher development come from the United States) – both observations suggest powerful areas for future research in Europe. And in all the research and development that we do, learners must be central – as indeed they are in all the papers here. I trust that these volumes will give readers as much pleasure and food for thought as the conference gave the participants.

GREG BROOKS
(President, IDEC, 1998-2002)
University of Sheffield School of Education
England
June 2003

Reviewers

The Editors wish to acknowledge the assistance of the following in reviewing papers:

Greg Brooks, University of Sheffield
Tony Doyle, Mary Immaculate College, Limerick
Tina Hickey, Institiúid Teangeolaíochta Éireann, Dublin
Eithne Kennedy, St Patrick's College, Dublin
Mark Morgan, St Patrick's College, Dublin
Finian O'Shea, Church of Ireland College, Dublin
Mary Thompson, St Patrick's College, Dublin

SECTION 1

Keynote Addresses

1 Irish Literature: Excavating the Past

Declan Kiberd, Ireland

Literature has never been a marginal adornment but always a central and defining element of Irish life. This has been the case for two millennia. Writers like Swift, Yeats and Joyce have featured on the banknotes of the modern nation; and the recent Nobel Prize for Seamus Heaney was the lead headline on TV news programmes and in the Sunday papers. The source of that authority is very ancient. In the oral culture of Gaelic Ireland, a word was itself also an action, a deed; and the filí (poets) had the power to bless and to curse.

It was the poet who ceremonially handed the chieftain his rod of office at investiture; and it was the poet who had the duty to adjudicate thereafter whether this was a good or a bad reign. The first recorded file (poet) was Aimhirgin who lived in the first century AD. His duties were to tabulate and apply all laws, *and* to tell imaginative stories (a conjunction which suggests that Irish cynicism about the law predated colonial days). 'What you have told us is incredible, Aimhirgin', the sardonic men of Ulster would guffaw in response to his latest fable, 'but we believe you because you are a poet, and when a poet says a thing, it must be true'.

In this way, people recognised the power of words not so much to reflect as to transform reality – an aesthetic theory developed many centuries later by Oscar Wilde who asked 'What is a good lie?' and answered 'That which is its own evidence'. No wonder rulers and princes went in awe of the poets, rewarding them with rich fields or fat cattle for their panegyrics. For the bards were the publicists and press agents of their day and a successful leader needed them to promote his cause.

After the defeat of Gaeldom at the Battle of Kinsale in 1601, the English planters targeted the poets as defenders of the old order and, by implication, subverters of the new. With the Flight of the Earls in 1607, most Gaelic poets lost their patrons and were reduced to hawking their songs to the masses. Their self-image remained aristocratic, even as their actual lives became desperate. Some were little better than beggars; yet they were also the first dandies of modern European literature, which is to say courtiers without a court. Their position was rather like that of today's Ph.D.s who cannot find academic employment and drive taxies in order to make a living.

These ruined bards became exemplary artistic figures for many subsequent Irish writers of English. The tramps in Samuel Beckett's *Waiting for Godot* wear the dented bowler hats and shabby morning suits of a former gentility, as when one says to the other, 'You should have been a poet,' the reply is 'I was once. Is it not obvious?' Poets like WB Yeats, and writers like JM Synge identified with these displaced Gaelic artists, seeing in their plight a pre-configuration of the crisis which overtook the Anglo-Irish aristocracy at the end of the nineteenth century, leaving its imaginative sons and daughters suffering from feelings of deracination and displacement. They were all 'tramps' now.

The poetry produced by the Gaelic bards after 1601 was a powerful lament for the death of the old culture; yet the very energy with which the diagnosis was made suggested that the culture wasn't dead, merely undergoing a further transformation. What dies was not Gaeldom, but a Gaelic aristocratic class. The Gaelic tradition lived on in the vary laments for its passing; and the account of the apparent death of its one aristocratic order became the master-narrative of its successor.

Even afterwards, Irish writers from Jonathan Swift to Samule Beckett took a certain pleasure in starting with the worst, but in stating it so superbly well as to rob it of half of its power to depress. 'Do you believe in the life to come?' someone once asked Beckett, only to be told, 'Mine was always that'. This aperçu found its way not only into one of his famous plays, but also onto a wall of graffiti in West Belfast during the recent violence: 'Is there a life before death?' Death and dying became regular paradigms of Irish culture. The Irish language, like the rural arts of thatcher or weaver, has been officially 'dying' for centuries, and much lamented in brilliant texts – yet it is still in a remarkably rude state of health, with more than four hundred books published in it each year. This might be termed the 'Elvis Presley' theory of culture, based on the notion of early death as the ultimate career move.

Once the English colonists tightened their control after 1601, the poets of the Gael had to become journeymen, day-labourers, itinerant teachers, even mendicants – yet in another sense they became more important than ever, for they were now expected to maintain the consciousness of a proud, if dispossessed, people. Words were the only weapons of the disarmed; and the telling of lies to scouts of the occupying armies might save a whole townland from devastation. Hence, the love of word-play, deceit and irony in the writing of the colonial period. Gaelic poets lamented the felling of the woods, but these woods turned out on inspection to be protectors of rebels on the run. They sang love-songs urging maidens to shelter gallant lovers from the storm, but the lovers always turned out to be insurgents and the storm was the gunfire of an English soldiery. Artists were learning how to say one thing while meaning quite another.

On the English side, the same penchant for irony took hold. *A Modest Proposal* by Swift was the classic exercise in the mode; its jocular suggestion that Irish children under the age of six be supplied as roasting meat to English tables was intended as a metaphorical account of the realities of English policy at the time, but it was taken literally by some London readers.

There were always two versions of reality in colonial Ireland, neither wholly successful. The English had power, but the Irish had numbers. It was less a case of official versus unofficial, than of unofficial versus unofficialer. Writers became as interested in ways of seeing as in the thing seen. So in *Gulliver's Travels*, Swift made great play of how differently the world appears to little and to big people; it all depends on perception. The Anglo-Irish, such as Swift, came increasingly to feel themselves a spiritually hyphenated people, seen as forever English in Ireland and forever Irish in England. This led to anxiety about their own identify, but it was a state conducive to the production of great literature. Most of the major writers of comedy in England came from this background: Congreve, Farquhar, Goldsmith, Sheridan, Shaw, Wilde. The secret of their dramatic success was that they were sufficiently like the English to be acceptable as valid commentators on the London scene, yet if they went too close to the bone or said too much, they would be dismissed as brainless Paddies and purveyors of Celtic whimsy.

Feeling themselves neither fully Irish nor fully English, Anglo-Irish writers adopted a rather detached approach to the world. If life is a comedy to the person who thinks and a tragedy to the one who feels, they were more likely to write comedy. Some of their greatest geniuses, from Swift to Beckett, took their detachment so far that as to write about man in a near-anthropological mode, as if he were a non-human witness to himself.

By the nineteenth century, literature was still of huge importance as a source of self-recognition to both Anglo-Irish and to the mere Irish as they took on the English language. A novel by Jane Austen was read, not just for its story, but as the model of a possible society and culture; people read such books in order to learn how to conduct themselves in polite company or how to address a noble lord.

The literature produced by the ordinary Irish now carried inscribed within it all their hopes. These people could not identify with the law, the army, the police, the state service, but literature remained the sole social institution (along with the Catholic church) through which they felt able to explore and express an identify and a longing for expressive freedom.

It followed that the literature produced by the coloniser and the colonised had a strong utopian element. Over time, both the Anglo-Irish and the Gaels came to identify a common plight, as the Anglo-Irish began to feel neglected and misunderstood by their lords and masters in London. Like the Gaelic bards, they also felt themselves to be upholders of valuable but imperilled traditions. Some, from Swift to Yates, created audacious experimental forms in which to protect their ancient ideas, while others, like Sheridan and Maria Edgeworth, used familiar forms in which to promote some modern democratic ideas.

Because Ireland was a colony, it was treated as a laboratory in which experiments could be tried by English social engineers too timid to attempt such things in the first instance at home. So a whole series of modernising changes was introduced initially in Ireland – a postal system, a scheme for national schools, disestablishment of the relation between church and state, the expropriation of aristocracy. Ireland became in consequence a crucible of modernity.

The adoption of English by the masses was part of that process; and it led to the emergence of a poetic new hybrid, Hiberno-English, spoken by those who were still thinking in Irish while using English words – 'Is it you that's going tomorrow?' Out of this dialect, figures such as JM Synge and Augusta Gregory would forge the basis for a revival of national literature in English, albeit in an English as Irish as it is possible for that language to be.

After the Great Famine in the 1840s, the modernisation process gathered pace. People who had started their lives in windswept Neolithic villages in the west of Ireland ended them in places like Hammersmith or Hell's Kitchen; even those who remained at home began to feel like strangers in their own land, as they sought to view it through the newly-acquired English language. By a curious paradox, English became the language in which the Irish case for a separate, distinct nationhood was put, and put so well that it was finally conceded in 1921.

Although the Literary Revival of the previous decades masked itself as a return to the Gaelic values, it was from start to finish wholly revolutionary in its understanding of tradition. If the leaders of 1916 Rising invoked ancient Gaelic values as a way of underwriting their commitment to modern social democratic ideas, James Joyce could gift-wrap the most innovative prose narrative of the twentieth century, *Ulysses,* in one of Europe's oldest tales, *The Odyssey* of Homer.

The sheer pace of change had made the Irish futurologists of necessity; and so they consoled themselves once again with suggestions that seemed a radical departure from what would actually be a revival of something old and long-familiar. Such tactics persist in the land of the Celtic Tiger, but they should not mislead anyone into thinking of the Irish as conservative people.

What the Irish worship is not so much the past as their own power over it. A people who could, for the most part, dispose of their native language in the nineteenth century when it no longer seemed of practical use, seemed by the close of the twentieth to be bidding farewell to those two elements which had filled the ensuing space – the Catholic religion and a belief in political nationalism. In the even vaster space left by these disappearances, it is possible that literature will become an even more important source of identity and self-description than it has been in the past. It is certain that the most recent waves of immigrants from overseas will bring cultural forms which, when blended with the Irish ones, may lead in time to even greater innovations. And that is really saying something.

2 Early Literacy Stimulation in a Preventative Perspective

Bente E. Hagtvet, Norway

Over the years teachers have used creativity, ingenuity and even threats and tricks to motivate children to read. In the main Oslo newspaper, *Aftenposten*, in May 2000, we could read another impressive story about a teacher's personal contribution to her students' literacy development. The story goes that the teacher, Ms Pedersen, a 37-year old, made a bet with her 28 sixth-graders the previous September that if they read 70,000 pages of books during the school year, they could give her a yoghurt bath in May. If, on the contrary, they lost the bet, the children would have to sing *Ba Ba Black Sheep* and *Incy Wincy Spider* with movements in front of all the pupils and teachers at the school. Needless to say, both teacher Pedersen and the dedicated readers were held in awe and admired by their fellow pupils. And Ms Pedersen got her message across – that reading skill is to a large extent a result of how many words and pages one reads.

The story about Ms Pedersen – and other similar stories – have a number of additional lessons to teach teachers and researchers of reading. First, there is a lesson about the challenges involved in motivating sixth-graders of today to read. Second, it points to the importance of motivation and positive affects in the development of reading skills. Third, and by implication, it suggests that if positive emotions are built into written language instruction from the first day in school, there may be less demanding ways of developing good reading skills than taking yoghurt baths. We should also remind ourselves that while an important majority of the pupils in Ms Pedersen's class presumably raised their reading scores considerably by means of their large amount of reading, the poorest readers may not have profited that much. They probably contributed fewer pages of reading to the overall class pool of pages read. After six years of low scores and feelings of inferiority, it usually takes more than a motivational kick to raise their competence and self-esteem. Rather, research indicates that their predicament might be much better handled by preventative means.

Poor readers and the prevention of poor reading are at the core of this paper, which regards early literacy stimulation in a preventative perspective. First, I discuss *why* early and preventative literacy stimulation are important. Second, I reflect on the impact that emotions appear to have on literacy development as the emotional correlates of success and failures are crucial when prevention of written language problems is discussed. Third, I present a general framework for early literacy stimulation that also includes emotional growth, and show *how* the framework can be implemented.

The Importance of Preventing Reading Failure

It is a well-established fact that failing to read and write properly damages a child's total development and may lead to reduced life opportunities in a great number of areas. In a review article on the socio-emotional consequences of having a reading problem, Bryan and Bryan (1990) identify a number of variables that are often associated with poor reading skills: test anxiety and problems of controlled attention, behaviour problems, tendency to give up when confronted with challenges, and tendency to be ignored by teachers as well as by friends, to mention only a few. If combined with poor environmental conditions, the list of correlates also includes school dropout, unemployment, depression and involvement in criminal activities (Maughan, Gray & Rutter, 1984). While reading problems cannot be seen as *the* cause of serious behaviour problems, they represent a serious at-risk factor. In this perspective, the prevention of reading problems contributes to the prevention of emotional instability and great human losses.

A second reason for preventing reading problems is related to the issue of time. Poor and slow reading skills tend to be more or less cemented after only a few years in school. This was documented in a study by Badian (2000) who examined the stability in reading scores across a span of nine years. Children who were poor readers at the end of grade three were typically poor readers at the end of grade eight as well, suggesting that kindergarten and the first years in school are critical for developing good reading skills.

Successful intervention may take place with older children. However, one then, typically, has to work through a complex composition of negative emotions and lost self-esteem. Also, inefficient learning strategies have to be eradicated and new ones encouraged. For these reasons, late intervention is often too late, or at best costly in terms of money, time and effort. Successful later intervention typically implies intensive and costly remedial treatment, for example, in special schools for dyslexic children (e.g., Finucci, Gottfredson & Childs 1985; Gaskins, 1998).

A third reason for preventing early reading problems is that a great number of recent studies on literacy training document that prevention works. Children who receive good early literacy training have proved to be better readers after a few years in school than groups of control children with less systematic literacy training. Indeed, a broad range of studies focusing on how children come to terms with the alphabetic script show this (for overviews see Badian, 2000; Snow, Burns & Griffin, 1998). The studies have been carried out in English as well as in languages with more regular orthographies, but they have a common theme. At some stage in the programme, they direct the learners' attention to the sound structure of oral language, and in most cases also to the connection between phonemes and graphemes (e.g. Ball & Blackman 1991; Bradley & Bryant 1983; Hatcher, Hulme & Ellis 1994; Lundberg, Frost & Petersen 1988; Landerl, 2000).

In sum, two developmental patterns are prominent when studies of reading and writing development are scrutinised. One is surprisingly negative: a 'minor' difficulty with learning to read and write often develops into a long-term and hard-to-remediate reading problem which typically generalises into a whole range of cognitive, social and emotional problems. The other pattern is surprisingly positive: early instruction that is appropriate to the child's developmental needs appears to lead to positive literacy development, even in children at risk of developing reading problems. Crucial elements in training studies associated with success stories are phonemic awareness and awareness of how phonemes and graphemes are connected. To achieve functional reading ability, attention should furthermore be paid to the integration of semantics and phonology. This yields a balanced approach integrating elements from training studies focusing on phonemic awareness and elements from 'the tradition of whole language' as the optimal approach to early literacy stimulation in a preventive perspective (Snow et al., 1998).

The Impact of Emotions on Reading Development

The tendency for a reading problem to impact on other cognitive and social realms of functioning has been attributed to factors like poor reading comprehension due to decoding problems, low motivation for school work and also to the emotional burden of perceiving oneself as a failure (Bryan & Bryan, 1990). This is a retrospective line of argument that at best is an inaccurate and superficial description of how language and emotions interact during development. There has been much less scientific concern with the complex set of potential elements of successful prevention, and why success creates more success. The intricate developmental interplay between language and emotions that appears to play a crucial role in narratives of both success and failure is simply not well understood. This may explain why early reading instruction tends to be rather technical and at best language – oriented, but most typically with no in-built emotional component. This may also explain why discussions of reading instruction often become superficial debates between right or wrong methods, between whole words versus phonics, between the use of authentic versus artificial texts etc.

Whether I study child language research, research on reading instruction or psychiatric research, or whether I look at psychologists working with reading-disabled children or teachers in special needs education, I tend to see experts who deal with either emotions or reading and language skills. Speech therapists and cognitive psychologists deal with language, clinical psychologists and psychiatrists deal with emotions, and teachers deal with subjects. And we are well trained to respect the limits of our professional competence. We do not even attend the same conferences. Few teach – or treat – language and reading against a background of professionally empowering children emotionally, and few deal with emotions while at the same time strengthening the language and reading skills of children in a professional way.

There are of course important exceptions to this. The Benchmark School in the U.S.A., for example, which is a special school for children with reading impairments, strongly emphasises the importance of including the child's emotional well-being in their instructional programme (Gaskins, 1998). On the assumption that it is crucial to a student 'to be seen', each teacher is nominated as a mentor for a small group of children, with a personal responsibility to make each of these students feel esteemed and cared for emotionally every day.

In an ongoing intervention study focusing on children with serious reading problems, we are regularly reminded of the importance of having a double glance at language and emotions. Last spring we worked with a case, David, who was then in sixth grade and who comes from a family with a history of reading problems (father, sister and grandfather read extremely poorly). David has participated in a longitudinal project we have run for more than seven years, that includes children between five and nine years old who have parents with dyslexia (Hagtvet, Horn, Lassen, Lauvås, Lyster & Misund, 1999). The intervention was designed to offer educational support to those children in the longitudinal study who did not learn to read and spell in school.

In sixth grade (i.e. at the age of eleven), David read five years below his classmates and had developed a mode of behaviour that was extremely irritating to teachers. When we first started to collaborate with the school to design a reading programme for David, the principal presented him as a complete nuisance. 'He is mentally absent in class, lies to teachers, spits at other pupils, has no or few friends, and is attracted to older children involved in criminal activities,' he stated. Interestingly enough, the poor reading was not referred to by either the principal or the teachers, despite the fact that David labelled himself as 'word blind' – a label which legitimised individualised work outside the classroom on his personal PC. The teachers, however, paid little attention to David's interaction with the computer. It was as if his behaviour problems had attracted their full attention.

We went back to the videotapes we had taken during assessments at the institute in his pre-school years, and observed an open co-operative and interested little boy. Somewhat slim and short for his age, above average intellectually (according to the Wechsler scales), a strong motive for achievement, and loving parents that David appeared attached to. The only at-risk signs we could detect in his pre-school records beyond the family history, was a subtle phonological weakness (i.e., identifying sounds in words at ages five and six) and a rather serious problem in the rapid naming of pictured objects.

We appealed to the teachers to 'set aside' ten weeks where everyone assumed that David's behaviour problems were consequences of the reading problems. During those ten weeks we worked with David's reading as well as his self-confidence. The expectation was that the behaviour problems would be reduced as the reading abilities improved.

For an hour a week for those ten weeks we worked with David's reading and spelling in a small group which included two other children at his age. We used a balanced and integrative reading programme focusing on both reading for meaning and analysing and manipulating segments in words (Frost, 2000). In particular we had David analyse syllables in words, as he needed to speed up his reading of long words. At the same time, we strengthened David's self-esteem through dialogues and creation of success experiences in the classroom and at the reading course. Because he was a fast and imprecise reader, we also focused on strengthening his metacognitive awareness by, for example, commenting favourably every time he applied a reading strategy that contributed to a more accurate reading. For example, he was praised when he stopped himself by applying the rule, 'not too fast'.

In the classroom, David's teachers were encouraged to give him manageable tasks in every subject – tasks he could master. We encouraged them to structure his work, and praise him for good attempts, and also to recognise improvements. In short, the teachers were encouraged to create successes and point them out to David, work on his learning strategies, and support his reading for comprehension by means of reading material adapted to his reading level.

The change in David's performance was evident after only a few weeks. At the end of the course his behaviour was described by his principal as 'normal'. 'I never have to deal with him anymore,' he proclaimed. David's reading skills had likewise improved. They were approaching a Grade 4 level. 'From presenting us with a behaviour problem, he has become an academic challenge,' the principal poignantly stated.

Again, David's story is a story about things having gone wrong. Things had in fact developed into something so extremely negative that a double view on emotions and language was forced on us. I shall now discuss how language and emotions appear to be related during early development – before things go wrong. I shall argue that such a double view is part and parcel of literacy stimulation with a truly preventative perspective.

The Dynamics of Emotions and Learning to Read and Write

My own interest in the interplay between language and emotions took off some 15 years ago when we did a longitudinal study of the oral and written language development of 70 randomly-selected children from age four until age nine (Hagtvet, 1996). Being a norm sample of four-year-olds when we standardised the Norwegian version of the *Reynell Developmental Language Scales*, all children were at the outset perceived by their parents to be functioning normally in terms of oral language mastery. However, when assessing the children's oral and written language skills by more precise testing, there were considerable differences within the group at more subtle oral language levels, in particular in language awareness and mastery of decontextualised language. At ages six, seven and nine there were also significant within-group differences in written-language mastery. In addition to language variables, emotional status was assessed clinically and by means of a checklist focusing the extent to which the child's functioning was on or off task (Hagtvet, 1996; 2000).

The average developmental profile of 13 children who became poor readers was compared with that of average readers and a group of so-called early readers, i.e. children who taught themselves to read before they started school. Three main characteristics stood out as striking:

• First, the relative achievement levels of the three groups were stable across time. The group of poor readers scored below the average readers, who, in turn, scored below the early readers on almost every language variable at every age-level from age four to age nine.

• Second, the only two variables on which the poor readers scored higher than the comparison groups were test anxiety and off-task-behaviour. This was evident both before and after starting school (starting-age in Norway at the time was seven).

• Third, there was a negative correlation between most language scores and 'anxiety level'. Children who had a good command of oral language at age four were in general less emotionally aroused. In more concrete and positive terms they were more persistent when performing different tasks, were more able to sit still on the chair and more verbally outgoing. They even took greater pleasure in telling jokes, had a better command of verbal jokes and were better at telling jokes with a point or a punch line. On the other hand, the children who scored low on oral and written verbal variables in pre-school, were also more highly aroused emotionally.

It is noteworthy that this correlation was observed even *before* the children experienced failure in learning to read and write in school. At least some of the children therefore started school with a double vulnerability – in the emotional and the linguistic domains. It is also noteworthy that this was observed in a group with no documented problems in oral language, suggesting that even a subtle language weakness may be associated with feelings of worry, anxiety and stress in the pre-school years. The early readers, however, showed an emotional strength, which in combination with their strong verbal abilities, in particular in manipulating linguistic segments and using and comprehending language in decontextualised ways, appeared to act as a resilience factor (Garmezy, 1993) in learning situations in school.

Being the poor readers' 'weaknesses' and the early readers' 'strengths', emotional variables appear of particular relevance to written language mastery.

Correlations as well as average group scores refer to general developmental patterns and functioning that may conceal within-group variations. For this reason the individual developmental patterns of the 13 poor decoders identified at age nine were retrospectively scrutinised (Hagtvet, 1996).

It then emerged that the four poorest readers at age nine also scored the lowest on the *Reynell Developmental Language Scales* at age four, and they were at all ages also highly aroused emotionally. The negative correlations between language variables and stress/anxiety were in other words higher in the group of extremely poor readers.

Co-occurrence does not of course necessarily imply causal patterns. We do not know whether the primary cause of low functioning was to be found in a language weakness or in the emotional system or the child's temperament. In a developmental and educational perspective the primary cause may also be of less importance than the mechanisms by which the two factors develop and interact.

McGee *et al.,* (1986) postulate a developmental pattern characterised by an *interactive* spiral where language and emotions constitute two cornerstones mutually reinforcing each other. They based their reasoning on a longitudinal study of reading disabilities and behaviour problems in boys from New Zealand aged five to eleven years, and found that 'behaviour problems pre-date reading disability, while reading failure further exacerbates the existing problem behaviour' (McGee, Williams, Share, Anderson & Silva, 1986, p. 597).

Our study with its dual focus on language and behaviour before the introduction to literacy makes the 'opposite' causal path just as plausible. The seriously poor readers showed signs of oral language weakness *and* an increased tendency to engage in off-task-behaviours, relative to comparison groups of average and good readers, before they started school and failed in learning to read and spell.

There was furthermore, as was also the case in the New Zealand study, a tendency for increased 'stress level' at age nine. One probable hypothesis that should be tested in future research is the assumption that a negatively working interactive spiral was initiated at a very early age, or as soon as a child started to feel insecure in linguistically demanding situations.

Complementarily, one might presume positive interactive spirals – or resilience – in the child with an advanced command of language, even before (s)he starts school. This appears to have been the case for the 'early readers' whose advanced language skills accelerated in both the oral and the written modality, as did also their emotionality level and ability to focus on task.

The observation that subtle oral language weaknesses in pre-school children are associated with later written language problems have been documented in a number of studies over the last decade, first and foremost by Scarborough (1989) in her seminal study of children of dyslexic parents. In this study she found that about 60% of the children from these families developed written language problems and that they had weaknesses in both phonological and syntactic areas as early as at age 2 ½.

The causal path might, of course, work differently for different children, starting in socio-emotional restlessness in some children, and in language weaknesses in others. The important point is that language and emotion appear to be strongly related.

After these rather striking findings in a study of a 'normal' and randomly selected samples of children, I studied the library systems to look for developmental studies that treated language and emotions as two sides of the same coin, so to speak. My suspicion was confirmed.

The relation between language and emotion in early development is an underdeveloped area of research. In one perspective, this is only natural when it comes to written language development, since the relation between emotions and written language problems cannot easily be studied until *after* the reading problems have entered the arena, i.e., after the child has failed to learn to read normally in school.

However, when looking at another arena where children are novices – at babies – it is well established that language competence develops in an emotional space created by the child and his/ her caretaker. Mothers' talk to children (baby talk) is loaded with affect, typically conveying closeness and warmth (Ferguson, 1977). Early mother-child communication is in fact to a large extent a matter of communicating feelings (e.g., Bateson, 1975; K. Bloom, 1977, 1990). The early interchange of emotions in gaze and vocal sounds (proto-conversation) is based on a sensitivity to timing which is extremely emotional and constitutes the ground on which the later verbal turn-taking is built.

On this basis, the relative lack of continued interest in how language develops in emotional space after the first year in a child's life is noteworthy. This lack of interest in first (oral and written) language learning is in some contrast to second language learning, where the relation *is* emphasised. In fact the emotional engagement of children learning a second language appears to be vital, since second-language learning appears inefficient when the language-learning situation is detached from emotional involvement and social interaction.

Immigrant children who are not integrated in the social-emotional networks of the native speakers only insufficiently pick up the semantic, syntactic and prosodic nuances in school (Krashen, 1982). And Dutch children do not appear to learn to speak German from watching television with only German speech (Snow, Arlman-Rupp, Hassing, Jobse, Joosten and Vorster 1976).

I shall next discuss an educational programme in which both affect and literacy are emphasised. The programme was originally tried out on Norwegian six-year-olds in kindergarten. Fifty children participated in a 10-months programme over a three-year-period (16 to 18 children each year) during the year before they were formally introduced to reading and writing in school. The programme has later been adapted to both younger and older children. I have labelled the programme, Ego-Based Literacy Stimulation to emphasise the importance of bridging the child's feelings and literacy development.

An Ego-based Literacy Stimulation Programme

A basic aim of the programme was to prevent written language problems while at the same time offering rich learning opportunities to all children (Hagtvet, 1988, 1990). Written language was discovered – or constructed – in play-oriented or daily routine activities, greatly inspired by both 'the language experience approach' and 'the emergent literacy tradition'.

The focus of stimulation was *communication*, rather than isolated letters and letter-sounds. This focus was based on the assumption that a basic motivation for reading and writing in young children is the discovery that texts have meaning, that ideas may be converted into text and that written language is of use in everyday life.

Influenced by dyslexia research and the tradition of phonics, we at the same time offered a play-oriented program stimulating phonological awareness (Frost and Lønnegaard, 1996; Tornéus, Hedström & Lundberg, 1986).

At a general level the content of the programme focused on four educational key areas:

* linguistic awareness (the ability to view language from an observer's point of view)
* decontextualised language (language detached from situational context)

- writing ('communicative drawing', pretend writing, dictating, conventional writing)
- reading ([pretend] reading, conventional reading aloud by adult to child)

To engage the children emotionally in literacy activities, efforts were made to ground the activities in the children's own experience, interests, needs and feelings. We also paid due attention to the *didactic challenges* of implementing these constructs into educational activities. Traditionally teachers have tended to focus on procedures and activities, e.g. 'read to your child', 'play with rhymes', 'discuss ideas in the text with your pupils during reading'. Relatively little attention has been paid to the importance of the emotional and social mood in which procedures are carried through. This may have left an extremely important component open to accidental acts and subjective judgement. This goes directly into the emotion/language issue, as it is the *way* activities are performed rather than their content that determines the emotional and cognitive impact those activities will have on the children. I shall now briefly give a few examples of the kind of 'meta-educational' reflections I have in mind.

Inclusion of activities stimulating linguistic awareness, and, in particular, phonological awareness, was motivated by research suggesting that sensitivity to the phonological structure of language is associated with good reading and writing abilities and vice versa (Bradley & Bryant, 1983; Frost, 2000; Hatcher, Hulme, & Ellis, 1994; Lundbeg, Frost, & Petersen, 1988; Snowling, 1987). But, if these activities are carried out by teachers who are not committed to them, or as teacher-driven routine duties, the effect may be the creation of reading failure.

Therefore, linguistic awareness skills were 'trained' by means of musical activities emphasising the rhythm and segmentation of language at a syllabic level. The programme also involved games focusing on, for example, first, last and middle sounds in short words, games such as sound subtraction ('What is the first sound in Anna?', 'Which word do you get if you remove /t/ in /tin/ or /s/ in /sand/?'). Via pleasant and motivating activities, the children thus increased their linguistic awareness while at the same time creating good feelings about language and linguistic activities.

Corrections of mistakes by the teacher were to be avoided. Rather, a central aim was to strengthen the child's self-confidence by emphasising what was good about an initiative or answer and by recasting a child's response or initiative into something promising and constructive.

The children were also encouraged to 'talk in monologues', e.g. by creating and retelling stories and jokes, or by dictating to an adult who wrote the monologue/text down while the child was watching. The idea was that this would contribute to the development of decontextualised language. Speaking in monologue is, according to Moffett (1968), the first step towards writing because the child now has to take on speaker responsibility and create a text without dialogue support, as is also typically the case when writing.

Influenced by the emergent literacy tradition, the children were also invited to (pretend)read and (pretend)write (Sulzby, 1986). Many have over the years emphasised the power of storybook-reading to create interest in literature, and in letters themselves. Storybook reading may also create emotional bonding, or attachment between child and the adult reader. Creating texts in connection with wordless picture books is another activity that is frequently recommended for children at this young age. But few activities have as strong a potential for getting children into the alphabetic principle as has writing, and in our programme the children wrote a lot. They scribbled, used their own secret signs and explored the alphabetic system in play and routine-like activities by taking notes and writing messages.

Writing furthermore starts inside the author's head and in a fundamental sense promotes ego involvement. As opposed to reading, writing starts with a familiar topic and also with the letters and words the writer knows. One may write a lot with the letters of one's own name and those of mom's and dad's, in particular if combined with pretend letters or 'alternative' signs if knowledge of the alphabet is limited. Writing also offers time to dwell on the taste of the sounds and to feel their articulatory position in the mouth. Writing thus has some unique qualities that contribute to anchoring the written language system inside the child, in his and her feelings, head and articulation system.

But, even as promising an activity as writing may be killed if the teacher does not *see* the author. Young authors need praise, encouragement and guidance in insightful ways and within each child's zone of proximal development (Vygotsky, 1962).

Vygotsky and related western theorists have designed general paradigms within which a didactics of individualised ego-based literacy instruction may be nicely framed. Ideas like 'scaffolding' and 'guided participation' together with the idea of 'zone of proximal development' underscore the importance of the ego via concepts like 'dialogue', 'graded help' and 'individual learning zones'. But some bridging appears to be needed between the rather general guidelines offered by a theorist like Vygotsky and the implementation of such ideas into practical acts, e.g. as practical instructions given in manuals for reading instruction. This bridging is crucial in an ego-based literacy stimulation. It is constituted by the forces that *empower* the child to success while at the same time learning to read and write. It appears to be deeply emotional and it is as much a matter of *how* the teacher behaves as *what* (s)he says or do.

I will illustrate some elements in this 'bridging' with reference to examples from four-to-seven year olds, who have participated in projects we have carried out in Norway and Sweden.

Some Crucial Elements in Ego-based Literacy Stimulation

First, we consider the issues of individualised progression and content. Not only was progression in our project defined by the individual child rather than by a prefabricated plan or method, but the 'Me' of the child was also in focus in most of the child's writing.

As mentioned above, the children were not formally introduced to the alphabet. Written words and sentences were, however, generously visible in the environment as signs, memos and text commentaries. The teacher furthermore answered questions when a child asked for the name or form of a letter when reading or writing, and she would also encourage a child to use more letters. She was in other words an active mediator of learning.

A 'This is Me' book was in continuous use. In this book the children would write down – by drawing, pretend writing or using alphabetic letters – 'foods I like and dislike', 'things I like and do not like to do', 'things which make me happy, unhappy and angry', etc. The children's feelings were thereby made a central focus. First, they were discussed orally, e.g., with reference to pleasant and unpleasant experiences in class, or with reference to pictures of children expressing emotions. Then feelings were explored and expressed on paper. In most cases the children did not know the letters as alphabetic entities, for which reason they tended to 'pretend write' by using their own 'secret signs'.

The children wrote about past events, future events or daily life events – events that were important to them. By means of writing, they reflected on personal experiences, emotional reactions and their relations to other important persons. In this way, writing became a means of 'marking' the individual child. It also made the children more aware of themselves – which presumably contributed positively to their identity formation. Next to his picture, Peter, age 6, wrote, 'My little brother (lillebroren min) stands (står) in the window (i vinduet) and looks at me (og ser på meg)'. This simple text expresses a moment of closeness between two brothers, and one might speculate that expressing this in writing makes Peter more aware of the importance of their relationship.

A crucial element in an ego-based literacy instruction is the idea that children should feel *no emotional pressure* in connection with learning to read and write. The fact that the children in our projects used and explored written language with *no pressure* to learn was probably a most important factor, in particular to the slow developers. So was the fact that much writing took place in groups and social settings – in role play, when groups were designing theatre performances and also when groups were writing memos and reports of projects and excursions. Written language was therefore based in social settings where play in a broad sense was an important element. It is the magic of play that things happen at a 'pretend level', and that failing then does not matter so much. One may take chances when playing, as play is not serious.

Another important element concerns teachers' ability to create *experiences of mastery.* Corrections took place in the form of reframing and rephrasing with no confrontation of failure, but rather by offering appropriate help. A central aim was to strengthen the child's self-confidence by emphasising what was good about an initiative or answer and by recasting poorly-formed sentences or reactions. The main idea was to create success and feelings of mastery in the children, and if needs be – if a task was too difficult – to make sure that every child succeeded by means of guided participation.

I am not arguing that individualised progression and content, avoidance of emotional pressure, and creation of experiences of mastery are innovative and new concepts. They are as old as history of education itself. What I am arguing is that these elements – and some others – are crucial in preventive literacy instruction.

Do children learn to read and spell in such a child-driven educational context where the letters are not even introduced systematically?

First, the programme I am advocating is not completely child-driven. In the project with the six-year-olds, the children to a large extent decided on topics and style of writing, but the teachers were active mediators in each child's zone of proximal development. Secondly, the teachers did initiate many games stimulating linguistic awareness, and many activities stimulating decontextualised language. And the children did slowly break the alphabetic code, but most typically with little awareness about their great achievement.

The majority of the children developed into alphabetic writers during the 10 months in which they participated in the programme. At the end of the year, 86% of the sample (N=43) wrote alphabetically. This is in some contrast to comparison groups of Norwegian children where around 20 percent of the children wrote alphabetically before starting school at age seven (Hagtvet, 1996). Even the poorest reading child who did not break the alphabetic code until May in Grade 1 – and with considerable individual tutoring by her teacher – kept her joy of writing. In Grade 3 she was still a fairly slow reader. She wrote extensively, however – and with great motivation.

Fifteen years have passed since we did the project with the six-year-olds. In 1997 an important school reform enabled Norwegian children to start school at the age of six rather than seven, and the new plans for Grade 1 include many of the elements mentioned above. This last spring I visited a number of first-grade classrooms in connection with a big evaluation scheme where we evaluated the so-called 1997 reform.

My preliminary impression is quite clear: few Norwegian children experience literacy stimulation which bridges the cognitive/linguistic and affective domains. Rather, phonemes and letters are typically taught in 'school-like' ways, e.g. by means of work sheets, while ego-involved play is used to stimulate social, motor and oral language development. Elements from the type of ego-based literacy stimulation I have discussed above were rather rare.

In the introductory part of a new book from 2001, *Literacy and Motivation*, the editors – Ludo Verhoeven and Catherine Snow – proclaim that the central issue of their book is how a world of engaged readers can be created. 'Promoting literacy acquisition requires interventions that address attitudes and beliefs as much as interventions that assure cognitive changes in the learners,' they claim (p. 2).

I would move a step further and argue with Vygotsky that language and emotion are so close that they should be treated as one unity of meaning. Or with L. Bloom that children simply do not learn language when their emotional systems are not receptive. Or with myself, that prevention of reading disability presupposes early literacy stimulation anchored in positive emotions. After all, it was also Ms Pedersen's recognition of the importance of play and humor that made her sixth-graders read 70 000 pages of books while she – the 'bet-loser' – was forced to take a yogurt bath to the delight of her pupils.

REFERENCES

Badian, N.A. (2000). Do preschool orthographic skills contribute to prediction of reading? In: N.A. Badian (ed.), *Prediction and prevention of reading failure.* Baltimore, Maryland: York Press.

Ball, E.W. & Blackman, B.A. (1991). Does phoneme awareness training in kindergarten make a difference in early word recognition and developmental spelling? *Reading Research Quarterly, 26 (1),* 49-66.

Bateson, M.C. (1975). Mother-infant exchanges: The epigenesis of conversational interaction. In D. Aaronson and R. Rieber (eds.), Developmental Psycholinguistics and Communication – disorders. *Annals of the New York Academy of Sciences, Vol. 263.*

Bloom, K. (1977). Patterning of infant vocal behaviour. *Journal of Experimental Child Psychology, 23,* 367-377.

Bloom, K. (1990). Selectivity and early infant vocalisation. In J. Enns (ed.), *The development of attention: Research and theory.* New York: Elsevier North-Holland.

Bloom, L. (1993). *The transition from infancy to language.* Cambridge: Cambridge University Press.

Bradley, L. & Bryant, P. (1983). Categorising sounds and learning to read - a causal connection. *Nature, 301,* (899), 419-421.

Bryan, J.H. & Bryan, T. (1990): Social factors in learning disabilities: Attitudes and interaction. In G.T. Pavlidis (ed.), *Perspectives on dyslexia, Vol 2* (pp. 247-281), London: Wiley.

Clay, M.M. (1975). *What did I write?* Auckland, New Zealand: Heinemann.

Ferguson, C. (1977). Baby talk as a simplified register. In C.E. Snow & C. Ferguson (eds.), *Talking to children.* New York: Cambridge University Press.

Finucci, J.M., Gottfredson, L.S. & Childs, B. (1985). A follow-up study of dyslexic boys. *Annals of Dyslexia, 35,* 117-136.

Frost, J. & Lønnegaard, A. (1996). *Språkleker.* Oslo: University Press.

Frost, J. (2000). From 'Epi' through 'Meta' to Mastery. The balance of meaning and skill in early reading instruction. *Scandinavian Journal of Educational Research, 44,* 2, 125-144.

Frost, J. (2001). Phonemic awareness, spontaneous writing and reading and spelling. *Reading and Writing: An Interdisciplinary Journal, 14,* 487-513.

Garmezy, N. (1993). Vulnerability and resilience. In E. Funder, R. Parke & C. Tomlinson-Keasey (eds.), *Studying lives through time.* Washington: American Psychological Association.

Gaskins, I. (1998). There's more to teaching at-risk and delayed readers than good reading instruction. *The Reading Teacher, 51 (7),* 534-547.

Hagtvet, B.E. (1988). *Skriftspråkutvikling gjennom lek*. (Literacy stimulation via play) Oslo: Universitetsforlaget.

Hagtvet, B.E. (1996). *Fra tale til skrift*. (From oral to written language) Oslo: Cappelen.

Hagtvet, B.E. (1990). Emergent literacy in Norwegian six-year-olds. In F. Biglmaier (ed.), *Reading at the crossroads* (pp. 164-179). Berlin: Frei Universität Berlin.

Hagtvet, B.E. (2000). Prevention and prediction of reading problems. In: N.A. Badian (ed.), *Prediction and prevention of reading failure*. Baltimore, Maryland: York Press.

Hagtvet, B.E.; Horn, E., Lassen, L., Lauvås, K., Lyster, S. & Misund, S. (1999). Developing literacy in families with histories of reading problems. *European Journal of Special Needs Education, 2,* 29-39.

Hatcher, P.J., Hulme, C., & Ellis, W. (1994). Ameliorating early reading failure by integrating the teaching of reading and phonological skills: the phonological linkage hypothesis. *Child Development, 56,* 41-57.

Krashen, S. (1982). *Principles and practices of second language acquisition.* Oxford: Pergamon Press.

Landerl, K. (2000). Influences of orthographic consistency and reading instruction on the development of nonword reading skills. *European Journal of Psychology Education, 15,* 3, 239-257.

Lundbeg, I., Frost, J., & Petersen, O-P. (1988). Longterm Effects of a Preschool Training Program in Phonological Awareness. *Reading Research Quarterly, 28,* 263-284.

Maughan, B., Gray, G. & Rutter, M. (1984). Reading retardation and antisocial behaviour: A follow-up into employment. *Journal of Child Psychology and Psychiatry, 26,* 5, 741-758.

McGee, R., Williams, S., Share, D.L., Anderson, J., & Silva, P.A. (1986). The relationship between specific reading retardation, general reading backwardness and behavioural problems in a large sample of Dunedin boys: A longitudinal study from five to eleven years. *Journal of Child Psychology and Psychiatry, 27,* 5, 597-610.

Moffett, J. (1968) *Teaching the universe of discourse.* Boston: Houghton Mifflin.

Scarborough, H. (1989). Prediction of reading disability from familial and individual differences. *Journal of Educational Psychology, 81,* 1, 101-108.

Snow, C.E., Arlman-Rupp, A., Hassing, Y., Jobse, J., Joosten, J. & Vorster, J. (1976). Mothers' speech in three social classes. *Journal of Psycholinguistic Research, 5,* 1-20.

Snow, C.E., Burns, M.S.& Griffin, P. (1998). *Preventing reading difficulties in young children.* National Research Council, USA.

Snowling, M.J. (1987). *Dyslexia.* Oxford. Basil Blackwell.

Sulzby, E. (1986). Writing and reading. Signs of oral and written language organization in the young child. In W.H. Teale & E. Sulzby (eds.), *Emergent literacy. Writing and reading*. Norwood, NJ: Ablex.

Tornéus, M., Hedström, G. & Lundberg, I. (1986). *På tal om språk. Lekar och övningar*. Uppsala: Almqvist & Wiksell.

Verhoeven, L. & Snow, C.E. (2001). *Literacy and motivation. Reading engagement in individuals and groups*. New Jersey: Lawrence Erlbaum.

Vygotsky, L.S. (1962). *Thought and language*. Cambridge, Mass: M.I.T. Press.

3   Literacy in Developing Countries: Why Not?

Vincent Greaney, Ireland

Illiteracy is both a cause and consequence of slow economic growth. Countries cannot develop their economies without capable human resources to provide basic services. Developing countries need people who are sufficiently numerate and literate to deal competently with commercial transactions, understand rules, regulations and contracts, create communication systems, and know how to provide basic services in health and education.

Literacy empowers the poor and their communities (Lauglo, 2001) and contributes to more productive agricultural techniques (Carron, Mwira & Righa, 1989). Female literacy is particularly relevant to health, has been associated with improved mothers' child-rearing practices, family health and population control (Greaney, 1996).

Definitions of literacy differ in many countries and from time to time within individual countries (Greaney, 1994). There is now a growing realization that the dichotomy, literate/non-literate, is inadequate and that literacy should be viewed as a continuum. The 1990 Jomtien World Conference on Education for All extended the view of literacy to incorporate that of basic learning competencies, which include in addition to the three Rs (reading, writing and arithmetic) general knowledge, problem solving and life skills. The addition of problem solving and life skills suggests that the tasks used to determine what constitutes a literate person will vary by location; life skills which are essential in one geographical economic context will be quite different in other contexts.

Given the confusion over what constitutes literacy, no one definition is appropriate for all situations. Literacy statistics will inevitably vary according to the definition used. UNESCO literacy statistics for various countries are based on different definitions and measurement approaches. Given these serious limitations, literacy/illiteracy estimates should be treated with considerable caution. UNESCO (2002) estimates that there were 887 million illiterates in 2000. The illiteracy problem is most pronounced in developing countries; recent data suggest that in developing countries 27 per cent of the population is illiterate, the majority of them being female. Not surprisingly, the greatest numbers of illiterates (71% of the total) are found in the most populous regions of East and South Asia. Illiteracy is particularly pronounced in Sub-Saharan Africa; among people aged 15 years and over, in excess of half the countries have illiteracy rates of 40 per cent +, while over one third have rates in excess of 50 per cent (Lauglo, 2001).

The reasons for the relatively high illiteracy rates are complex and inter-related. They stem in the main from conditions inimical to the development of literate populations. In this brief paper, we focus on five such conditions: (1) poverty, (2) inadequate education quality, (3) conflict, (4) poor governance, and (5) poor health.

Poverty

Inadequate National Finances

Poor countries tend to lack income generation capacity and face huge demands for scarce financial resources. They tend to lack such basic necessities as clean water, sanitation, electricity, and communications, roads and telecommunications systems. Lack of adequate roads, for instance, makes it difficult if not impossible to get agricultural produce to lucrative export markets. Lack of natural resources limits the potential for generating revenue. Lack of energy sources makes the production of materials highly labor-intensive. Recent economic and political developments do not suggest that the situation is about to improve. Over the last decade the price of some basic commodities (e.g., coffee, tea, cotton, minerals) has declined. While OECD countries in general during the 1990s experienced improvements in their GNPs, many of the poorer countries (e.g. Kenya, Ethiopia, Zambia, Central African Republic and Sierra Leone) have experienced declines in their wealth.

Family Poverty

Today over half the world's population lives on less than US$2 per day and over 1.2 billion on less than US $1 per day. Most of the poor reside in rural areas. Frequently, children have little option but to work. Recent estimates (World Bank, 2001b) suggest that in developing countries the number of children between the ages of 5 and 14 who are working is about 250 million, of whom 120 million work full time. Africa has the highest incidence of child labor (about 40 per cent) while Asia and Latin America have about 20 per cent rates. A working child gives up childhood and future prospects and foregoes the opportunity of becoming literate so that his/her family can eat and, in some cases, so that younger brothers and sisters can attend school.

Inadequate Education Quality

Schooling is a necessary but not sufficient condition for literacy development. The limited objective comparative evidence from the existing national and international studies of educational achievement (e.g. Ross et al., 2000, Martin, Mullis et al., 2000) indicates that the level of learning achievement of students in participating developing countries tends to be low. Evidence from Bangladesh (Greaney et al, 1999) suggests that school attendance was virtually essential to achieve even minimal literacy levels, but that mere enrollment was insufficient to achieve literacy. Among those who left school after three years the majority were unable to recognise letters, or complete simple number and word identification tasks. Problems in promoting literacy through schooling include high levels of grade repetition at the junior grade levels (most notably in Francophone African and in some Latin American countries), and early dropout.

By OECD standards, many teachers have low professional qualifications. Teachers entrusted to give instruction have qualifications, as low as third grade primary school (e.g., Maldives), primary school completion (e.g., Madagascar) or less than ten years of schooling (India). Much instruction is of the chalk and talk variety with a great deal of emphasis being placed on rote learning. Not surprisingly, many teachers are seriously deficient in subject matter mastery. Lack of textbooks and teaching aids ensures that many children do not have access to quality education materials to support meaningful instruction and learning.

While governments recognise that education has the potential to alleviate poverty and promote development, some countries cannot afford education systems. Countries with a gross national income per capita (formerly gross national product) of less than US$ 300 include Cambodia, Central African Republic, Chad, Eritrea, Ethiopia, Ghana, Madasgascar, Malawi, Mali, Mozambique, Nepal, Nigeria, Rwanda, Tanzania, Togo, and Uganda (World Bank, 2002c). Despite their best intentions, these countries plus many others may not be able to devote adequate resources even to basic education. In Haiti, 80 per cent of students are enrolled in private schools, simply because the state cannot afford to provide public schooling. Even where schools exist, many parents cannot afford the costs of sending children to be educated. Prohibitive costs include books, uniforms, travel, supplementary fees to support teacher salaries and examination fees. In China the high cost of textbooks has contributed to the inability of some parents to send their children to school (Greaney, 1996). Girls have more difficulty than boys in acquiring a good quality education. Fewer girls are likely to complete primary education. In India whereas 81 percent of males aged 15 to 19 have completed grade 1, only 58 percent of females did so (World Bank, 2002b). In some Muslim countries, social attitudes do not permit school education for girls on the conviction that it might lead to sexual exploitation by male teachers.

The situation is not improving. Currently, the international community is striving to achieve the Education for All (EFA) goal of having access to and completely free compulsory primary education of good quality. Some 83 countries are on track to achieve Education For All (EFA) by the deadline of 2015 set at the 2000 World Education Forum in Dakar (Senegal). However, on present trends, more than 70 other countries will not make it, and some are even regressing (UNESCO, 2002).

Conflict

Literacy cannot be fostered in times of armed conflict. Widespread conflict undermines the capability of governments to deliver basic services, including education. Over 50 countries have experienced significant armed conflicts since 1980 (World Bank, 1998). The number of wars between countries has dropped considerably. In the 1990s, conflicts between countries killed about 220,000 people, a drop of nearly two-thirds from the 1980s, while about 3 million died in wars within states and the number of refugees and internally-displaced persons increased 50% (UNDP, 2002). Short (2002) reported that 20 per cent of Africans are affected by conflict. The vast majority of armed conflicts in recent times involved internal conflicts (e.g., Sri Lanka, Bosnia Herzegovina, Rwanda). Thirty countries experienced displacement of more than 10 per cent of their populations through conflict (Bush & Saltarelli, 2000). Education has been a major casualty; eleven countries identified as being unlikely to achieve universal primary education by 2015 (Matsuura, Wolfensohn, Obaid, Bellamy, & Malloch Brown, 2001) were bogged down in conflict and have to face the additional problem of educating war-orphans and child soldiers. Close to half of Mozambique's primary schools were destroyed during its war. Rwanda lost two-thirds of its teachers through death or emigration; the economy was decimated and over 300,000 children killed. In the past decade, over 2 million children have been killed and 6 million injured as a result of armed conflict (World Bank, 2001a). Currently there are nearly 300,000 child soldiers actively participating in armed conflict around the world; many of these have had their formal education and chances of becoming literate prematurely ended.

Poor Governance

Corruption hurts the poor most severely as it diverts scarce funds for public services including education from those who most need them. In developing countries there is widespread evidence of corrupt government administration including purchasing of government positions, and misuse of funds. In education for instance, the needs of politicians rather than the distribution of school-age children may often determine where new schools are constructed. Students in remote areas are often denied access to trained teachers due to political influence, which allows excess teachers to work in urban schools. In some instances cooperation between administrators and/or politicians permits scarce educational funds to be directed towards non-existent schools ('ghost schools') and teachers ('phantom teachers'). Monopolistic national textbook boards, lacking incentives to produce quality textbooks, can be a particular source of corruption. Evidence of poor governance brings with it additional costs. The perception that politicians and civil servants in poor countries are corrupt undermines international public support for development assistance by creating the erroneous impression that all assistance is affected by corruption.

Poor Health

Over 180 million preschool children under the age of five, or 33 per cent of children under five in developing countries, are stunted or chronically undernourished (UN ACC/SCN, 2000). Nearly 30 million children born every year suffer from inadequate foetal nutrition and are disadvantaged at birth (UN ACC/SCN, 2000). Over 100 million children are affected by Vitamin A deficiency alone (UNESCO, 2003). In 1998, approximately 11 million children died from preventable and treatable diseases such as diarrhoea, measles, malaria and pneumonia, over 50 per cent of which are attributable to malnutrition (UN SCC/SCN, 2000).

The HIV/AIDS epidemic underlines the extreme vulnerability of the economies of poor countries. In 1999, AIDS killed almost 3 million people worldwide. More than 5 million were newly infected with HIV in 2000, almost 80 per cent of them in Africa. The twenty countries with the highest prevalence rates are all located in Sub-Saharan Africa. Over one third of the adult population in Botswana is infected. HIV/AIDS is on the increase in Eastern Europe and in East and South Asia. The education sector is seriously affected by this disease (World Bank 2002a). Teachers tend to have high infection rates. In the worst afflicted African countries, it is estimated that 10 per cent of teachers will die from AIDS over the next five years. Current data suggest that, by 2010, 14,500 teachers will have died from aids in Tanzania, and between 88,000 and 133,000 in South Africa. Teacher deaths in Zambia in 1998 were equivalent to the loss of two-thirds of the annual output of newly qualified teachers. Inevitably, teacher illness and absenteeism leads to a decline in educational quality, an increase in illiteracy rates and deterioration in the number of skilled workers. Additional teachers have to be trained from already meagre and strained national education budgets. It is anticipated that HIV/AIDS will also contribute to school dropout and the diversion of financial resources to support orphanages. Girls are more likely to drop out of schools to look after sick relatives or younger children.

The Challenge

Existing international data suggest that illiteracy rates have been on the decline in all regions of the world in recent decades, due in great part to an increase in access to primary education. The estimated absolute number of illiterates, however, has declined only marginally, partly due to the rapid increase in population especially in developing countries. Illiteracy data continue to be subject to much debate due to problems of definition and measurement. UNESCO data for OECD countries are no longer considered appropriate measures in modern industrialised countries, which tend to have higher literacy expectations than mere mastery of word recognition and simple writing tasks. The International Adult Literacy Survey for instance defined literacy as the ability to understand and employ printed information in daily activities, at home and in the community, a definition that requires much higher achievement levels than has been the case in UNESCO statistical reports to date.

Developing countries face great challenges as they strive to empower their citizens through making them literate. Far too many lack the human, financial, and material resources to tackle illiteracy in a large scale meaningful way, and will need external support. This support and assistance can be given in the form of grant aid, technical assistance and concessional funding that allow for the development of sustainable and affordable activities. Changes in current economic policies can help some of the poorest countries.

Debt relief remains a severe challenge for many countries. Between 1990 and 1998, overseas aid to Africa had fallen drastically from $32 per head in 1990 to just $19 in 1998. Some progress has been made in tackling debt in the World's most heavily indebted countries. The United Nations has set a target of 0.7 per cent of GNP for aid for developing countries. In 1999, four countries surpassed the UN target: Denmark, Norway, The Netherlands and Sweden, followed in order by Luxembourg, France, Switzerland, Canada, Finland and Ireland; the United Kingdom ranked 15th and the United States 20th in terms of official aid support (Morrissey, 1999). Industrialised countries spend more than US $300 billion dollars a year on agricultural subsidies, a figure that is roughly equal to the GNP for all of Sub-Saharan Africa. In addition, OECD countries provide about one billion U.S. dollars on a day in domestic agricultural subsidies, more than six times what they spend on official development assistance for developing countries (UNDP, 2002). On average, industrial country tariffs on imports from developing countries are four times those on imports from industrial countries.

The quality of most current national and international literacy data is less than satisfactory. Rather than depend on estimates or indirect measures such as years of schooling, valid measurement requires some form of performance assessment of literacy levels. Modern sampling test development approaches, such as used in the International Adult Literacy Study (Murray, Kirsch & Jenkins, 1997) can make this form of literacy assessment more valid, reliable, timely and efficient than the present inadequate approach.

Literacy is central to personal development and to economic prosperity as it greatly enhances peoples' abilities to absorb knowledge and raise their living standards. The scope of the problem is so great in many countries that it will require strong national leadership and considerable external support. Governments in developing countries need to devote more of their scarce resources to promoting education, and ensure that children have access to and avail of quality basic education. This may require adopting strong political stances including prioritising primary education over other levels, stamping out cronyism and corruption, and limiting expenditure on military and on expensive non-productive schemes (e.g., national airlines, conference centres and grandiose public buildings). Citizens in developed countries can develop a deeper understanding of the plight of their fellow humans living in less fortunate circumstances, and give support in the form of aid and technical assistance. They can also try to influence legislators and others to remove or minimise economic policies that discriminate against poorer countries and support educational programmes and initiatives in countries lacking the resources and capacity to promote literacy.

Lack of education and access to printed materials has condemned far too many people to lives of ignorance and poverty. Future historians will judge the response of individuals, national governments and organisations and international bodies to the major challenge of eradicating illiteracy.

REFERENCES

Bush, K. & Saltarelli, D. (2000). *The two faces of education in ethnic conflict: Towards a peace-building education for children.* Florence: UNICEF Innocenti Research Centre.

Carron, G., Mwira, K., & Righa, G. (1989), *The functioning and effects of the Kenya literacy programme.* Paris: International Institute of Education Planning.

Greaney, V. (1994) World Literacy. In F. Lehr and J. Osborn (Eds.). *Reading language and literacy: Instruction for the twenty-first century*, Hillside, NJ: Lawrence Erlbaum 217-38.

Greaney, V. (1996) Reading in developing countries: Problems and issues. In V. Greaney (Ed.), *Reading in developing countries.* Newark, DE: International Reading Association (Ed.), 5-38.

Greaney, V., Khandker, S., & Alam, M. (1999). Bangladesh: Assessing basic learning skills. Dhaka: University Press and the World Bank.

Lauglo J. (2001) *Engaging with adults: The case for increased support to adult basic education in sub-Saharan Africa.* Washington DC: The World Bank

Martin, M. O., Mullis, I V.S. et al. (2000). *TIMSS 1999 International Science Report.* Boston: International Association for the Evaluation of Educational Achievement (IEA) and Boston College.

Matsuura, K., Wolfensohn, J., Obaid, T., Bellamy, C., & Malloch Brown, M. (2001). Harness the power of Education for all: Joint statement on the first anniversary of the Dakar World Education Forum, Press release April 27.

Morrissey, D. (1999). Ireland Aid: Bucking the trend. *http://europa.eu.int/comm/development/publicat/courier/courier178/en/en_020_ni.pdf.*

Murray, T.S, Kirsch, I. S., & Jenkins. L. (Eds.). 1997. *Adult literacy in OECD countries: Technical Report on the First International Adult Literacy Survey.* United States Department of Education, Washington, DC.

Ross K. N. (Ed.) et al. (2000). Translating educational assessment findings into educational policy and reform measures: Lessons from the SAQMEQ initiative in Africa. Paper presented at World Education Forum, Dakar, Senegal 26-28 April.

Short, C. (2002) UN Aid Target Column: 875W EU Development Assistance [26 Jun]. *www.parliament.the-stationery-office.co.uk/*

UN ACC/SCN [United Nations Administrative Committee on Co-ordination/ Subcommittee on Nutrition]. (2000). *Fourth report on the world nutrition situation, nutrition throughout the life cycle.* Geneva: ACC/SCN in collaboration with the International Food Policy Research Insatitute.

UNDP [United Nations Development Programme]. (2002). *Deepening democracy in a fragmented world: Human development report 2002* New York: Oxford University Press.

UNESCO. (2002). *Education for all, Global monitoring report. Is the world on track?* Author: Paris.

UNESCO. (2003). *Vitamin A deficiency - a cause of child death that can be easily prevented.* http://www.unicef.org/vitamina/

World Bank. (1998). *Post-conflict reconstruction: The role of the World Bank.* Washington DC: Author.

World Bank. (2001a). Great Expectations, *Spectrum*, Winter, 14.

World Bank. (2001b). The Global Fight against Child Labor, *Spectrum*, Winter, 13.

World Bank. (2002a). *Education and HIV/AIDS: A window of hope.* Author: Washington.

World Bank. (2002b). *http://www1.worldbank.org/education/edstats/index.html.*

World Bank. (2002c). *The little data book.* Author: Washington.

SECTION 2

Assessment of Literacy

4 Adolescents' Responses to Fiction: Qualitative Aspects of a Quantitative Reading Literacy Survey

Astrid Roe, Norway

The OECD Programme for International Student Assessment (PISA) is a new regular survey that assesses the competence of 15-year olds in three domains of literacy: Reading Literacy, Mathematical Literacy and Scientific Literacy. The first assessment was carried out in 32 countries during 2000 and comprised 180,000 15-year olds. Reading literacy was the major assessment domain in 2000. Reading materials consisted of 37 passages and 137 items. Nearly 50% were open-response items, which, in some cases, invited a large variety of responses, particularly where questions asked for interpretation or reflection.

This paper examines the responses of 115 students to one of the items in the study. The item is a question based on a short story. As a comparison 26 graduate students of literature, who were regarded as reading experts in this connection, also read the story and answered the question. The paper focuses on how 15-year olds respond to fiction. Outcomes are considered in terms of the students' overall reading achievement and their gender. Differences between the responses of 15-year olds and students in the graduate group are also investigated.

The PISA Reading Literacy Framework

The PISA reading material is designed to represent the kinds of literacy that 15-year-olds will face in the future. Reading literacy is defined as the ability 'to understand, use and reflect on written texts in order to achieve one's goals, to develop one's knowledge and to participate in society' (OECD, 1999, p. 20). Students are expected to demonstrate their proficiency in retrieving information, understanding texts at a general level, interpreting texts and reflecting on content and form of texts in relation to their own knowledge of the world.

It is clearly stated in the PISA Reading Framework that reading literacy is to be understood in a broad sense rather than in a technical sense. Furthermore, readers should be able to construct, extend and reflect on the meaning of what they have read across a wide range of texts associated with a variety of situations. The theory behind the reading framework is based on cognitive views of reading literacy, emphasising the interactive nature of reading and the constructive nature of comprehension. The framework regards reading as a process in which readers generate meaning in response to texts, by using their prior knowledge and understanding.

There is wide agreement on the view that understanding a written text is more than just understanding the meaning of the words. Reading is a result of cognitive and verbal processes that are influenced by the reader, the context and the text itself. Readers will have different levels of prior knowledge and experience. Texts can affect different readers in different ways. Thus the process of reading and understanding becomes different from one reader to another (e.g. Fish 1987, Beach & Hynds, 1991).

Two-Digit Coding

Marking and coding open responses in PISA is sometimes quite demanding, and a detailed marking guide with strict rules for coding of answers had to be followed. For most of the items, the codes 1 or 0 were used for credited and non-credited answers. If an item called for advanced interpretation, code 2 (full credit) was given to the best answers, and code 1 (partial credit) was given to simpler or shorter answers. The codes make only a rough categorisation of all the various answers arising from some of the questions. As the codes are transformed into score values for statistical analyses, the qualitative aspect is totally lost. To preserve some of this qualitative aspect, the Norwegian PISA Project Group developed a two-digit code system to categorise the responses into groups, defined by content for diagnostic use. This was done for ten of the main study items and was used in Norway only (Roe, 2000). The development of two-digit codes for reading was inspired by the work done by the Norwegian Maths and Science groups, who developed two-digit codes for their domains after the field trial in 1999 (Kjærnsli, Lie & Turmo 1999). Two-digit codes are the official codes in PISA mathematical and scientific literacy – based on the experience from the Third International Mathematics and Science Study (TIMSS), where such codes were used for diagnostic purposes (Lie, Taylor & Harmon 1996).

The item to be presented is based on a short story about a woman and a panther. The two are trapped in a house surrounded by floodwater. The woman is inside the house, while the panther has jumped from a floating tree onto her porch. It is hungry and threatening and the woman considers shooting it. At the end she puts the gun aside and feeds the animal with what is left of the ham that she has just cooked for herself. The next morning the flood is gone and the only trace of the panther is the white gnawed ham bone on the porch. Seven questions are based on this text, of which four are open-ended. The following item is chosen for this paper:

> Here are some of the early references to the panther in the story.
> 'the cry awoke her, a sound so anguished...': (line 32)
> 'The answer was a repeated cry, but less shrill, tired sounding...' (line 44)
> 'She had...heard their cries, like suffering, in the distance.' (lines 52–53)
> Why do you think the writer chooses to introduce the panther with these descriptions?

The question requires the student to demonstrate ability to detect nuances in language, which colour interpretation. It is categorised as 'reflecting on the form of a text'. For full credit (code 2), the student '... must recognise that the descriptions are intended to evoke pity or to prepare for the woman's later compassionate behaviour when she feeds the cat'. For partial credit (code 1): the student '... must refer to the author's intention of creating suspense or mystery or to the literal information given in the quoted descriptions' (PISA Marking Guide, 2000). Table 1 gives the two-digit codes which were developed:

TABLE 1: TWO-DIGIT CODING SYSTEM

Score	*Code*	*Example*
Full Credit	21	To evoke pity
	22	To prepare for the woman's later behaviour
	23	The panther is in the same situation as the woman/They both fight to survive
	29	Other
Partial Credit	11	To create suspense
	12	Because this is how wild panthers cry
	13	To make the setting mysterious
	19	Other
No Credit	01	Vague
	00	No answer (missing)

For most responses, the codes worked well. Most of the student responses contained only one element, for example: 'To make the reader feel sorry for the animal' (code 21) or 'To tell us how a panther sounds' (code 12). 17% of the answers contained elements from two code categories. Giving the higher code solved the problem, although this conceals one of the two elements that the student has mentioned. In future analyses, such answers will probably be given all relevant codes to preserve the qualitative aspect to a greater extent.

Results

Table 2 shows how the responses are distributed. The majority of the credited answers focus on suspense (code 11) or pity (code 21). It is also noticeable that very few students mention the author's intention to prepare for the woman's later behaviour (22) or the comparison with the woman's situation (23), which require the ability to draw an inference from the arrival of the panther to what happens later in the story. The most striking result, however, is the gender differences in the non-credited and 'missing' categories.

TABLE 2: DISTRIBUTION OF RESPONSES – PERCENTAGES OF STUDENTS

Codes	Girls	Boys	Total
No credit	9	24	17
Code 11	27	20	23
Code 12	10	8	9
Code 13	17	11	14
Code 21	25	16	20
Code 22	-	2	1
Code 23	6	-	3
Missing	6	19	13
Total	100	100	100

The International Association for the Evaluation of Educational Achievement (IEA) International Reading Literacy Study for 14-year-olds also revealed a small gender difference favouring girls for the narrative domain (Elley 1992). In the IEA report *Are Girls Better Readers?*

(Wagemaker, 1996), Munck and Taube suggest that the content of reading materials has a differential influence on males' and females' reading comprehension. They refer to a hypothesis suggested by Chipman, Marshall and Scott (1991), who claim that students simply shy away from or have difficulty dealing with subject matter that is regarded as the territory of the other sex. It is also argued that female students are less sensitive to the reading content than boys are, which might imply that boys would experience stronger affective reactions against typical feminine literature than girls against masculine literature. As the main character in the PISA short story is a woman, the above theory could be one explanation of the fact that girls outperformed boys in all seven items based on the story.

A cognitive explanation of the gender difference might be the degree of familiarity of the content of a text. If boys are only interested in masculine contents, and girls have broader interests, girls perform better. The reading comprehension of boys in comparison with that of girls can also be seen as a product of boys' slower maturation rate relative to girls, and their lower cognitive abilities at the age of 15 (Kimura, 1999). Many of the items require written answers, which may explain why girls perform better, given the fact that girls' writing skills generally are better than boys'. Motivation may also be a gender-related factor.

Figure 1 shows students' achievement in each response category. Overall reading scores are standardised to mean of 0 and a standard deviation of 1. The bars show standard errors of the mean. There is a clear tendency for students who relate the description of the panther to the author's intention 'to evoke pity', or to 'the woman's situation' to achieve better than students who focus on more general aspects that are not related to what happens later in the story, like 'suspense' or 'the way panthers scream'. The four students in the code 23 category (one student was coded 22 and two were coded 23, the four appear together as code 23 in the diagram) seem to be among the best achievers. The most common code 21-answer, 'to evoke pity' may reflect the ability to draw an inference from the arrival of the panther to the woman's situation; however, it may just as well represent an interpretation of the part of the text referred to in the question stem. Code 12, which seems to comprise the lowest achievers among those who get credit for their answers, represents a literal retrieval of the quoted passages in the stem. Responses in the categories 11 and 13 reflect an understanding of the author's intention to influence the reader in a certain way. Students who give answers that are not accepted or who do not answer are among the lowest achievers.

FIGURE 1: STUDENT RESPONSES BY READING ACHIEVEMENT LEVEL

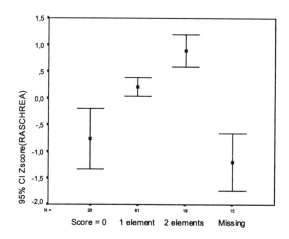

The expert responses did not fit very well into the code system, first of all because most of them contain more than one, and often three or four, elements. Expressing more than one interpretation probably reflects ability to see more nuances in the text. This hypothesis was confirmed when we looked at the achievement levels of 15-year-olds who mention one versus two elements who include varying numbers of elements in their answers (Figure 2).

In general, the expert responses contain various explanations that focus on the symbolic or the thematic meaning of the text. These experienced readers show the ability to infer relations between events and facts in systematic ways. They include the identification and representation of both referential and causal/logical relations in text, which are regarded as essential components of reading comprehension. They also show high standards for coherence, which are necessary for successful comprehension. Very few 15-year olds' responses reflect these standards and abilities. According to van den Broek (2000), the standards for coherence differ widely as a function of the skill level of the reader, and skilled readers are driven by a desire to grasp the referential and causal/logical antecedent of the current sentence. Less-skilled readers may relax totally and abandon the need for such coherence. The standards that readers adopt differ by such factors as metacognitive skills, motivation, reading goals and pragmatic concerns (p. 7).

FIGURE 2: NUMBER OF ELEMENTS IN STUDENTS' RESPONSES BY READING ACHIEVEMENT LEVEL

The quotations below will illustrate how the two groups of readers actually expressed their responses. The students' responses also serve as examples of how the two-digit codes were used.

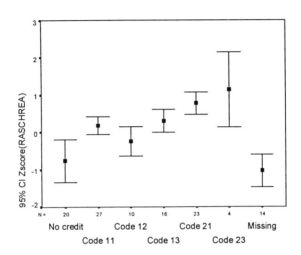

Students:
- To show that the panther suffered because of the flood too (code 23).
- To explain why she gave it food instead of killing it (code 22).
- To create suspense and because the reader will feel sorry for it (code 11 and 21, was coded 21).
- To establish a relationship between the panther and the reader so the reader hopes she doesn't kill it (code 29).
- Because she has never seen a panther in her life, and the reader can learn how a panther really is (code 12).
- To make it more mysterious as she did not know where the cries came from (code 13).
- He wanted to create suspense by describing the animal gradually (code 11).
- No it was very surprising. I would never thought of it (code 01).
- I don't know. You have to ask him yourself (code 01).

Experts:
- The way the panther is described through the sounds that it makes, makes it more alien. The woman had never seen the animal, and may not know for sure what it is. The alien can be connected to something sacred, and the food then becomes a sacrifice.
- The panther's life is threatened, and its predicament compares with the woman's situation. At the same time, there is a battle of survival between the animal and herself.
- The panther is presented as human. It represents the desperate in her and her surrounding's situation. There is a touch of empathy in the description.

Final Reflections

This analysis shows that expert responses to a fictional text are dominated by inferences and understanding beyond the literal meaning, whereas 15-year olds generally focus on the surface or literal meaning of the text. Further analyses of open response items might add interesting information that could elaborate on the pattern that has so far emerged. The use of two-digit codes will be a helpful tool in these analyses, which again can contribute to better understanding of how adolescent readers respond to texts. Finally, it is our hope that this work can lead to better teaching of reading in secondary schools. Studies have shown that secondary school teachers pay little attention to actually teaching reading, unless the student suffers from dyslexia or has other special needs – although students have to read a lot in secondary schools (Lundberg, Tønnessen & Høien, 1993). If teachers knew more about how different groups of students read, they might be better able to teach reading strategies to help them go beyond the surface meaning of the text, to analyse, evaluate and extend the ideas presented in the text, to draw inferences, to read between the lines and to grasp symbolic meaning, metaphors, or irony. Reading strategies are needed, not only when reading fiction, but also when reading newspapers, magazines, textbooks and the diversity of electronic texts that young people are increasingly exposed to. Young adults need to be aware of how texts are constructed and how texts may actually influence people's perspectives on the world.

REFERENCES

Beach, R. & Hynds, S. (1991). Research on response to literature. I.R. Barr, M.L. Mosenthal & P.D. Pearson (Eds.) *Handbook of reading research* (Vol 2). New York: Longman

Chipman, S.F, Marshall, S.P., & Scott, P.A. (1991). Content effects on word problem performance: A possible source of test bias? *American Educational Research Journal, 25,* 145-55.

Elley, W. (1992). *How in the world do students read?* The Hague: International Association for the Evaluation of Educational Achievement (IEA).

Fish, S. (1980). *Is there a text in this class?* Cambridge, MA: Harvard University Press.

Kimura, D (1999). *Sex and cognition.* Cambridge Mass.: The MIT Press.

Kjærnsli, M., Lie, S., & Turmo, A. (1999). *Two-digit codes for science and mathematics. Results from a Norwegian workshop.* Oslo: University of Oslo. Faculty of Education.

Lie, S., Taylor, A., & Harmon, M. (1996). Scoring techniques and criteria. In M.O. Martin & D.L. Kelly, *TIMSS Technical report volume l: Design and development.* Boston: Center for the Study of Testing, Evaluation and Educational Policy, Boston College.

Lundberg, I., Tønnessen, F.E., & Høien, T. (1993). *Norsk leseundervisning i internasjonalt lys.* Stavanger, Norway: Senter for leseforskning.

Munck, I. & Taube, K. (1996). Gender differences at the item level. In H. Wagemaker (Ed.), *Are girls better readers? Gender differences in reading literacy in 32 countries.* Amsterdam: International Association for the Evaluation of Educational Achievement (IEA).

OECD. (1999). *Measuring students knowledge and skills. A new framework for assessment.* Paris: Author.

OECD. (2000). *Reading marking guide 2000.* Melbourne, Australia: Australian Council for Educational Research.

Roe, A. (2000). *Two-digit codes for reading.* PISA Report No. 8. Oslo: University of Oslo. Faculty of Education.

van den Broek, P. & Kremer, K.E. (2000). The mind in action: What it means to comprehend during reading. In B.M. Taylor, M.F. Graves, F. & P. van den Broek (Eds.), *Reading for meaning. Fostering comprehension in the middle grades.* New York: Teachers College Press.

Wagemaker, H. (Ed.). (1996). *Are girls better readers? Gender differences in reading literacy in 32 countries.* Amsterdam: International Association for the Evaluation of Educational Achievement.

5 National Assessments of English Reading Literacy in Ireland

Jude Cosgrove and Patrick Forde, Ireland

The aim of this paper is to review the outcomes of recent national assessments of reading literacy carried out in Ireland and to reflect on their implications for policy and teching practice. The paper concludes with a discussion of future directions for national assessments of English reading.

In 1972, the first formal assessment of English reading was carried out by the Department of Education as part of a broader system designed to monitor educational achievement (Kellaghan, 1997; Cosgrove, Kellaghan, Forde, & Morgan, 2000). Since then there have been four national assessments of English reading (Table 1). All of these assessments were implemented at primary level, and involved pupils from 4th and 5th classes (grades). The assessment instruments used overlap from one assessment to the next so that it is possible to examine trends in performance over time.

TABLE 1: NATIONAL ASSESSMENTS OF READING IN IRELAND, 1972-1998

Year	Age or class	Respondents	Test instruments*
1972	10-year olds	4,500 pupils in 300 schools	NS6; Schonell (A), Kingston
1980	4th and 5th class	2,000 pupils in 100 schools	NS6; Schonell (A)
1988	5th class	2,200 pupils in 120 schools	NS6; D88; ST88
1993	5th class and 11-year olds	4,000 pupils in 150 schools	NS6; TARA
1998	5th class	4,000 pupils in 150 schools	TARA

*NS6=National Survey Form 6; Schonell (A)=Schonell Test Form A; D88=Adaptation of Drumcondra Attainment Test in Reading Level III; ST88=Material developed by the assessment of performance unit of the Department of Education of England and Wales; TARA=Tasks for the Assessment of Reading Achievement.

Single indices, based on the number of correct responses on the assessment as a whole, were used as outcome measures up to the 1993 assessment. Since then, pupil achievement in English has been reported by sub-domain. This shift in reporting practices occurred in line with developments in international assessments, including the 1991 International Association for the Evaluation of Educational Achievement's Reading Literacy Study (IEA RLS; Elley, 1992; Martin & Morgan, 1994).

The main instrument used in the 1993 and 1998 assessments (Tasks for the Assessment of Reading Achievement, or TARA; Martin, Forde, & Hickey, 1991) was developed between 1989 and 1991 specifically for use in national assessments of English reading. Similar to IEA RLS, TARA assessed pupils' performance in three separate but related sub-domains: narrative or story texts, expository or information texts, and documents or non-continuous texts. Results were also reported as a weighted aggregate of these three subscales (documents was assigned half the weight of the narrative and expository scales, which were assigned an equal weighting).

In the 1993 and 1998 national assessments, reading literacy was defined as '... the process of constructing meaning through the dynamic interaction among the reader's existing knowledge, the information suggested by the written language, and the context of the reading situation' (Wixson & Peters, 1984; see also Robeck & Wallace, 1990). The importance placed on comprehension and the constructivist nature of the reading process is evident in this definition.

In order to collect information about aspects of pupils' environments that are relevant to achievement, all national assessments of English reading included questionnaire measures. In the 1993 and 1998 surveys, for example, questionnaires were administered to pupils, teachers, parents and principals.

Achievement in Reading

Some of the main findings from national assessments of English reading are summarised in this section. While trends in achievement since 1980 are reviewed, the emphasis is on outcomes of the 1993 and 1998 assessments (see Cosgrove et al., 2000 for more details).

Trends in Overall Achievement

Improved reading scores were observed between 1972 and 1980, with gains equating to 10 months in reading age (Kellaghan & Madaus, 1982). Improvements in reading standards of Irish pupils were also recorded in smaller-scale studies of schools in Dublin around this time (Travers, 1976; Ward, 1982). Since 1980, overall standards of reading have not changed. Overall mean reading scores on the TARA measure in the 1993 and 1998 assessments were almost identical.

Performance by Sub-domain

In the 1993 and 1998 assessments, scores on the documents scale were marginally lower than on the narrative and expository scales. This finding may be linked to the relatively lower emphasis given to documents text in the national English curriculum for primary schools (which was revised recently; Ireland, 1999), and is consistent with findings from IEA RLS (Martin & Morgan, 1994).

Descriptions of Achievement

Using data from item analyses, it was possible to describe the achievement of pupils. Questions involving the following types of task were answered correctly by most 5th class pupils: use of a TV guide; simple cross-referencing in a timetable; identification of highest rates on a graph; and straightforward location of information in both continuous and non-continuous texts. Questions involving the following types of task, on the other hand, posed difficulties for many 5th class pupils: distinguishing between active and passive voice; distinguishing between concepts such as title, theme, protagonist and content; distinguishing between motive and outcome; inferring meanings of unfamiliar words using context clues; integrating prior knowledge with information explicitly mentioned in the text; understanding and inferring causality; dealing with more complex use of index, glossary and dictionary; and complex cross-referencing of tables.

Gender Differences in Overall Achievement

In 1993, no significant gender differences were found when the total (aggregate) scale scores were compared. However, in 1998, girls scored significantly higher than boys on reading assessment as a whole. In 1993, no significant gender differences were found when the mean scale scores of each of the sub-domains were compared. In 1998, in contrast, girls scored significantly higher than boys on the narrative and documents scales.

Trends in the Distribution of Achievement

The percentages of pupils scoring two or more standard deviations above and below the mean in the three domains and on the overall test (about 2.5%) did not differ significantly between 1993 and 1998, nor did the percentages differ by gender. However, the 1993 data indicate a non-significant difference in the percentage of boys and girls scoring two or more standard deviations below the mean (3.4% compared with 1.7%). The corresponding percentages in 1998 were 2.3% and 2.6% respectively.

Martin (1996) analysed the distribution of achievement in IEA RLS by identifying the upper and lower performance quartiles of boys and girls and comparing the means of these groups. Results indicated that, in many countries, gender differences favouring girls were more pronounced in the low-scoring than the high-scoring group, with Ireland showing the second highest mean difference at age 9 and the highest difference at age 14. Previous analyses of 1991 IEA RLS data (Martin & Morgan, 1994) revealed that three times as many Irish 14-year old boys as girls had reading scores two or more standard deviations below the mean. When these results from IEA RLS are compared with the outcomes of the 1993 and 1998 national assessments of reading literacy, they suggest that the gender gap at the lower end of the achievement distribution has narrowed somewhat.

In contrast, if we compare teachers' ratings of boys' and girls' achievement in 1998, we find a statistically significant difference favouring girls. For example, while teachers classified 12.4% of boys as 'weak/inadequate' readers, only 8.5% of girls were so classified. Similarly, while 10.9% of boys were rated by their teachers as having a reading proficiency of '3rd class or lower', only 7.4% of girls were judged to be at this level. When teachers were asked about pupils' preparedness for everyday demands in reading they indicated that 14.5% of boys but only 10.2% of girls would 'need assistance'.

School Resources for Teaching Reading

Three important findings relating to school resources emerged from analyses of the 1993 and 1998 reading assessments. Firstly, although the number of library books per pupil varied substantially across schools (the range in 1998 was 0.4 to 58.6), overall, the average number per pupil per school doubled between 1993 and 1998 (from 4.4 to 8.7). Secondly, there has been an increase since 1993 in the provision of learning support. In 1993, 9.5% of boys and 7.1% of girls were in receipt of learning support; in 1998 these figures rose to 14.8% for boys and 9.5% for girls. Thirdly, on average, pupils receiving learning support scored about one standard deviation below the mean in both 1993 and 1998. However, 1.9% of the pupils receiving learning support in 1998 were found to have reading scores that were one to two standard deviations above the mean, while a further 37.7% scored within one standard deviation of the mean. Of pupils not receiving learning support, 1.0% had reading scores that were two or more standard deviations below the mean, and 10.9% had reading scores that were one to two standard deviations below the mean. These findings have implications for allocation of learning support facilities between and within schools.

Correlates of Achievement in Reading

In this section, variables associated with the reading achievements of pupils in recent national assessments are considered.

Pupil Correlates

Frequency of leisure reading was quite high in both 1993 and 1998, while the frequency with which pupils read books in their leisure time did not change since 1993: over 40% of pupils (45.1% in 1993 and 43.8% in 1998) read books almost every day or daily. Large gender differences were associated with leisure reading. For example, in 1998, 53.4% of girls, but only 34.0% of boys, read books almost every day, and 17.4% of boys compared with 6.9% of girls indicated that they thought reading was boring. These findings are important as both the frequency of leisure reading and a positive attitude to reading correlated positively with reading achievement (r for leisure reading and achievement = .32; r for attitude to reading and achievement = .25).

In both 1993 and 1998, correlations between time spent watching television/videos and reading achievement were not statistically significant, and the correlations between time spent playing computer games and reading achievement were weak but significant. There was large variation in the amounts of time spent watching television and videos (e.g., in 1998, 29.6% of pupils watched one hour or less per school day, compared with 19.1% watching three hours or more). Pupils did not play computer games as frequently as they watched television and videos; only 9.1% claimed that they played 3 or more hours of computer games a day at the weekend. Of these 'heavy computer game users', 7 out of 8 were boys.

Home Background Correlates

The high response rates for the parent questionnaire in both 1993 and 1998 (over 95% in both years) suggests a high degree of interest and involvement on the part of parents in their children's education. Many home background factors were found to be associated with reading achievement. Pupils living in lone parent families scored, on average, one-fifth of a standard deviation lower than pupils in families where both parents were present. Pupils of lower socio-economic status, as indicated by possession of a medical card, scored two-thirds of a standard deviation lower than pupils whose parents did not possess a medical card. Access to a range of study aids in the home was significantly correlated with achievement also ($r = .43$), as was number of books in the home ($r = .44$). These two indicators may be regarded as a proxy for positive home educational climate and the finding is consistent with analyses of the 1991 IEA reading literacy survey (Martin & Morgan, 1994). Indeed, Martin and Morgan (1994) suggest that one of the most striking findings of IEA RLS was the consistent association between reading achievement and access or exposure to print.

The frequency with which parents read to their children during preschool years was also associated with achievement ($r = .33$ in 1998), indicating the important role parents play in shaping their children's reading skills. Parental academic aspirations for their children were also associated with pupils' achievement ($r = .51$ in 1998), suggesting once again that parents do play a central role in their children's academic progress.

Implications of Recent National Assessments

The finding that there has been no change in overall reading standards between 1980 and 1998 may appear surprising to some, given that school resources (as evidenced, for example, in the increase in the number of books in school libraries and the increased number of learning support teachers) have improved noticeably since 1993. However, it may be that the impact of these resources will not be translated into improved test scores so soon. The next national assessment of English reading, which will be implemented in 2004, will allow for a further analysis of the impact of resources on achievement. It is also possible that the measurement of resources has been inadequate in previous surveys, and that indicators of school resources should include a measure of resource use as well as resource availability.

Further, it is possible that standards in other curricular areas have improved, although in the absence of trend data in other curricular areas we cannot know whether this is the case or not. Also, the recent replacement of the 1971 curriculum (Department of Education, 1971) with a substantially revised curriculum (Ireland, 1999) which emphasises meta-cognitive skills in reading, may be expected to have an impact on achievement in time.

Another factor to take into account when considering the lack of change in standards is the fact that pupil achievement is not determined by school factors alone, and several variables relating to home background and pupil habits and attitudes were found to be associated with achievement. These included the frequency with which pupils read in their leisure time, their attitude to reading, the level of access pupils have to books and study aids at home, whether pupils live in a lone- or dual-parent family, parental involvement in their children's education, parental academic aspirations for their children, and socio-economic status.

Given the associations between achievement and home background, it is possible that the lack of change in standards may be associated with overall decreases in favourable home circumstances, although the 1993 and 1998 data do not allow definitive comparisons of home circumstances to be made.

Several other findings give rise to concern. One is the comparatively low achievement of boys, who performed more poorly on the test overall in 1998. Boys' reading skills were also rated significantly less favourably than girls by teachers, a finding which also emerged in the 1993 survey. Given that boys spent less of their spare time reading, and that seven out of eight pupils who may be classed as heavy computer game users are boys, the findings taken together suggest that all pupils, and boys in particular, need to be strongly encouraged to take an interest in reading, and to read widely. Schools should develop an atmosphere conducive to valuing reading skills and their enhancement (through, for example, reading corners in classrooms, a well-resourced class library, or use of reading as a reward). Teachers should encourage pupils, especially boys, to read widely, both inside and outside of school, and use lessons in all subject areas to develop vocabulary, oral skills, reading skills and writing skills. These may eventually crystallise into ability to research, argue and persuade; essential skills in today's society which is replete with texts.

Findings suggest that greater involvement of parents is needed, with an emphasis on their role in their child's educational development, especially in formative and habit-forming ways.

Analyses of the provision of learning support in English indicate an overall increase. However, there is evidence to suggest that learning support resources, where available, are not allocated in an optimal manner. These findings are consistent with a recent study of learning support provision in Irish primary schools (Shiel, Morgan & Larney, 1998) and suggest that the criteria for selecting pupils for learning support may need clarification.

Analyses of pupils' strong and weak points indicate that some pupils are still in need of assistance with the most basic aspects of reading, but that the vast majority of pupils appear to have mastered basic reading techniques. Clearly, more emphasis is needed on developing skills to enhance higher order reading strategies. (For a more detailed description of skills development see, for example, Edwards (1999); Pearson, Roehler, Dole & Duffy (1992)). These include:

- Vocabulary development, which is a prerequisite for comprehension.
- Activities such as the identification of key points in texts, and distinguishing between central and peripheral points, including summarising texts and discussion of main ideas.
- Identification and understanding of story grammar, including concepts such as plot, character, motive, causality, and narrative devices and their purposes.
- Encouragement to use meta-cognitive (self-monitoring) strategies whilst reading, including self-questioning to check understanding and clarify that goals for reading are being achieved.
- Awareness and appreciation of differences in content/process in narrative, expository and documents texts. Such awareness may be developed through activities which require pupils to present the same information in different formats.
- Identification and understanding of structure, sequence and organisation of expository and document texts and their uses. This may be enhanced through information presentation activities, with an emphasis on use of authentic, relevant texts.

Conclusion

Although the 1993 and 1998 assessments of English reading can be considered adequate and up-to-date in the sense that they form part of a larger systematic system of monitoring the educational achievements (Kellaghan, 1997), and they exploit modern item response modelling techniques, there are several areas which appear to require further development.

First, recent advances in reading theory, as evidenced in assessment frameworks such as those for the Programme for International Student Assessment (PISA; OECD, 1999) and the Progress in International Reading Literacy Study (PIRLS; Campbell, Kelly, Mullis, Martin & Sainsbury, 2001) need to be incorporated into future national assessments of English reading. The assessment also needs to be revised to reflect recent changes to the English language curriculum (Ireland, 1999). This implies that new reading material will need to be developed and incorporated into the assessment design for the next national assessment of English reading.

Second, the analyses in reports of national assessments carried out in Ireland to date have relied primarily on single-level univariate or bivariate analysis techniques. This is problematic because characteristics of individual students are not independent but rather nested within schools. Moreover, univariate and bivariate analyses are not adequate for describing the complex interplay between the many background variables which underlie student achievement. Clearly, more sophisticated multivariate techniques, which include interaction terms, are needed to describe these complex personal and social realities in a more accurate manner.

Fortunately, a number of multilevel, multivariate modelling techniques have recently become available (see, for example, Hox, 1995), which allows one to overcome both of these shortcomings. Such techniques allow one to separate variance at the student level from variance at the level of the school (or indeed from many other additional levels), and the multivariate nature of the techniques means that one can begin to take into account some of the complex interactions that occur between contextual variables. Smyth (1999) recently used these techniques to examine school effects on a number of different types of student outcome at second level in the Irish context, and these techniques have been used in both international and national analyses of the PISA data (see OECD, 2001; Shiel, Cosgrove, Sofroniou & Kelly, 2001).

A further aspect of national assessments of English reading that requires attention is the possibility of developing nationally-defined proficiency levels. While we know the proportion of pupils at various points of the reading scales (for example, the proportions scoring two or more standard deviations below the mean), we cannot say with any accuracy what kinds of reading tasks individuals located along the reading achievement scale are likely to be able to do. Using nationally-defined proficiency levels would allow us to anchor specific points of the scale to curricular objectives associated with different class or grade levels. The development of proficiency levels for future national assessments of English reading may be particularly timely in light of the recent implementation of the revised primary English curriculum. However, if proficiency levels are developed, the problems associated with them will need to be clearly spelled out in resulting reports.

A fourth aspect requiring attention is the lack of information on writing standards. Hartnett, Shiel and Murphy (1998) have noted that the majority of studies on children's writing in Ireland have tended to focus on the extent to which the objectives of writing instruction and strategies for the development of writing skills (as described in the curriculum) are implemented. However, there is little information on standards of writing; i.e., the quality of children's writing in primary schools. Linked with this, little is known about the link between reading and writing skills of pupils in Irish primary schools. Lack of information about standards in writing is particularly problematic at this time, as schools and teachers begin to implement the revised primary school curriculum for English. Therefore a short assessment of writing skills will be developed in 2002 with a view, in the longer term, to implementing the assessment as part of the next national assessment of literacy.

REFERENCES

Breen, R., Hannan, D.F., Rottman, D.B., & Whelan, C.T. (1990). *Understanding contemporary Ireland: State, class and development in the Republic of Ireland.* Dublin: Gill & Macmillan.

Burstein, L.. (1992). *The IEA Study of Mathematics III: Student growth and classroom processes.* Oxford: Pergamon.

Campbell, J.R., Kelly, D.L., Mullis, I.V., Martin, M.O., & Sainsbury, M. (2001). *Framework and specifications for PIRLS assessment 2001.* MA, USA: PIRLS International Study Center, Boston College.

Cosgrove, J., Kellaghan, T., Forde, P., & Morgan, M. (2000). *The 1998 assessment of English reading (with comparative data from the 1993 assessment).* Dublin: Educational Research Centre.

Department of Education (1971). *Primary school curriculum. Teacher's handbook.* 2 Vols. Dublin: Author.

Department of Education. (1995). *Report on the national survey of English reading.* Unpublished report. Dublin: Author.

Edwards, S. (1999). *Reading for all.* London: David Fulton Publishers.

Elley, W.B. (1992). *How in the world do students read?* The Hague: International Association for the Evaluation of Educational Attainment.

Hartnett, M., Shiel, G., & Murphy, R. (1998). Reading and writing in the primary school: How are they related? In G. Shiel and U. Ní Dhálaigh (Eds.), *Developing language and literacy: The role of the teacher.* Dublin: Reading Association of Ireland.

Hox, J.J. (1995). *Applied multilevel analysis.* Amsterdam: TT-Publikaties.

Ireland (1999). *Primary school curriculum: English language. Teacher guidelines.* Dublin: Author.

Kellaghan, T. (1997). *Proposal for a system of monitoring national educational achievements.* Dublin : Educational Research Centre, St Patrick's College.

Kellaghan, T., & Madaus, G. F. (1982). Trends in educational standards in Great Britain and Ireland. In G. R. Austin and H. Garber (Eds.), *The rise and fall of national test scores* (pp. 195-214). New York: Academic Press.

Martin, M.O. (1996). Gender differences among high and low performers. In Wagemaker, H. (ed.), *Are girls better readers? Gender differences in reading literacy in 32 countries* (pp. 36-41). Amsterdam: International Association for the Evaluation of Educational Achievement. .

Martin, M. O., Forde, P. D., & Hickey, B. L. (1991). *Assessment of reading comprehension in primary school. A development project. Summary report.* Dublin: Educational Research Centre.

Martin, M.O., & Morgan, M. (1994). Reading literacy in Irish schools: A comparative analysis. *Irish Journal of Education, 28,* 3-102.

Organisation for Economic Cooperation and Development (1999). *Measuring student knowledge and skills: A new framework for assessment.* Paris: Author.

Organisation for Economic Cooperation and Development. (2001). *Knowledge and skills for life: First results from PISA 2000.* Paris: Author.

Pearson, P.D., Roehler, L.R., Dole, J.A., & Duffy, J.J. (1992). Developing expertise in reading comprehension. In S.J. Samuels & A.E. Farstrup (Eds.), *What research has to say about reading instruction* (pp. 145-199). Newark DE: International Reading Association.

Robeck, M. C., & Wallace, R. R. (1990). *The psychology of reading. An interdisciplinary approach* (2nd ed.). Hillsdale NJ: Erlbaum.

Shiel, G., Cosgrove, J., Sofroniou, N., & Kelly, A. (2001). *Ready for life? : The Literacy achievements of Irish 15-year olds with comparative international data.* Dublin: Educational Research Centre.

Shiel, G., Morgan, M., & Larney, R. (1998). *Study of remedial education in primary schools. Summary report.* Dublin: Stationery Office.

Smyth, E. (1999). *Do schools differ? Academic and personal development among pupils in the second-level sector.* Dublin: Oak Tree Press/ESRI.

Travers, M. (1976). A second replication of a survey of reading comprehension in Dublin city national schools. *Irish Journal of Education, 10,* 18-22.

Ward, N. (1982). A fourth survey of reading comprehension in Dublin city national schools. *Irish Journal of Education, 16,* 56-61.

Wixson, K. K., & Peters, C. W. (1984). Reading redefined: A Michigan Reading Association position paper. *Michigan Reading Journal, 17,* 4-7.

6 Making Literacy Learning and Teaching Creative: Feedback Portfolios

Svetlana Ushakova, Russia

Changes are common in education, but at no time in history has change moved ahead at quite the pace that it does today. The rapid increase in knowledge has changed the content in subjects taught at school; changes in understanding how children mature and how learning occurs have led to changes in teaching methods. In addition, technology has brought new methods and vast amounts of information to the classroom, and has created new avenues for individualising instruction.

The process of globalisation and international marketing makes us all think today: What does it mean to be a teacher and a student in the 21st century? How could school prepare the students for the new forms of social participation, citizenship, for the new work environment, consumption, and leisure? These are just a few of the questions which make all of those involved in education think about the future of literacy, and the possible ways that teaching and learning might develop.

The participation in the international project on authentic assessment, which started in 1999, helped the teachers of Linguistic School 1531, Moscow, Russia to look from a different angle at the processes of teaching and learning, while working together with the students on feedback portfolios.

Beginning the Work

When work on feedback portfolios started at the school there were also changes in curriculum and instruction, with a shift from a teacher-centred approach based on the transmission of facts, to a student-centred approach based on inquiry processes. Then it was realised that the traditional forms of assessment and the methods used to collect information needed to be revised. It became clear that it was necessary to change the level of teacher and student involvement to one in which both are viewed as active creators of knowledge.

The students in our portfolio project – 12-to-13 year olds – had already had some experience of work with portfolios so this contributed to maintaining their motivation. A very real problem was that students in the high to average achievement range seemed unable to engage in self-assessment. These students believed in rapid learning, which led to poor performance on mastery tests, and over-confidence about performance. It was also evident that, in order to develop into independent life-long learners, the students would have to learn to assess the learning situation, set their own purpose, choose the most effective actions and evaluate their success. Besides, effective instruction is informed instruction. The teacher needs information on children and their progress. Therefore, data from a number of assessments were required. In as much as the feedback portfolio is created to work out effective learning and instruction strategies and to foster the development of adequate self-assessment, our main goal as teachers was to promote an ongoing and broad view of student learning.

Effects of the Feedback Portfolios on Teaching and Learning

The work on portfolios proceeded alongside efforts to make the processes of teaching and learning more strategic, with teachers being encouraged to scaffold instruction so that the students could become aware of and competent in applying learning strategies.

A teacher who aims to encourage student development should organise the process in such a way that different types of student thinking can be encouraged, depending on whether new material is being processed, or new learning is being consolidated with earlier learning. Practice showed us that that the development of strategic learners can take a substantial amount of time, that teacher and students must be committed to strategy instruction, and that instruction should include not only the definition or 'what' of a strategy but also relevant procedural and conditional knowledge. When the students have procedural knowledge, they understand the steps or processes involved in using a strategy. Conditional knowledge requires students to know why, where and when to select and apply a strategy as well as to evaluate its effectiveness. Sufficient practice in strategy usage was deemed to be important so that students would know enough about their learning strategies to approach different assignments flexibly and adaptively. Students should become sophisticated enough to ask questions about a novel task, use and adapt strategies to meet the demands of the task. For example, while reading text, students can come across a concept that is too difficult to grasp, they may have a difficulty with word identification, or they may be unable to identify the important ideas. If these problems are left unattended, the student's attempts to get the gist of the text or to construct meaning can fail. In dealing with these problems students were offered six research-based questions to help monitor comprehension:

1. Are there any words I don't understand?

2. Is there any information that doesn't agree with what I already know?
3. Are there any ideas that don't fit together because I can't tell who or what is being talked about?
4. Are there any ideas that don't fit together because I can't tell how the ideas are related?
5. Are there any ideas that don't fit together because I think the ideas are contradictory?
6. Is there any information missing or not clearly explained?

Another way to help students think about what they do is to use an inventory. It can serve as a vehicle for modelling and demonstration. It can give students a concrete idea of important strategies.

Strategy instruction makes teaching explicit by helping not only to show students *what* to do, but also *why*, *how* and *when*. Among the strategies widely used by the students are KWL (in reading as well as grammar learning), RSG (in the work with the text: retelling, summary, gist), What's new? (developing speaking skills in a foreign language), and RAFT (for teaching writing). The students collected the descriptions and steps of strategies in the part of their portfolio called 'collector'. By the end of this school year they had collected the following strategies for reading: KWL, KWL-Plus, Question-Answer Relationships, Inquiry Charts, Anticipation Guide, Chapter Tours, Mind-Mapping, Story-Mapping, Pyramid Diagram, and Power Notes. By using classroom strategies that teach students to activate, focus, select, organise, integrate and apply as they learn, the teacher can foster the development of individuals who are purposeful thinkers and independent learners. The materials that reflect students' work with adapting a strategy are presented in the section of the portfolios called 'working materials'.

From 'I'm the Best' to 'I'm OK'

The way to achieve the goal of empowering students to take responsibility for their own learning is through reflection. Reflection is the process of thinking about how you have learned, what you have produced and where you will go next. Turning to their portfolios for real evidence of what they have already learned, they can set goals for future learning. Following four components of strategy instruction: assessment, awareness, modelling and demonstration, and application, students learn to reflect on what, how and why they're doing this or that activity and then choose use this or that strategy. In our case, special attention was paid to the assessment component for reasons given earlier.

The teacher completed presentation of a strategy with some key questions, and asked the students to respond in writing. The questions generally included the following: What did you do to fulfil this assignment? What did you do to find the main ideas (in a reading or listening task)? Did you find it difficult or not? Why? In the awareness step, these reflective responses to the written questions were used to discuss the assignment, which then led to the stage of a discussion of why a strategy is useful and what rules, guidelines or procedures are successful with the strategy. In modelling and demonstration, a think-aloud procedure helped to model how to use the strategy.

After each practice the students reflected on the process again answering the questions: Did you follow the steps? How successful were you? What caused difficulty for you? What would you change if you did this activity again?

Reflection followed regular class assignments encouraging strategy application. In organising different class activities where reflection was to be included I used pair and group work, feeling that the most productive approach to developing reflection is the work of a group of three students.

At the end of a term the students were asked to respond to the following questions:

1. What did I learn this term?
2. What have I done really well?
3. What helped me to do it well?
4. What strategies can I use?
5. I'm really proud of...
6. I still need help with...
7. One goal that I would like to reach by next term is...

Students organised a class library and borrow a book once a month. They worked on it independently. While reading, they keep a book diary that that they can draw upon later to share information with their classmates. The following is a sample of one student's reflection on her individual reading:

> This work shows my result in reading. It's a book diary based on *Desert, Mountain, Sea* by Sue Leather. While working with this book. I learned how to work out the main idea of three different stories which are included in one book. The use of the strategies 'Follow the Character' and 'Chapter Analysis Grid' helped me to write complete characteristics of the characters. It's my favourite part of my work

now. I think it can also help me to understand real people. I enjoy working with the text looking for evidence of this or that idea. I'm really proud of my work. I still have to work on writing book reports and book reviews. I want to find the ways to make them so interesting that my friends would choose the book to read too, so that we could have a reading conference on them.

After a year of work with strategies and collecting portfolios the students who had said 'I'm the best' started to say 'I'm OK'. A change in their level of self-understanding was evident. This was coupled with a change in students' questioning behaviours. From the questions 'What do I read?' the students started to ask more often 'How do I read?', reflecting the strategies they used. Changes in reflection put forward a question 'What should I do in my free time to become a successful learner?' As a result, this work helped to maintain motivation in students, reinforced independence and developed greater responsibility for their own learning.

Conclusion

The work with portfolios helped to involve students in the process of assessment. This collaborative work strengthened the bond between student and teacher and established partnership relations in teaching and learning. The meaningful dialogue about the criteria and process used in evaluation provided students with an important model and helped the development of self-evaluators and independent learners. It helped to work on the development of individual learning style for each student and changed the style of teaching. Both learning and teaching have become more reflective, providing creative and critical thinking development.

BIBLIOGRAPHY

Buehl, D. (2001). *Classroom strategies for interactive learning (2nd ed.)*. Newark, DE: International Reading Association.

Courtney, A.I., & Abodeeb T.L. (1999). Diagnostic-reflective portfolios. *Reading Teacher*, 52(7), 708-715.

Millar G.J., Heffler B., & Mereweather K. (1995). *Student-led conferences using portfolios to share learning with parents*. Ontario: Pembroke.

Serafini M. (2000/2001). Three paradigms of assessment: measurement, procedure, and inquiry. *Reading Teacher, 54(4)*, 384-388.

Simpson M.L., & Nist S.L. (2000). An update on strategic learning: It's more than textbook. *Journal of Adolescent and Adult Literacy, 43(6)*, 528-538.

SECTION 3

Children's Literature

7   La Bible dans la Littérature pour Enfants en Pologne

Grażyna Lewandowicz, Pologne

Le choix du sujet résulte d'une part de l'intérêt pour le contenu et le message de la Bible, et de l'autre part pour la littérature pour enfants. La Bible est un livre extraordinaire et fascinant, et des motifs bibliques sont présents dans la culture et la littérature polonaises depuis des siècles. D'ailleurs, toute la culture européenne s'appuie sur deux piliers: celui de la culture antique et celui de la culture chrétienne avec son livre sacré – la Bible.

Le sujet principal de notre travail concerne les liaisons entre la Bible et la litterature pour enfants, la présence des motifs et des allusions bibliques dans des publications destinées aux jeunes lecteurs. Pour les fins de 'analyse, nous avons choisi 50 romans, provenants aussi bien de la littérature polonaise que de la littérature anglophone. Ces livres ont été édités en Pologne à plusieurs reprises, la plupart d'entre eux étaient recommandées pour l'usage scolaire. Dans les livres retenus, nous avons cherché des citations, des allusions et toutes sortes des renvois à la Bible. Nous avons également dressé une liste de la phraséologie biblique dans la langue polonaise. Il est utile de préciser que dans la langue polonaise il existe quelque 400 tournures bibliques, tandis dans la langue allemande il y en a plus de 500 et dans la langue anglaise environ 800. Le plus grand nombre de tournures bibliques vient du Pentateuque et des Evangiles. Dans notre travail, nous les avons comparées avec le texte de la Bible. Dans les romans pour enfants analysés, nous avons trouvé seulement 70 allusions et tournures de provenance biblique. Parmi les plus fréquents il y a: l'arche de Noé, être un rocher, ténèbres égyptiennes, plais égyptiennes, filles sages et bêtes, sage comme Salomon, un jugement de Salomon, le Verbe fut chair, être comme une colonne de sel, ton trésor est là, où est ton cœur, trompe de Jéricho. Parmi les personnages bibliques les plus connus, à part ceux qui ont été mentionnés ci-dessus, il y a: Adam et Eve, Joseph de l'Egypte, Moïse, David et Goliath, Job et dans le Nouveau Testament, Jésus et Hérode.

La seconde étape du travail a consisté à définir les fonctions de ces allusions et citations bibliques dans une œuvre littéraire. Le plus souvent, elles ont été utilisées en tant que des unités phraséologiques, mais dans certains cas des renvois à la Bible étaient importants pour le contenu du roman. Dans notre analyse, nous avons distingué les fonctions suivantes de l'application des allusions et des citations bibliques. (Exemples choisis) :

1. des allusions bibliques en tant que les *titres des chapitres* dans les romans: Par exemple, dans le livre de Kornel Makuszynski 'Une dispute pour Basia', un des chapitres est intitulé 'Le nouveau jugement de Salomon'. Le contenu du chapitre se reporte au jugement rendu par le roi dans un conflit entre deux femmes qui se disputent un enfant. Dans le roman de Makuszynski, il y aussi deux parties qui veulent garder Basia, l'héroïne principale du livre.

Egalement Astrid Lindgren dans le roman 'Madika de la Colline de Juin' a intitulé un des chapitres 'Joseph dans le puits', lequel décrit un jeu inspiré par la Bible. Madika – le personnage principal joue une scène de Genèse, présentant Joseph jeté dans un puits par des frères jaloux.

2. à travers des allusions bibliques, les auteurs des romans *caractérisent leurs personnages:* C'est un procédé utilisé le plus souvent. Les personnages ont été comparés, par exemple, au David et Goliath (être fort comme Goliath, poilu comme Ezaw), à l'alpha et l'oméga (savoir), ou encore à Salomon (être sage comme Salomon). Les auteurs des romans caractérisaient de cette façon aussi le savoir-faire des personnages et leur comportement.

3. des allusions bibliques ont servi aussi pour *caractériser des objets et des animaux:* Kornel Makuszynski dans son livre 'Le Grand Portail' a comparé une automobile à un char de feu du prophète Elie, et dans un autre livre le même auteur compare une voiture avec des meubles avec l'arche de Noé. Dans un roman de L. M. Montgomery 'Anne à l'Université', il y a deux chiens en porcelaine qui portent les noms de Gog et Magog – deux personnages bibliques puissants. Dans un autre roman de Kornel Makuszynski, 'Un voyage de chien', un chien, son personnage principal, est comparé à la bête de l'Apocalypse.

4. *caractéristique de la situation dans laquelle se trouvent les personnages:* Assez fréquemment, les situations dans lesquelles se trouvent les personnages des romans sont commentées par des renvois à la Bible. Dans une situation de stupéfaction, on les compare souvent à la femme de Lot, et dans des luttes avec soi même à la bataille de Jacob avec

l'ange. Une scène biblique sérieuse, dans ces romans est juxtaposée avec une situation joyeuse, voire triviale. Par exemple, une scene de dénoyautage des cerises est comparée avec le massacre des innocents, et un nuage de poussiere soulevée par des camions avec celui qui a accompagné les Israélites après leur exode de l'Egypte.

5. *émotions des personnages*: Egalement, les émotions des personnages sont accompagnées par un commentaire biblique. Peur, incertitude, tristesse, sont présentées par des expressions imagées comme : "ses cheveux ont raidi", "protéger comme sa prunelle", "Dieu a donné, Dieu a pris" (Job), la colère envahit comme la Mer Rouge, la joie est comparée à la danse de David devant l'arche, un cri fort au son des trompes de Jericho.

6. *prière:* Des fragments entiers de la Bible sont évoqués dans des moments très importants pour les personnages, quand ils prient pour la santé de leur proches, comme le fait Anne Shirley, quand elle prie Dieu pour la santé de Gilbert gravement malade, avec les mots du Psaume 30, ou encore quand ils remercient Dieu pour la guérison, comme le font les personnages du "Jardin mystérieux" de F.H. Burnett, qui démontrent leur joie, en chantant le Psaume 95.

7. *détermination du temps :*Pour souligner le fait que quelque chose s'est passé il y a longtemps, les auteurs servent de l'expression 'depuis le temps d'Adam et Eve', l'âge mûr des personnages est souvent comparé à l'âge de Noé. C'est le cas, par exemple, chez Montgomery où le petit Thomas se plaint à Anne Shirley (citation): 'Madame Linde s'est fâchée contre moi, puisqu'un jour je lui ai demandé si elle se rappelle l'époque de Noé. J'espérais qu'elle allait me le raconter, comment c'était avant. Anne, est-ce qu'elle vivait déjà, à cette époque?'

8. *rencontre avec la Bible:* Les scènes qui décrivent la façon dont les personnages prennent connaissance de la Bible sont très intéressantes. Le plus souvent, elles se passent à l'école, pendant les classes de religion. Les personnages doivent s'y préparer, en apprenant par cœur des fragments de la Bible, ce qui mène parfois aux situations comiques, comme dans 'Les aventures de Thomas Sawyer'. Les histoires bibliques sont racontées par les parents, les grand-mères, les servantes. La Bible est souvent lue par les personnages eux-mêmes, et certains possèdent leur propre exemplaire de la Bible.

9. *construction de l'histoire :* Une citation de l'Evangile selon Jean 'ton trésor est là, où est ton cœur' est un élément structurel de l'histoire dans le roman de Zbigniew Nienacki 'Monsieur Automobile et les templiers'. Cette citation revient plusieurs fois dans le roman (plus de 20 fois), et tout le suspens est construit autour. L'action du roman se concentre sur la recherche d'un trésor caché par les templiers et la citation biblique en est le mot clé.

La problématique présentée suscite certaines constatations générales. Les auteurs habilement utilisent des citations et des allusions bibliques. Ils ne les prennent ni littéralement, ni avec trop de respect. Les écrivants puisent dans cette source, pour enrichir et rendre plus attractives leurs histoires, en créant des jeux de mots, des renvois, des oppositions. Souvent, des tournures et expressions de provenance biblique déchargent une situation difficile, atténuent le contenu, introduisent un élément d'humour, si apprécié de lecteurs. On remarque que les auteurs anglophones utilisent plus souvent des allusions bibliques, et même des citations de la Bible, ce qui résulte probablement de la tradition protestante.

La seconde partie du travail concerne le problème de l'adaptation de la Bible aux enfants. On peut distinguer trois principales périodes dans la publication en Pologne non seulement de la Bible, mais aussi des livres religieux en général. La première période, ce sont les années d'avant la II guerre mondiale, quand le marché des livres était libre. La seconde période, ce sont les années de la République Populaire de Pologne, jusqu'aux années 80, quand il n'y a pratiquement pas eu de littérature religieuse pour enfants. La troisième période, ce sont les 20 dernières années. Des changements intervenus sur le marché du livre religieux ont été liés avec l'élection du pape Jean-Paul II et avec la création de la 'Solidarité'. Il faut remarquer que le plus grand nombre d'adaptations de la Bible aux enfants a eu lieu dans les 10 dernières années. Cela est lié aux des changements politiques et économiques (arrêt de censure, arrêt de la réglementation du papier) qui ont rendu possible la création du marché libre du livre. Cependant, la bibliographie des adaptations de la Bible aux enfants publiées au XXeme siècle a démontré une présence permanente, même si variable selon les décennies, du message biblique adressé à l'enfant.

Les adaptations de la Bible, qui paraissent sur le marché polonais, sont, en grande partie, des traductions des langues étrangères, surtout de l'anglais. Le contenu biblique est présenté en histoires, comme des contes, avec une linéarité des événements. Pour les enfants, on ne fait pas de distinction entre les Evangiles selon Mathieu, Mark, Luc et Jean. On leur présente un seul évangile, lequel raconte la vie et l'activité de Jésus. Certains éléments de l'original sont omis dans ces adaptations, cela est valable surtout pour des scènes cruelles de l'Ancien Testament. D'autres scènes – de la joie, de la victoire - sont à leur tour très exposées. La langue d'une adaptation est simplifiée, plus moderne, avec l'introduction des dialogues. La distance entre les personnages bibliques et l'enfant est réduite. Il est difficile de savoir si ces premières rencontres avec la Bible, à travers ses adaptations, influencent une lecture ultérieure, à l'âge adulte de la Bible. Néanmoins, Il est certain qu'une offre riche des telles éditions permet d'éliminer des lacunes dans l'éducation biblique, en ce qui concerne la connaissance des faits et de l'histoire biblique, et constitue une incitation générale à la lecture de l'original à l'âge adulte.

8   Marginalisation and Irish Children's Literature: A Personal View

Finian O'Shea, Ireland

In 1997 a special edition of the American children's literature publication, *The Lion and The Unicorn* was dedicated to Irish children's literature. In the editorial, Celia Callett Anderson and Robert Dunbar, write:

> A recent Irish novel for young adults – Gretta Mulrooney's *Crossing the Line–* carries on the blurb, the sentence 'not since *Forever* has a teenage novel explored first love and sexuality so openly and honestly.' This is the sort of development in contemporary Irish writing for young adult readers which may well come as a considerable surprise to those who previously thought of the terrain as the preserve of leprechauns, fairies and talking donkeys. It is, however, merely one of the indications of how, over the past three decades, Irish society itself changed and how that change is being reflected in the children's books being written and published there.

This is a view echoed in several recent publications on children's literature in Ireland including *Realistic Fiction for Under Twelves* where Liz Morris chronicles how literature for children has changed to reflect a more realistic view of Irish society. In a paper, *Circles and Triangles, Sharks and Wishbones: The World of Irish Young Adult Fiction*, Robert Dunbar (2001) investigates contemporary themes within fiction for young adults published in Ireland. Carol Redford (2000) looks at contemporary issues in *Difference and Conformity: What Do We Tell the Children?* All three writers see the changes in societal mores and attitudes being evidenced in the kinds of literature which are being produced for our young readers. In this paper, I explore one aspect of that change – marginalisation as a theme in Irish literature for children.

I began by listing every possible circumstance under which marginalisation could be seen as a theme and began to list the books that fitted into each category. But that was not what I wanted to do. So I selected books that mattered to me – a totally selfish premise I realise, but the one I chose , none the less!

I had intended to begin with a definition of marginalisation. But seeking some parameters in which to explore the theme proved a far better ploy. In an essay entitled *Take Your Time,* the late Virginia Hamilton talks about herself as 'being part of a parallel culture – of a minority group, in a sense in opposition spiritually and societally to the empowered American culture'. The characters in her books reflect this view of the world. 'They are uncertain of their position in society', she says. 'They move through life and time with dis-ease. They seek some relief from the conflict'.

In *Gates Of Excellence,* Katherine Patterson echoes this sentiment when talking about 'the outcast child looking for a place to stand'. It is a combination of both of these points of view, that of the 'dis-ease' and of the 'seeking a place to stand' that I feel offers me the parameters within which to look at marginalisation as a theme of some Irish published books.

Irish History

Morgan Llywleyn's *Strongbow* is the first book I want to refer to. Irish history has provided a rich and varied tapestry for our writers to use as a backdrop for their narratives. In this case, Llywelyn tells the tale of the Norman conquest of Ireland. Aoife, daughter of the king of Leinster is forced to marry the Norman Stongbow as part of a fragile alliance between the Irish and Normans. Both Strongbow and Aoife are marginalised within a historical context. What is interesting about the narrative is that alternate chapters are told from Aoife's point of view and Strongbow's. How those quite disparate political and cultural points of view (the dis-ease) become a shared vision (the finding a place to stand) is the impressive strength of this novel. It is also one of a minority of books for children to have a genuine political context.

Under The Hawthorn Tree by Marita Conlon-McKenna is set against the background of the potato famine of 1846. It looks at the plight of a marginalised, dispossessed race suffering the effects of poverty and starvation. The tale is told through the eyes of Peggy, Michael and the remarkable Eily, all of whom survive at the margins of society before finding a safe haven with Nano and Lena, their grand-aunts.

That period in history also provides a backdrop for many stories about the famine and about emigration. Marie Louise Fitzpatrick's *The Long March* takes a different starting point. The tale here is told of a group of Choctaw Indians in America collecting $170 from their meagre resources to send as famine-relief to Ireland – one marginalised people reaching out to another. The author magnificently illustrates the simple and powerful tale.

Recent International History

History in the twentieth century is the setting for *Angels without Wings*. This has to be one of the most compelling and complex novels for young adults to emerge from Ireland in recent years. I am an unabashed champion of its author Mark O' Sullivan, three of whose books I will refer to here. *Angels without Wings* is set in Germany in 1934. It centres on the Lingen Gang, Siegfried, Greta, Anna and Dieter. These are the main protagonists in a series of popular adventure stories written for children by Axel Hoffen. Axel, however, is now being coerced to write the next book in the series in line with the ideals set out by the Nazis. There is no place for Jewish Anna and for one-armed Dieter in the new order.

Tortured and forced to watch his characters conform to ideals of the Reich, Axel begins to suffer terrible cruelty both physically and mentally, at the hands of the SS. The four protagonists in the story step from the pages of the book and become 'angels without wings'. They attempt to rewrite the narrative, save Axel and the 'Lingen Gang'. It is a wonderfully crafted piece of writing, highly political and a challenge to the reader.

Gregory Maguire uses the Second World War as the backdrop for his novel set in occupied France in *The Good Liar*. It examines the dilemma posed by the friendship between two young brothers, Rene and Marcel, and Monsieur Soldier, a young German in the occupying army. The marginalisation of the characters is subtler here and involves them in positioning one another in order to keep secrets secret, especially about the Jewish family being hidden in the boys' home!

Indeed one of Maguire's earlier novels *I Feel Like A Morning Star* deals with marginalisation in a more overt way. Here society in a post-apocalyptic world is lived in vast underground biospheres. Three children defy the Council of Elders to find their way to the surface and, as in *The Good Liar*, the characters become marginalisd by their own concept of truth and so give the readers a range of moral dilemmas to deal with!

The Jewish refugee theme finds an interesting voice in Marilyn Taylor's *Far Away Home* – the tale of Jewish children from continental Europe who were sent to the UK to escape the war. Marginalised in their own country, Karl and Rosa arrive in Northern Ireland from Vienna and have to adjust to life away from their parents, in a new country.

Mark O Sullivan's most recent novel, *Silent Stones,* introduces Robby, a young man trapped between the worlds of his embittered grand-uncle Eamonn and the shadow of his dead IRA father, Seán. The appearance of Razor McCabe, a terrorist on the run, and a family of New Age Travellers sets a chain of events in motion between all of these characters on the margins of society, a narrative which is really worth reading.

Bullying places people on the margins of society – often with tragic consequences. Maeve Friel's *Charlie's Story* and Maria Quirk Walsh's *Searching for a Friend*, provide some of the most powerful examples of this. More recent novels to deal with this issue include Patrick Deeley's *The Lost Orchard* where Paul is intimidated by bully Raymie Boland and *Stretford's Enders* by Trevor J Colgan where Swayne the school bully makes Luke's new life in Dublin's southside even more problematic that it might have been.

Ireland's pluralist society is not really well reflected in contemporary reading lists – John Quinn's *Duck and Swan* was a brave attempt at looking at racism, but our multi-cultural society needs to be reflected in a more realistic depiction of life for many of our migrant, refugee, and asylum-seeker fellows. Colgan's *Stretford's Enders* does make an attempt at this, with characters from diverse backgrounds and nationalities making up the narrative.

Minority Groups

Disability is another invisible theme in children's literature here – Mark O' Sullivan's character Gary in *The Wishbone* (from *Two Islands*) is blind, and so living on the margins of the sighted world which he negotiates with some deftness. Learning difficulties find their way into the opening of Deeley's *The Lost Orchard* where Raymie is struggling to read the word 'attempt' aloud in front of the class – Mr. McGrane, the teacher, facilitates Raymie's marginalisation and perhaps gives him little option to save his self-esteem other than to be the bully – another interesting sub-theme perhaps?

Our own minority population of Travellers have, for many years been marginalised within society and kept firmly apart from mainstream society – very few books have really looked at this. Marita Conlon-McKenna's award-winning *The Blue Horse* tells the story of Katie, a traveller child, and her encounters with the attitudes of both the settled and travelling communities, as the family struggle to become members of the settled community. *Finnegan's Wind* by John Wood looks at the life of Callum, a traveller boy and his encounters with the settled community – it portrays how each has to stretch to accommodate an understanding of the other – a process which is realised by the end of the narrative.

White Lies again by Mark O' Sullivan is the first novel for young adults where Seánie, a gay character 'comes out' to his friends Nance and OD. What is interesting about it is that the coming out of a gay character is not the marginalised aspect of the book – that theme might best be explored in relation to the character of OD and his family circumstances. Seánie's being gay is incidental to the story.

Gay and lesbian issues are evidenced in two books from the O' Brien Press – *Allison* by Tatania Strelkoff and the adult book *When Love Comes to Town* by Tom Lennon. I am including the latter in this discussion as it is finding its way more and more into the preserve of the young adult list. Both books look at how the main characters come to terms with their sexuality and how their families and friends react to this. Both Allison and Neil become alienated and eventually marginalised by their coming out, and the unfolding narrative develops around how they deal with this.

Social Problems

Ecstasy and Other Stories is a collection of short stories first published in Irish by Ré Ó Laighléis and translated by the author into English. The stories range across the social spectrum to look at marginalised people in many situations – gambling addiction, homelessness, alcoholism, AIDs and crime. They are powerfully written and present a bleak and unforgiving look at Irish society. Jane Mitchell's *When Stars Stop Spinning* also looks at the debris of life as indeed does Martina Murphy's *Dirt Tracks*.

Breaking The Wishbone by Siobhán Parkinson is an attempt at a similar exposé of Irish society. It deals with homeless youth in an urban setting, and is interesting in that it presents the narrative in the form of a monologue.

People can slip into the margins of society and no one realises it until they are gone. June Considine's Ally in *Flower Child* is a wonderful example in this gentle sensitive story. Sarah, the main character in Jane Mitchell's *Different Lives* is another example of a protagonist who slips out of the lives of her family and into the margins of life in London. There is a wonderful ending to the story where the resolution is that there isn't one!

Though I acknowledge that there is need for social realism as a backdrop for a literature for our young readers, I agree with Betty Marion Brett when she writes 'literature will use social issues as the raw material of an artistic creation, ... *(but)* going beyond the issue to illuminate life and the human condition... is the other necessary ingredient in the process'.

It is interesting to see that Irish writers and their publishers are now looking outside of Ireland for the settings for their novels. Aubrey Flegg's *Cinnamon Tree* set in Africa and Siobhán Parkinson's *Call of the Whales* which is set in the Arctic are two recent examples. Maybe this turn-of-events can be seen in terms of a maturity on our part, that we are not longer navel-gazing!

But I think that there are still stories in Ireland that need to be told and indeed heard - maybe most importantly how we in Ireland appear to those from outside our land and our culture who are now making a valuable contribution to our lives and society.

REFERENCES

Articles
Anderson, C.A., & Dunbar, R. (1997). Editorial. *The Lion and the Unicorn*, 21 (3). Hopkins University Press,

Brett, M. (1989). Selecting children's books: The rarest kind of beast. In J. Hickman and B. Cullinane (Eds.), *Children's literature in the classroom: Weaving Charlotte's web*. Boston: Christopher Gordon.

Dunbar, R. (2001). Circles and triangles, sharks and wishbones: The world of Irish young adult fiction. In G. Shiel and U. Ní Dhálaigh (Eds.), *Reading matters: A fresh start* (pp. 91-100). Dublin: Reading Association of Ireland.

Hamilton, V. (1987). Take your time. In B. Harrison and G. Maguire (Eds.). *Innocence and experience: Essays and conversations in children's literature*. New York: Lee and Shepherd.

Morris, L. (1996). *Big guide to Irish children's books*. Dublin: Irish Children's Book Trust.

Redford, C. (2000). *Difference and conformity: What do we tell the children?* In V. Coghlan & C. Keenan (Eds.), *The big guide to Irish children's books II*. Dublin: Irish Children's Books Trust.

Patterson, K. (1981). *Gates of excellence. On reading and writing for children.* New York: E.P. Dutton.

Books for Children/Young Adults
Colgan, Trevor J. (2001). *Stretford Enders*. Dublin: Red Fox.

Conlon-McKenna, Martia. (1990). *Under the Hawthorn Tree*. Dublin: The O'Brien Press.

Conlon-McKenna, Marita. (1992). *The Blue Horse*. Dublin: The O'Brien Press.

Considine, June. (2000). *Flower Child*. Dublin Poolbeg Press. From Pelly Nelan (Ed.) *Flume Angles*. UK: Mammoth Books.

Deeley, Patrick. *The Lost Orchard*. Dublin: The O'Brien Press.

Fitzpatrick, Marie Louise. (1998). *The Long March*. Dublin: The Wolfhound Press.

Flegg, Aubrey. *The Cinnamon Tree*. Dublin: The O'Brien Press.

Friel, Maeve. (1994). *Charlie's Story*. Dublin: Poolbeg Press.

Lennon, Tom. (1993). *When Love Comes to Town*. Dublin: The O'Brien Press.

Llywelyn, Morgan. (1992). *Strongbow*. Dublin: The O'Brien Press.

Maguire, Gregory. (1989). *I Feel Like A Morning Star*. New York: Harper and Row.

Maguire, Gregory. (1995). *The Good Liar*. Dublin: The O' Brien Press.

Mitchell, Jane. (1997). *When Stars Stop Spinning*. Dublin: Poolbeg Press.

Mulrooney, G. (1997). *Crossing the Line*. Dublin: Poolbeg Press.

Murphy, Martina. (2001). *Dirt Tracks*. Dublin: Poolbeg Press.

Ó Laighléis, Ré. (1996). *Ecstasy and Other Stories*. Dublin: Beacon Books.

O'Sullivan, Mark. (1997). *Angels Without Wings*. Dublin: The Wolfhound Press.

O'Sullivan, Mark. (1997). *White Lies*. Dublin: Wolfhound Press.

O'Sullivan, Mark. (1999). *Silent Stones*. Dublin: Wolfhound Press, Dublin 1999.

O'Sullivan, Mark. (2000). *The Wishbone*. Short story in *Two Islands. Stories for Young Readers from Ireland and Australia*. Australia: Fremantle Arts Centre Press.

Parkinson, Siobhán. (1999). *Breaking The Wishbone*. Dublin: The O' Brien Press.

Parkinson, Siobhán. (2000). *Call of the Whales*. Dublin: The O' Brien Press.

Quinn, John. (1995). *Duck and Swan*. Dublin: Poolbeg Press.

Strellkoff, Tatania. (1998). *Allison*. Dublin: The O'Brien Press.

Taylor, Marilyn. (1999). *Far Away Home*. Dublin: The O'Brien Press.

Walsh, Maria Quirk. (1993). *Searching for a Friend*. Dublin: Attic Press.

Wood, John. (2000). *Finnegan's Wind*. Dublin: Wolfhound Press.

9 Know Your Place: Identity and Place in Children's Novels

Mary Thompson, Ireland

We have little direct access to that place or state called Ireland, compared to the abundance of ways we inherit of *knowing* Ireland, of reading the great book that is Ireland. We may know the air and physical configuration of the parish in which we were born, the suburb we now inhabit, the towns and beauty spots we visit, but Ireland? Not even an inveterate traveller would claim to know every inch of the physical landscape. If we do know Ireland, it is through the media of the arts (sculptures, poetry, the range of narrative forms, music and song); the critical discourses of politics and culture, including religion and economics (speeches, theories, essays, literary or otherwise); scientific (archaeology, cartography) and ethical enquiry, the media, and so on. The modes of knowing as well as the types of knowledge are incorrigibly plural and dispersed. They insist that we know Ireland in their terms.

There are two forces at work when we struggle to understand our relationship to place. First, we know it more from the interplay of texts and discourses about it than we do from our physical experience of it. Second, when we read or tell stories about place, the conventions of narrative and what we already know about places from other stories shape the telling.

Let us take some examples from across the discursive spectrum of how our notions of place are represented and yoked together. It is almost impossible for readers schooled in English departments of Irish universities to read Irish rural realist novels without exploring their relationship to other familiar discourses of place. I cannot read, for example, John McGahern's *Amongst Women,* without linking it to the familiar paradigms of Daniel Corkery's influential book *Synge and Anglo-Irish Literature* (1931). In this, Corkery outlined the forces he believed should be represented in Irish literature, namely, religion, nationalism and the land. I might also recall Eamon De Valera's now cliched 1943 St Patrick's Day articulation of frugal, bucolic Irishness or John Hinde's carefully arranged and tinted postcard pictures.

In addition to siting new stories about place within the context of the discourse of place, most seasoned readers contextualise each story they read within recognisable story forms and conventions. We make sense of the places we inhabit by relating them to the places we have encountered in fiction, and the way characters connect with places in stories. Even young schoolchildren do this. They note what Bakhtin (1937-38) calls the 'spatial situations' such as the forest or the mountain or – most popular in children's literature, the sea – and the semantic function which they serve within the story. Children have a prior knowledge of the sea and the forest as literary constructs. They may not have articulated this knowledge in conceptual terms, but from their reading of Little Red Riding Hood, Hansel and Gretel and numerous other literary encounters, they know something of the danger that is synonymous with the forest. A forest is a physical location but it is also an unmapped metaphoric territory, outside the walls and therefore resonating with danger, evil and personal challenge. The particular stories about the forest or the sea – such as, say, Eoin Colfer's *Benny and Babe* (1999), or Will Gatti's *Sea* (1999) – interact with these models of knowing. In this way the reader may form expectations about what is likely to happen next, either in the real world, or in the world of the text. Reading place then implies reading literary conventions as well as literal spaces.

However, the significance of place does not stop there. The relationship between individuals and Ireland is complex. What is the process by which children evolve a sense of self, and what role does place play in that process? Let us begin by tracing one example of a stereotypical oppositional representation of Ireland as the locus of tradition that resists modernity, and examine its implications in terms of constructing selfhoods.

Dualistic Representations of Ireland

Patriotic romanticism has imbued the Irish landscape with great significance since the late eighteenth century. As recently as 1916, writers are drawing on images of an elemental Irish landscape that could erase individualism and, in the process, individuality. Douglas Hyde's determination to de-anglicise Ireland was a mode of reconstructing it in opposition to the imperially, monolithic other that was Britain, of the process of definition through differentiation. The frugal virtues that were exalted by Hyde and what Kevin Whelan calls de Valera's 'intolerably dreary Eden' were an extension of Hyde's separatism. The aestheticised western landscape became a synecdoche for Ireland. The process continued, but was modified in the 1950s when Bord Fáilte attempted to represent Ireland both as an industrialist's tax-free haven and an unspoilt landscape that was the repository of romantic selfhoods.

The pattern of projecting traditional images of Ireland, reconstructed according to these familiar templates, continues. Bord Fáilte's current advertising campaign exhorts us to 'rediscover the magic' of Ireland, eliding the urbanisation, and the sophisticated economy that are the Irish hallmarks. A recent edition of the *Irish Times* (9 June, 2001) carries two articles that serve to illustrate how today we perceive the landscape of Ireland from a tangle of opposing traditionalist and progressivist perspectives. Eileen Battersby's 'Resisting the rules of the roads' (p. 7) explores the impact of road building on important archaeological excavations, and underlines the tension between the idea that roads are arteries pulsating with progress and the archaeologists' vertical probing into the past. In the same edition, Gordon Deegan's aptly entitled article, 'Back to the future in the Burren' (p. 9), recounts the Mullaghmore saga, which ended with the government demolishing the £3m car park on foot of a High Court order. In this article, a local spokesman, John O'Donoghue, remarked that the local opposition to the car park 'was motivated by an old-fashioned, almost innocent love of the mountain'. Brendan Daly TD summarised the opposing point of view when he perceived the same mountain as 'solid gold'. Deegan, the writer of the article, gazing on the landscape from which all evidence of the mooted interpretative centre had been erased, commented that 'the virgin fields give little indication of the battle that has raged over the site'.

The rhetoric of the three commentators, Deegan, O'Donoghue and Daly, reconstructs the site and the controversy in familiar idioms: virginal Ireland, untainted, embattled, the object of 'innocent' – meaning uncorrupted – love, and Ireland, a raw material that may be processed to yield profit. Daly's crass commercialism vies with John O'Donoghue's romanticism, and Deegan's mythologising. Deegan's nostalgic diction – his re-virginising the landscape – and O'Donoghue's mystification give primacy to it and not to the individual or the community. It implies a yearning for unmediated contact with the natural object – similar to that of Romantics such as Wordsworth, Holderlin, Rousseau or early Yeats.

We might enquire what relationship is implied between these two polar representations of Ireland and the citizens who construct their Ireland in that way. The relationship might be seen in terms of a trajectory that extends from passivity (tradition) to possessive control (modernity), from being spoken to by the landscape to speaking of it in alien terms. An extreme critic of the Mullaghmore defenders might hold that the place constitutes a complex shifting force field in which the individuals and community were caught up and their identity dispersed within it, in which the boundaries between Mullaghmore and their individual selves are indeterminate. A puritan might accuse them of remorselessly seeking the pleasure of place to the exclusion of necessary progress, trapped in what might be called in Freudian terms a pre-Oedipal state of citizenship, that is, not having achieved a critical distance from it. The State in the case of the Mullaghmore saga organised the energies that are diffused among its opponents from the locality, and adopted a patriarchal role. The affair becomes a synecdoche of the battle between nature and culture, between what is natural and the symbolic. Place as constructed within this model is essentially split, torn between the repressed and the real.

Such dualisms are, inevitably, replicated in children's novels as they are in publicly circulated stories for adults (novels, dramas and poems such as Patrick Kavanagh's *The Great Hunger*) published since the 1930s. It could be argued that narrative provides the most effective medium of transmitting complex ideas about relationships between people and place.

Self and Story

Narrative as a discursive mode is crucial to the process of creating a sense of self, and evolving a sense of self is inimitably the business of being a child. So it is that stories have become the conduit for complex apprehensions about place. As Kieran Egan (2001) has remarked, story 'is the only form of language that can fix the hearer's affective orientation to the events, characters, ideas, or whatever, that make it up. Stories, basically, are little tools for orienting our emotions.' Egan here focuses on how stories avoid the dualism of conventional rationality, because thinking and feeling are inextricably woven into their fabric.

Space does not allow a full exploration of the appropriateness of the form of story to understanding the dialectic between self and space. Stories propose modes of selfhood and ways of relating (to other people and to the environment) that are then imitated in the real world. Novels can be especially successful in achieving this, because they aim to represent the minutiae of the life we live and the place in which we live it. They constitute a form of representation in which complex tensions and problems can be presented, but in an accessible, pleasurable form. Built into them are the values, hopes and fears of society, guides as to how ideally we ought to relate to the past, the future and to other societies – and of course to the place itself.

But the value of story runs even deeper, because we order the events of our lives in accord with the principles of narrative. We know ourselves because of the stories we tell – to ourselves and to others – about our lives. Those stories share platforms with the stories of others whom we encounter and whose tales impact upon us. Stories can create order out of chaos – that was the great conviction of modernist artists (Yeats and T. S. Eliot spring to mind) – and they can find order where none is apparent. They can give form and meaning to experience.

In Ireland the landscape has been the lodestone of literature since the early middle ages. The stories we recount now engage intertextually with the wealth of tales in which Ireland – known so well as to be personified as Róisín Dubh, Gráinne Mhaol, an tSean Bhean Bhocht, the chief protagonists of innumerable tales. When the issues relating to place are recast in the form of story, they become amenable to wider audience. Indeed, in the words of the wise man of Cormac McCarthy's *The Crossing*, the world that 'seems to us a thing of stone and flower and blood is not a thing at all but a tale'. We need to tell Ireland's stories to know Ireland, and we need to tell new stories because a story always avoids closure, certainty, and can provide a fresh perspective on the familiar. Stories do not offer the last word, but the best word so far.

While stories have been told with a child audience in mind for at least the past three hundred years, publications have been sparse, at least until the last twenty years or so. That means that the stories that are available have potentially more impact.

Place in Children's Fiction

Let us look at how this conflict between place as the repository of history and place as the site of progress is played out as much in the stories of established – one might say canonic – writers such as Eilis Dillon and Patricia Lynch as in contemporary writers. Patrick Deeley's *The Lost Orchard* published in 2000 and shortlisted for the Bisto Book of the Year Award, is set near the Callows, dangerous wetlands that exert an intense attraction on their inhabitants. Full of quagmires and concealed dangers they exude a Hardyesque fertility and aesthetic; they are simultaneously seductive and sinister. The Callows is a place where time stands still (p. 71), a place that responds to natural, rather than human, rhythms. The Darkfield mining company – the correlative of Hardy's mail cart in *Tess of the D'Urbevilles* – embodies mechanical violation and the profit instinct, modernity and the hunger for gold replacing the respect traditional inhabitants accorded the place. 'I imagined an army of aliens come to claim the flat, defenceless fields of Darkfield', the narrator remarks. Extraordinary butterflies, emblematic of the natural, unforced aesthetic of the environment, contrast with the clanging, crushing mills that evoke the concept of progress. The novel ends on a pessimistic note, the Callows decimated but fighting back, reclaiming territory sterilised by the mining company. Hardly virginal as is Mullaghmore, still scarred, but enduring. A model of resilience, of elemental energy from which mere humans might learn lessons.

Similar binaries are established in Patrick O'Sullivan's *The Horses of Dereenard* (2000) and Michael Morpurgo's *The Ghost of Grania O'Malley* (1996). In the former, Rebecca's aunt values her isolation, her traditional farming lifestyle and her regard for the land is passionate. The horses that work on neighbouring Sam Staunton's traditional forestry acquire a certain dignity from their work, emphasising their anthropomorphic nature. The narrative elides the boundaries between people, animals and the land:

> It was nice, [Rebecca] thought, that the same families had been involved in the forestry for generations...There was a felling of family about it all, and the horses were part of the family too ...She heard the singing of the birds, and again the woody incense of the trees filled her nostrils. (pp 20-21)

Maurice and Luke who personify the brash selfishness of progressivists, provide the conflict of the plot. The story ends somewhat unconvincingly with victory to the conservationists and their unrepentant regressive sentiments.

Unlike the previous characters cited, Jessie, the protagonist in *The Ghost* who suffers from a physical disability – 'cerebral lousy palsy' – pits herself against the landscape rather than courts absorption into it. Her success in this personal contest enables her to empathise with Grania, the gendered iconic embodiment of ancient, beleaguered but resilient Ireland, now facing the threat of earth-diggers. Grania outlines the central tenet of her philosophy: 'None owns the land. You look after it, you protect it for those who come after you, that's all' (p 72). Morpurgo cautiously deconstructs his oppositions, accepting the inevitability of advancement. The ancillary character Jack, an American who is Jessie's partner against the earthbusters, is never happier than when he is tinkering with machinery, the byword for progress. Whereas the aggressive face of progress meets a sorry and ecologically incorrect end when they are unceremoniously cast over the cliff, the book avoids the sentimentality and unreality that characterises *The Horses,* for example, in its cautious affirmation of progress.

As the opening remarks of this essay suggest, the novels of Deeley, O'Sullivan and Morpurgo are situated in relation to the norms, patterns and processes of their literary and cultural antecedents, among them the narrow field of children's novels. Among these are the works of Patricia Lynch who began publishing books for children in the 1930s. In her depiction of place she admits to little of the contest between tradition and modernity that is apparent in the books cited so far. Her novels call upon the epithet 'snug' with unfailing regularity to describe her homes. Descriptions of dwellings might be interchanged from one book to the next. Typically, her homes merge with their natural surroundings, emphasising the characters' closeness to, rather than distance from, their environment. In *The Turf-Cutter's Donkey* (1934),

> The cabin was so low and the thatch so covered with grass and daisies, that a stranger would never have found it only the walls were whitewashed. (p. 1)

Michael from *The King of the Tinkers* (1938) lived . . . .

> in a stone cabin hidden away in the mountains. Even the roof was made of long slabs of stone. The house was painted green and had two windows on one side, one on the other. . . .The cabin was a long distance from the road and there wasn't another dwelling within sight or sound...Yet Michael was never lonely, for . . . . his mother told him stories. (1972, p. 9)

Long Ears: The Story of a Little Grey Donkey (1943) too has a 'snug' home:

> Once inside the green gate it was as snug a farm as you could wish to see. There was the house itself – low and built of great blocks of stone, whitewashed so smooth that the cracks were filled in and the walls as smooth as ice. (p. 62)

Home in Lynch's books provides a seductive oasis of security and certainty that comes from a perfect congruence between place and self. That certainty is of course threatened. Narrative implies plot and plot requires conflict. The opposing emotions to those evoked by home are induced when the protagonists abandon its security. The description of home offered above from *The Turf-Cutter's Donkey* continues

> The road ran past their home, right across the bog...There were treacherous green patches and holes so deep that there was no bottom to them, but there were paths for those who knew. (pp 1-2)

Egress is fraught with danger and the boundaries of home are well patrolled. Inevitably, characters do in the nature of narrative, leave home, often only to find themselves lost in an enveloping mist – as in *Long Ears: The Story of a Little Grey Donkey*. Kevin in *The Seventh Pig and Other Irish Fairy Tales* (1950) had the temerity always to imagine a world beyond his cosy home: 'Far beyond the grey curtain of rain and spray was Spain, where the sun always shone and grapes and oranges grew like blackberries on brambles.' (p. 73). But out in the dark, he is far from exhilarated by the freedom and unpersuaded by the attractiveness of uncharted space. Rather, when he watched the shadows while he was out in the dark, he found the moonlight was strange and confusing. The sanctuary of home is surrounded and underpinned by an entirely different reality, that of another world that answers to different laws. Mist blurs the borders and reality easily metamorphoses into a magical terrain, attractive but unreliable. Children negotiate the boundaries without confidence or understanding. Home is the only sanctuary.

Eilis Dillon, on the other hand, writing at the mid-century, is ambivalent about progress. Her *The House on the Shore* (1955), a rollicking, suspense-filled adventure sketches convincingly a backdrop of an isolated rural community on the cusp of progress, moving from a traditional, unchanging lifestyle to an acceptance of the merits of advancement. The main protagonist /narrator Jim inherits his uncle's land as his mother had hoped he would, and the young adventurer metamorphoses into a hardworking farmer, his lifestyle little different from that of his ancestors. However, a seaweed factory has brought great prosperity to Cloghanmore, and significantly, Jim refuses to rebuild the old family home, the locus of family memory. Jim manages both to sever his ties with the past, and to maintain them, suggesting something of the dilemma of progressive conservatives.

Macken's *The Flight of the Doves* was published in 1968, thirteen years after *The House on the Shore*, just as free education was about to transform Irish childhood and prosperity began to unfold. Its goal is a stereotypical generic place in which resides a granny who embodies security for the orphan whose access to tradition has been ruptured:

> A village of whitewashed thatched cottages, built with no definite order, you would think, in small stony fields, leading up to hills that became mountains, and backed in the distance by blue mountains far off, and in front of it the sea with many islands, and long beaches with white sand. (p. 142)

Sean O Faoláin, an iconoclast in the 1940s and 1950s when calcified representations of place dominated public thinking, has commented that we are drugged by the fear and reverence that the past engenders:

> We lived under the hypnosis of the past, our timidities about the future, our excessive reverence for old traditions, our endemic fear of new ways, of new thinking, the opiate of that absurd historical myth, and, the horror of the feeling of solitude that comes on every man who dares to push out his boat from the security of his old, cosy, familiar harbour into unknown seas. (1969, p. 162)

Note his pejorative use of the epithet 'cosy' whose synonyms are so beloved of Lynch, Macken and others. Note too his rejection of the filiative model of relationship, evident in his dismissal of reverence and security. As O Faoláin's comment implies, the discourse of place in these examples (both from children's books and from current affairs) is closely related to that of time, to the tension between or the confluence of past and future as they are embodied in the landscape. One method of evaluating the accomplishment of a novel, then, relates to how successfully, as Bakhtin puts it, 'space becomes charged and responsive to movements of time, plot and history' (1981, p. 84). In his opinion, 'Time, as it were, fuses with space' (1981, p 243). The challenge to a writer then is how to ensure that his narrative combines a temporal logic with a spatial one.

In the first two fictional examples offered above, space and time adhere to the laws of suspense. The characters are essentially static, the power and the initiative belong to chance as exemplified by nature or happenstance. Both Deeley and O'Sullivan posit a timeless zone threatened with rupture. However, while Deeley's novel is dense with detailed, loving description of this erotic, seductive place, O'Sullivan merely asserts Dereenard's attractiveness. In both cases the logic of the plot precludes the agency with which a contemporary realist novel might endow its characters. Dereenard is a monument to unchanging time, above temporal contingency. It is an example of perfect stability of being, capable of reclaiming territory lost to fires and poison, endlessly recycling the same time, the same character types. The mutable self mutates not at all either in *The Horses* or in the examples of Lynch's work.

However, Deeley's *The Lost Orchard* might be considered a transitional novel, not cast entirely in the adventure mode. In it there is an epiphanic moment in which the protagonist realises that 'everything must eat. The wasp must eat' (p 168). Humans are, the book implies, determined by instincts, by various hungers, and so our capacity for change is limited. However, the narrator is changed by virtue of that knowledge. In *Grania* the character Jessie moves – literally and metaphorically – in a social world charged with historical dynamics. She challenges the mountain and subdues it. The strength thus gained enables her to create an alliance with Grania, personification of the land, and subdue their joint antagonists. The twin episodes relate causally to each other.

The act of reading can consolidate nostalgia as a mode of engaging with place and is, by implication, ahistorical, traditional in the sense that it makes it possible to rethink the diffusion of history. Through a ritual of division, through the rite of exclusion, these books condemn one pole – 'progress' – and elevate the other, traditional pole. They present a unilateral view of Ireland that is already deeply pervasive and was the only view affirmed by institutions of power such as the Church and State in the decades of the mid-century. A combination of economic constraints, a censorious attitude in society at large and the Censorship of Literature Act of 1929 severely circumscribed the types and range of stories available to adults, and, even more particularly, to children. The very form of narrative was absent from readers authorised for use in schools, which presented only factual information. The genre of children's literature was scarcely recognised as such. But then childhood was an invisible, silent category in the Ireland of the twenties, thirties, forties and early fifties, such that Robert Dunbar identifies the stories of John McGahern about his mid-century childhood as 'an anguished scream at the absence of childhood/adolescent recognition'.[3] An aura of undignified silence surrounded childhood and still persists to a degree.

There were, of course, some children's stories in circulation, to be found in the threadbare public libraries, and they might have included the British children's classics, the Enid Blytons and the school stories, but in many respects the existence of these books only served to exacerbate the problem. Frank O'Connor in *An Only Child* has referred to the diet of

British comics that signalled to him his alienation from a normative childhood as represented for British children. Represented in them was an index only of his otherness. The New Zealand writer Margaret Mahy recounts a similar misapprehension a generation later. When she began to write fiction she found that she could not set her stories in familiar territory, because she perceived the normative setting for children's stories was England.[1]

Out of the pitifully few stories published at the mid-century, there was a handful that attempted a complex and richer apprehension of place. One example is a short novel by Francis MacManus, *The Flower Garden*, published in 1940. This story is a variant of the Cinderella theme, but told in an uncompromisingly realistic fashion. The main protagonist moves from her bourgeois home controlled by a brutal adult to her tearaway uncle's shop in Kilfinane. Here is presented a young protagonist who does achieve an affiliative stance in relation to place, who does not find consolation in cottages that merge with the landscape. Here is represented a realistic Ireland and a character who achieves a critical distance from it. The irony, of course, is that this and similar books were published only for adults. Today, children who struggle to find an ideal relationship with their changing environment are not constrained by the negative attitudes, the paucity of stories or the authoritarian attitudes of half a century ago. Yet nostalgia and old idealisations persist, such that both children and adults must maintain a critical, selfconscious attitude to how we relate to place.

NOTE

1. Comments made by Margaret Mahy after her lecture, 'Stories from under the table: the power of story in family life', Once upon a summertime Children's literature summer school 2001 Children's Books in Ireland Summer School, 18 May 2001.

REFERENCES

General
Bakhtin, M. M. (1937-38). Forms of time and of the chronotope in the novel: notes towards a historical poetics. In M. Holmquist (Ed.), *The dialogic imagination* (p. 97). Austin: University of Texas Press.

Corkery, D. (1931). *Synge and Anglo-Irish literature*. Cork: Cork University Press.

Dunbar, R. (1996). Children's fiction and the Ulster troubles. In P. Cotton (Ed.), *European children's literature (Kingston Hill Papers in Education)*. Kingston-Upon-Thames: Schools of Education at Kingston University.

Egan, K. (2001). Evolution and early understanding: We begin as poets. *Arista, 2 (1)*, 11-19.

O'Faoláin, S. (1969). *The Irish Harmondsworth*. London: Pelican.

Adult Literature

McGahern, John. (1990). *Amongst Women*. London: Faber.

Hardy, Thomas. (1981). *Tess of the D'Urberevilles*. London: James R. Osgood, McIlvaine & Co.

Kavanagh, Patrick. (1942). *The Great Hunger*. Dublin: Cuala Press.

McCarthy, Cormac. (1994). *The Crossing*. London: Picador.

O'Connor, Frank. (1961). *An Only Child*. London: Macmillan.

Children's Literature

Deeley, Patrick. (2000). *The Lost Orchard*. Dublin: O'Brien Press.

Dillon, Eilis. (1955). *The House on the Shore*. London: Faber.

Lynch, Patricia. (1934). *The Turf-Cutter's Donkey*. London: Dent.

Lynch, Patricia. (1938). *The King of the Tinkers*. London: Dent.

Lynch, Patricia. (1943). *Long Ears: The Story of a Little Grey Donkey*. London: Dent.

Lynch, Patricia. (1950). *The Seventh Pig and Other Irish Fairy Tales*. London: Dent.

Macken, Walter. (1968). *The Flight of the Doves*. London: Macmillan.

Morpurgo, Michael. (1996). *The Ghost of Grania O'Malley*. London: Macmillan Education.

O'Sullivan, Patrick. (2000). *The Horses of Dereenard*. Dublin: Woflhound.

10   The Multigenre Project

Patricia G. Smith, Australia

Multigenre research papers have taken us over. The discussion will be about how the multigenre concept of doing inquiry played out for my group of pre-service teachers and Lisa Keskinen's 4th grade of primary students. Be warned. You may be seduced, too, even though what follows is only a small 'grab' at what is possible. A good place to start is with Tom Romano's definition of multigenre:

> A multigenre paper arises from research, experience, and imagination. It is not uninterrupted, expository monologue nor seamless narrative nor a collection of poems. A multigenre paper is composed of many genres and sub-genres, each piece self-contained, making a point of its own, yet connected by theme or topic and sometimes by language, images, and content. In addition to many genres, a multigenre paper may also contain many voices, not just the author's. The trick is to make such a paper hang together. (Romano, 2000, p.x)

Success in introducing anything new requires enthusiasm. I am genuinely excited about the multigenre project's possibilities. I have read Romano's books with increasing avidity. I know that here is a dose of energiser for the teaching of writing in the classroom. At the very least, there is the opportunity to link writing and inquiry in a new framework. We started the project asking 'How could the students be infected? Would they want to write with the passion about which Romano was himself writing?'

Tom Romano's idea for the multigenre paper, he says, came from Michael Ondaatje's *The Collected Works of Billy the Kid* (1970). So it seemed sensible to copy him by using this book with the older students. Ondaatje wrote about the last years of Billy's life. The book is made up of songs, thumbnail character sketches, poems, a comic book excerpt, narrative, stream-of-consciousness passages, newspaper interviews, even photographs and drawings. Each genre is complete in itself, and is satisfying in itself, but unites with the others to create a single literary experience.

There are as many ways as there are teachers to introduce multigenre to suit issues of time and curriculum. The preservice teachers were enrolled in a subject called *Images of Reality in Young Adult Fiction*. We had spent a semester reading, discussing, writing journals and being involved in Literature Circles and Writing Workshop. Most students chose to answer the assessment questions with multigenre papers rather than conventional essays. This was not because they were easier. In fact, these students were themselves amazed at how detailed their research had been. They had become passionate about their inquiry.

Multigenre in Fourth Grade

Meanwhile, in the 4th grade classroom, Lisa had met the concept of writing with passion head-on. She asked her students to produce a writing project/folio on a topic or issue of their choice that was both interesting and important to them (a topic that they felt *passionate* about). This was probably the most important pointer to success. The children were passionate about many topics. Saving whales, using animals for cosmetics testing, cutting down rainforests, and animals in circuses were probably predictable, but Archimedes and jellyfish also made the list. One girl just wanted to find out more about Archimedes than 'the bath story'.

The jellyfish choice is very interesting. Ben had been on a big holiday to Broome in Western Australia and had arrived back with wide, red welts on his arms and back and still quite traumatised after he had been stung by a large jellyfish near the end of the trip. He brought a cream for Lisa to slather the sore spots when they became painful. Ben's research and writing helped him deal with the incident and also grow as a writer.

Lisa knew her students could do the multigenre project, but she also knew that they would need solid structure, direction, support and encouragement in order to do it really well. She came up with a fairly thorough plan for the process. They were to construct a folio. The folio was to include six pieces of writing, in six different genres. Together these pieces would construct a thorough picture of the topic/issue of the child's choice. The children chose to work on one piece at a time, or to move between several pieces. This flexibility enabled them to write in the style that appealed to them most on any given day. If they experienced 'writer's block' on a particular piece, they moved to another piece for the session, thereby maximising productive writing time.

Each child submitted a project proposal in which they detailed their focus and listed the genre they intended to cover. This proposal was to be used as a project planner and was not set in concrete. Students negotiated changes to their proposals as their ideas and projects evolved.

Lisa used the information on the proposals for planning Guided Reading and Writing sessions. For example, if five students planned to write a report, then she grouped them for a Guided Reading session where they read two examples of reports and discussed the features of each. A Guided Writing session followed, where perhaps the students would write a short report together, then begin writing their own, coming together regularly as a group to provide feedback and to support each other's efforts.

Multigenre in College

The equivalent reading and writing workshops in the preservice teachers' class were important in the process. Eman pursued a question about patterns in stories of survival. She used Brian Caswell and David Phu An Chiem's *Only the Heart*, Wendy Orr's *Peeling the Onion* and Fred D'Aguiar's *The Longest Memory* as references to explore the question. The contents of her paper, which was presented on various kinds of paper in a folder, along with a small Chinese box for the poem, included:

* Letter to the teacher
* Book review: Only the heart
* Diary entry by Phuong
* Councillor's report on Anna Duncan
* Reflection: poem by Anna Duncan
* Stream of consciousness: Whitechapel
* Survival kit.

Wanting to be sure that I had grasped why a student had chosen a particular genre, I borrowed another idea from Romano. The students were asked to write Endnotes for each piece that would be a reflection of why they had chosen a particular genre. The following is an example from Eman:

Endnote 3: Diary Entry by Phuong

Because of the book *Only the Heart,* I decided to write this entry as if I was Phuong. As you read you will see my intention to portray how Phuong developed, how she survived. The words are intended to display her feelings, how she's changed and what she's become. I've included words from the book such as 'shield of innocence' and 'wind up doll'. When I wrote the diary entry, I really wanted to express in the message her view that beauty is a curse and a constant reminder of how it has made life difficult to endure and better let go. Where else but in a diary would this be written?

Others used Endnotes that included creative and scholarly responses. They imagined, they quoted sources, included quotes from the work of others. For example Travis makes a point about realism in family stories:

> Endnote 3: Shows the reality rather than implicitly describing the point the writer wants to make. (Travis had written An Extract from Austin James Eighteenth Century Novel: *Tales for My Children* using an incident in *Lockie Leonard: Legend*).

This is a demonstration of how our Australian contemporary children's realistic family fiction has changed over the years. The style of writing is based on the type of language and style used in Charlotte Barton's (1841) *A Mother's Offering to Her Children* (the first published Australian book for children) to recreate a scene from *Lockie Leonard: Legend* (Winton, 1997, pp.104-5). This contrast shows the massive change that children's literature has undergone since its emergence in the 19th century. Saxby (1998) describes this early development of children's literature as:

> The story of family life grew out of the Puritan movement of the sixteenth and seventeenth century when children were seen as inherently evil and in need of salvation (Saxby, 1998, p.250).

A Mother's Offering to Her Children and *Lockie Leonard: Legend* are specific types of literature about families. One is dated and the language too constructed to be realistic, the tale too moral to be true and with explicit instruction present. The other is contemporary and speaks the reader's language. It is not preaching a message but presenting issues to be explored by the reader. It shows rather than tells. By not explicitly explaining what the author believes, but showing reality, the author leaves the door open for all readers rather than cutting out some of them.

Younger and Older Writers

While Lisa's 4th grade students took to the work with no qualms, in the preservice teachers' class there were many students who didn't regard themselves as writers even though they had managed a successful secondary education and gained enough points to get into teaching. I introduced writing workshops and multigenre proved to be a successful way for them to discover themselves as writers and also to explore themselves as individuals with ideas about important issues in their lives.

The notion of unity underlay much that went on. An ethnographic task helped students deal with this unity between what could be disparate pieces. They also learned to use the setting, and to write dialogue. Ethnography was a new term to most of them and they liked the idea that they were moving on to learn what seemed to them to be a higher level of writing and research. As undergraduates they were much taken with the view that I thought they could do 'real' research.

A brief explanation may be useful to illustrate a typical workshop. The preservice teachers were asked to draw a map of their home town/suburb and mark in some landmarks such as the school, the church, a tree they remembered, and so on. They wrote about something that had happened to them at one of the points. These stories were shared. Then they were asked to write as if they were spectators describing something that happened at another spot. These latter pieces were usually more powerful as they gained in confidence. We discussed how the place came alive through the action rather than an actual description, thus the need to avoid adjectives and adverbs. The idea of presenting dialogue exchanges as voices rather than with the 'said John' is very powerful. Work spent on writing dialogue is always time well spent in any writing workshop.

Finally, they were asked to spend three separate twenty-minute periods writing down observations and dialogue in a place where they meet in a group. Many work for a hamburger chain. Others chose their basketball team or health club. We did talk about strategies that would help their writing such as listing the five or six most important things for an outsider to know about your site and the people there. What ties these items together? Their ethnographies were published. This was the first time, in spite of all the years that the Writing Workshop has been around, that many of them had had work published. They were very readable and some would have been good enough for commercial publication as short stories.

Conclusion

What have been described are the efforts to help the students learn to combine research with experience. They have explored various genres used by authors and practised writing different genres themselves. John Marsden's Marina in *So Much to Tell You* writes a diary; Virginia Euwer Wolff's *Make Lemonade* is written in sixty-six chapters with text lines that break according to natural speaking phrases. These were new and startling genres within young adult literature, though not the varied genres found in Ondaatje's work. Most importantly, the students learned to write in other voices as well as their own. They made critical choices about what references they would use for the research and so learned about whose purposes were being served in the writing – their own and those of the source person. Finally they themselves breathed life into the multigenre concept when they became confident, after careful scaffolding, to engage in the writing.

Eman's list of contents represents a small part of the total of genres chosen. Many, like Eman, made careful selections about presentation. This was not an issue of making them pretty but an opinion about the multiliterate nature of texts. Business cards hold more meaning than the text on them. Type of card, colour, graphics all contribute to the meaning. The beautiful Chinese box was a special receptacle for the moving poem about a personal journey.

The 4th grade students thought carefully about the presentation of their final product, too. They were encouraged to be creative in presenting their folio. The final package included a contents page and the original project proposal sheet. Their writing was powerful, passionate, challenging and just wonderful! Feedback from the children, parents and other teachers was extremely positive. On our celebration day (completion) there was such excitement in the air. They all knew that they had achieved something very special, Lisa included.

The Multigenre Project provided a rich learning experience for us all. It was a truly 'open-ended' project that catered beautifully to a range of abilities and talents. We engaged in all aspects of language use, both spoken and written. The project encouraged dialogic and critical thinking. It also promoted creativity, as it embraced the use of various art-forms in presentation of the work, demonstrating transformation of knowledge. The project enabled students to follow their true interests and passions, therefore engaging them fully in the process. It allowed students to explore their own experiences, thoughts, feelings and ideas, thereby promoting deeper understandings of themselves and others.

REFERENCES

Barton, C. (1841). *A Mother's Offering to Her Children*. Sydney: The Gazette.
Caswell, B. & Chiem. D. P.A. (1997). *Only the Heart*. Sydney: UOQ Press.
Ondaatje, M. (1970). *The Collected Works of Billy the Kid*. London: Picador/ Macmillan.

Orr, W. (1996). *Peeling the Onion.* Australia: Allen and Unwin
Romano, T. (2000). *Blending Genre, Altering Style* Portsmouth: NH: Heinemann.
Romano, T. (1995). *Writing with Passion: Life Stories, Multiple Genres.* Portsmouth: NH. Boynton/Cook
Saxby, M. (1998). *Books in the Life of a Child.* Australia: Macmillan
Winton, T. (1997). *Lockie Leonard: Legend.* Australia: Pan Macmillan.

SECTION 4

Early Literacy and Family Literacy

11 The Voices of Beginning Reading Instruction: Families and Schools in Four European Countries

Marti Brugemann, U.S.A.

How do children learn to read? Theories, research and even written curricula only represent part of the answer. The voices of children, parents, teachers and administrators provide other perspectives on this complex accomplishment.

During a sabbatical from my university I was able to explore voices in Germany, Finland, Scotland and England. These countries were chosen for a variety of reasons. Finland has an extremely high literacy rate. In addition, most adults spoke English and I would have assistance interviewing children. My German is fairly fluent and I would be able to interview both children and adults myself. England's national curriculum assessment, and literacy hour provided a unique system. Scotland was an opportunity to investigate another type of English-speaking school. Colleagues were able to assist in making initial contacts in Germany, Finland, and England. My visits provided an opportunity to interview children and adults, read curriculum guides and related materials, peruse research and talk with university faculty.

Protocols for semi-structured interviews, distributed prior to my visit, were designed to reflect five major areas: assessment; curriculum; family involvement, reading theory; and instruction. An attempt was made to visit schools in both urban areas and smaller villages within each country. Five different classrooms were observed in Germany, Finland, and England; three in Scotland. Over 250 adults and children were interviewed directly with nearly equal numbers in each country.

Raw interview data collected was entered into the Nudist software programme for qualitative analysis.

Children's Favorite Stories

Children were asked to name their favorite story and/or author. I gave each classroom Jan Brett's *Gingerbread Baby*, which some children mentioned. However, the majority of children were not influenced by my selection.

Responses of children from all four countries indicate contemporary authors and/or books are favored. Only German children placed traditional tales (e.g., Grimm's stories) over contemporary authors. Finnish children mentioned classics and traditional tales least but were influenced by comics and movies (e.g., Donald Duck). Books based on movies (e.g., Batman and Pokemon) were popular in England. While all Scottish children responded with a favorite story and/or author, 16 percent of Finnish children, 13% of English students, and 25% of German children failed to name a favorite.

TABLE 1: PERCENTAGES OF CHILDREN INDICATING MAIN SOURCE OF FAVORITE STORIES OF CHILDREN, BY COUNTRY

	Traditional tales	Classics	Comics and movies	Contem-porary authors	Non-fiction	Many choices	Do not know
Germany	26	0	9	22	9	9	25
Finland	8	6	17	34	14	3	16
Scotland	8	15	23	31	23	0	0
England	17	7	21	26	13	3	13

Frequency of Family Reading to Child

Both children and parents were asked about bedtime reading routines. The analyses compared children's statements to their parents' reports. Some families did read at times other than bedtime. For example, one mother said she reads in the morning when her other children were gone to school so she could spend time alone with her youngest child.

TABLE 2: FREQUENCY OF FAMILY READING TO CHILD AS REPORTED BY PARENTS AND CHILDREN (PERCENTS OF PARENTS/CHILDREN)

		Often	Seldom	Never
Germany:	Parents	72	22	6
	Children	41	36	23
Finland:	Parents	45	23	33
	Children	50	36	14
Scotland:	Parents	88	0	12
	Children	77	11	12
England:	Parents	71	21	21
	Children	88	6	6

In Scotland, 88% of parents said they read often, while only 77% of children agreed. Children and parents were in agreement with regard to 'never' reading. Parents and children in England also provided conflicting responses, children said their parents read more frequently than their parents admitted.

In Germany, 72% of parents said they read often, while children only noted 41%. Twenty-three percent of children said their parents never read to them, while only 6% of parents reported that they never read to their children. In Finland, about one half of children and one half of parents indicated frequent reading. However, as in Germany, some parents stated that they stopped reading to the children when the children could read well on their own.

Children in all four countries indicated that they usually read to both parents. Finland, in particular, had over 60% in this category. In contrast, Finland had the lowest number of children reading to siblings, while Germany ranked the highest in this area. In both Germany and Finland, grandparents did not listen to homework. Most often, children were reading during homework, but on occasion, they read for the enjoyment of younger siblings.

How Children Said They Learned to Read

Next, children were asked, 'How did you learn to read?' Student responses to the questions were categorised into seven areas. The 'home' category means the child learned to read at home prior to coming to school, either through parental guidance or independently.

To provide a context, this section begins with an overview of the reading methods observed in the various schools and verified with the European Commission's document *Studies: Initial teaching of reading in the European Union* (1999). According to the document, Finland and Germany utilise two major theoretical approaches to reading. Though there are significant differences in the application, both countries employ a contemporary and a traditional basal method. Finland also uses a Swedish method, 'Reading through Talking', which begins with child-generated stories. In Germany, the Swiss 'Lesen durch Schreiben' (reading through writing) is used. Students learn basic phonemes with picture illustrations. In the context of class stories and related children's literature, teachers encourage children to write using the given sounds and invented spellings.

The school I visited in Scotland uses a phonics method and the Oxford reading scheme, but children are placed in a scheme that fits their learning style if the Oxford series is not successful. Scotland has detailed guidelines for curriculum and assessment.

While Finland does have national guidelines for devising curricula, local areas also engage in curriculum development and teachers freely choose methods and books.

England has a national curriculum and a mandatory literacy hour consisting of: class-shared text work, focused word work, and independent reading, writing, word and/or sentence work. The teacher works with small and large groups by reviewing, reflecting, consolidating teaching points and presenting work covered in the lesson.

Finnish children enter school at age seven. Not surprisingly, perhaps, 43% of Finish children reported learning to read before they came to school. Parents and teachers verified the children's responses. Children learn through reading comic books, using the computer, having the newspaper and stories read to them, and from the T.V. bylines. Children did not state that they learned to read by writing.

In Germany, children enter school by age six. Most German children reported that sounds and letters and spelling words helped them to learn to read. In Scotland, where schooling begins at age 5, children felt that sounds and letters (38%) and word-spelling (39%) accounted for their ability to read. None felt actual reading and writing contributed to their early reading ability. The majority of English children (43%) felt they learned through words and spelling plus sounds and letters (27%). Reading and writing at home were mentioned. No mention was made of school books.

How Teachers Say Children Learn to Read

Teachers and administrators were asked how they personally felt children learned to read. Teachers were also asked what they felt were the most important components for reading. The following is an overview of responses.

A teacher from Perth, Scotland said that learning to read involves a mixture of many skills: memory comes first, then phonics and looking for meaning. She felt the most important components of learning to read are motivation and phonological skills. The headmaster of her school believes learning to read is a complex link between thought and artifacts. He suspects that children initially associate the whole word shape with an explanation and later, upon instruction, develop individual letter sounds.

A teacher in Brentwood, England feels there is more than one way to teach reading: for some children reading just happens; other children require repetition and phonics; still others may need to create books. The school's head teacher and literacy specialist feels that, despite many kinds of strategies for teaching reading, children basically learn through enjoyment; children should be surrounded with books, catalogues, and signs. The school itself exemplifies the priority given to reading by placing its library in the entrance and in the hallways.

Teachers and administrators in other English schools believe schools must utilise a variety of methods in teaching reading because no single way is effective. Another teacher feels reading is a combination of strategies and children simply begin 'bubbling' on their own. The importance of language and communication was stressed.

A teacher in Kirchheim, Germany feels children learn to read by hearing, seeing, and handworking, along with a lot of practice with all kinds of reading materials. She stated that children need to read their own stories, literature books, and the fibel, as well as see adults reading. She believes that children recognise the power of reading and are naturally curious. She opines that the most important component of learning to read is to devour reading materials. She also feels that schools reflect and build on the early learning of the child's name and observations of words and letters by transferring them to other contexts.

In a traditional school in Frankfurt, Germany, the principal said children today do not have the same prior knowledge and vocabulary as in former years. She stresses the use of the five senses in learning and feels it is important to use different kinds of materials with a very structured approach which includes the fibel, worksheets, and phonics. Formerly, a more whole language approach was used.

A second school in Frankfurt used the 'Lesen durch Schreiben' method. The principal and all three beginning reading teachers believe children learn to read by first understanding that the text is speech written down; therefore, the text needs to be directly connected to the lives of the children. Sound/symbol relationship are also important for children to experience within their own writing experiments.

A headmaster in Hameenlinna, Finland opined that many children learn to read by themselves because they are interested; methodology is less important than desire. She feels they need to hear many stories and to think. Other Finnish teachers stated that children first need to be interested in written text in order to connect hearing and word structures with meaning. Another teacher feels there are many ways to learn to read. Some children learn more slowly; some need the ABC's and phonemes; some learn mechanically. Finally, some see whole words continually and remember. In her own family, reading 'just appeared'. Her daughter first learned to write and then read.

Another Finnish teacher feels that children learn to read because they are eager and curious about words and the reading materials of their parents. Children want to know. She believes the most important component is interest and eagerness. She stated that children learn to read if they are motivated and if there are motivating things at home. If parents read stories to their children and spend time with their children, the children become curious.

How Parents Reported Learning to Read

Another interview question probed how parents learned to read. The majority of English and Scottish parents felt they learned to read through reading schemes. Many parents could name specific characters. A small percentage of English parents felt either that their parents taught them to read (especially by writing) or that they learned by themselves. Scottish parents mentioned learning through use of letters, pictures, and words.

Finnish parents named syllables as being the primary unit of instruction. Fewer individuals mentioned letter names, pictures, sounds, or learning by themselves. Interestingly, a much smaller percentage of Finnish parents than of their own children read before coming to school .

German parents mentioned a wider range of instructional methods. The majority felt they first learned the letter names and the fibel or school but 20% felt they learned at home. This figure is half the percentage of parents who felt their children learned to read at home and half the percentage of children who reported learning at home.

Parent Perspective on How Their Child Learned to Read

The final area for review concerns how parents felt their children learned to read. English and Scottish parents were the most aligned with what I actually observed and read. The Scottish classrooms use a combination of phonics, schemes, sight words and stretch-out sounds. The major emphases in English schools include library books, scheme books, and sight words. Parents in these countries also appear more involved within classrooms. The few parents who did not know how their children learned to read were newly-arrived immigrants. German parents mentioned the whole-word spellings over specific books. Parents stated that they thought the whole-word spelling method superior to the older method of learning separate letters. Finnish parents felt 'gliding sounds' was the most effective approach (28%). They also stated that this procedure is better than learning separate sounds before blending them together. The next highest area was learning through children's literature. Nearly one-quarter of Finnish parents stated that children did learn to read before entering school.

Conclusions

A broader view of the data reveals some definite trends. First, movies and comics (especially Disney) play a significant role in what children read and *how* they learn to read. A second trend is the acknowledgement by parents, teachers, and administrators that children learn to read when they are motivated and curious, relegating the instructional method to a secondary status. Teachers and administrators strongly advocate reading to children and, encouragingly, bedtime-story reading has not vanished. In all four countries many parents still read to their children, regardless of the child's age. Likewise, European families listen to their children read on a daily basis. The role of siblings is significant.

A final observation is that most parents are informed about their child's reading instruction and recognise differences from their own instruction. They feel current methods are superior and children are learning more quickly.

REFERENCE

European Commission. (1999). *Studies: Initial teaching of reading in the European Union.* Luxembourg: Office for Official Publications of the European Communities.

12 Partnerships in Early Childhood: Linking Parents, Teachers and Academia to Improve Literacy

Catherine O'Callaghan, U.S.A.

As the twenty-first century begins, the structure of family life in industrialised nations continues to change. In the United States, more than 60% of mothers with children below the age of six can be found in the workforce, thereby forcing school districts to provide adequate childcare (US Bureau of Labor Statistics, 1999). In Europe, child care programmes have been seen as a public obligation for several decades (Kamerman, 1999).

In the United States, the National Research Council (2001) has just completed a major research review on the quality of early childhood programmes. The report indicated that there are several key features associated with effective programmes. Quality early childhood programmes develop the whole child and also provide excellent staff development opportunities. Teachers in these programmes are taught to respond to the needs of the child and his/her interests. However, many children living in poverty are denied these excellent educational opportunities.

Effective Intervention Programmes

Quality early childhood programmes are especially necessary for children at risk of academic failure due to poverty or family distress. Bloom (1964) was one of the earliest proponents of early intervention during the first five years of life for children who were at risk. Since Bloom first advocated for intervention, U.S. Federal Government programmes such as Head Start and Even Start have been developed to provide children from impoverished areas an enriched academic beginning. The research on the effectiveness of these early programmes has been mixed. There is a body of empirical evidence to show that these early intervention programmes produced gains in cognitive as well as socio-emotional development (White & Casto, 1985). The programmes which demonstrated the largest effects on learning illustrated many of the key features of quality programmes such as high staff-to-child ratios and highly qualified staff (Frede, 1998). In addition, research indicated that these programmes decreased grade repetitions and placements in special education over the long term (National Research Council, 2001). However, the impact of the programmes on IQ scores were not shown to have lasting effects. It is hypothesised that this may be due to the overall poor quality of schools in disadvantaged areas which graduates of Head Start or Even Start attend (Lee & Loeb, 1995).

Early childhood educators have affirmed the positive impact of intervention programmes for children at risk. In order to increase the effects of instructional time, several programmes have incorporated parental components. However, research has shown that parental programmes do not provide as strong an impact as models which involve children directly (St. Pierre, Layzer & Barnes, 1998). Therefore, effective early childhood programmes integrate parental components into instructional activities for the children.

Staff development, as well as parental involvement, is another key feature of effective early-childhood intervention models. Early-childhood teachers' intellectual abilities are strong predictors of how much a young child learns (Ferguson, 1998). As well as the teacher's knowledge base, the teacher's ability to respond to the student is another key component. Responsive teachers attend to the child's interests and developmental levels and adjust instruction accordingly (National Research Council, 2001). Research has indicated that specific teacher behaviours in early childhood, such as modelling communication skills and extending children's activities and problem-solving by providing prompts, all contributed to learning gains (Frede, Austin & Lindauer, 1993).

Therefore, according to research, for an early intervention programme to be effective, it must include the key features of quality programmes, such as high staff-to-child ratios and excellent staff development. Even Start, a federal early-childhood intervention programme, embodies these characteristics and offers an alternative model to Head Start by focusing on family literacy.

The Even Start Programme

Even Start is a family literacy programme that understands that the education of parents and children is interdependent. The model recognises that for parents to become the best primary teachers for their children, their own literacy skills must be improved. The model was created from systems theory which argues that for change to occur, all components impacting the child must work together. The four components of the Even Start Model are:

* Adult Education-GED workshops/English as Second Language training and job training
* Parenting workshops
* Early childhood education for children up to the age of eight; and
* Parent and Child Interaction Time (PACT).

For Even Start to succeed, the four components must work together on the same curricular goals. Therefore, as the adult is learning about community resources, the Even Start preschool classrooms are exploring the same topic. This allows the adults to act as models for their children as they learn subject matter together. The Even Start model was implemented in Downtown Brooklyn, New York, through a partnership between higher education and the New York City Board of Education. The local school district and St. Joseph's College in New York City have collaborated to intervene in the lives of families at risk.

The Even Start Tech-Link Model

Even Start Tech-Link is an intergenerational family literacy programme located in Downtown Brooklyn, New York. The programme is a collaboration between the New York City Board of Education and St. Joseph's College. This collaboration has been in existence for two years and implements the four Even Start components. There are co-directors from each institution administrating the programme.

The programme services approximately 55 families that qualify based upon economic need. The majority of the families are African Americans and Latinos residing in the Bedford Stuyvesant and Fort Greene areas of Brooklyn. These families are members of the working poor and many qualify for public assistance. The majority of adults participating in the programme have not attained their high school diploma.

Adult Education Component

The New York City Board of Education Adult Services office offers Even Start parents classes in adult basic literacy. Classes are offered every day to accommodate parents' work schedules. They are encouraged to attend as many sessions as possible to pass the high school equivalency examination. In addition to adult literacy, parents are able to participate in a 30-hour computer course. The programme's focus is on keyboarding, word processing and the use of the Internet to help parents prepare for the job market.

Parents who speak a second language are also offered courses in English as a Second Language through the New York City Board of Education. These courses are held several times a week and are designed to meet parents' immediate needs, such as filling out forms. Gradually, parents are introduced to more difficult components.

Parenting Component

St. Joseph's College offers a Family Literacy Fair in the Autumn and again in the Spring. Members of the Education department provide workshops for the parents on how to integrate literacy into their everyday lives. This year, parents were shown how to use family photos to tell family stories and to use cooking to develop vocabulary.

Parents were also visited twice a month in the home by family assistants to follow-up these parent workshops. These visits also connected families to the programme's social worker who would inform the parents of government services which they were entitled to receive. In addition, once-a-month group sessions of all Even Start parents were held to create a support network among the families. Guest speakers were often invited to address the parents on topics such as their neighbourhood library services.

Early Childhood Component

A major component of the Even Start Tech-Link programme is staff development. Teachers from the Even Start classrooms attended a Summer Literacy Institute at St. Joseph's College. Sessions were conducted by the faculty on topics such as Guided Reading, Learning Styles, Integrating Literacy with the Arts and Content Area Reading for Early Childhood. At the end of the Summer Institute, teachers were asked for topics they wished to explore during the academic year and these were presented in Autumn/Spring staff-development sessions. This year, teachers requested presentations on behaviour management, literacy for early childhood and instructional techniques for the inclusive classroom. The teachers were also able to observe the laboratory preschool classrooms on campus and to comment on the developmentally appropriate practices of the preschool teachers.

Follow-up observations of the Even Start Tech-Link teachers were also conducted by the college faculty. These visits were designed to assist the Even Start teachers in utilising the ideas they acquired during their staff development workshops. Teacher assistants and computer equipment were also supplied to the early childhood classroom through funding from the grant.

Parent and Children Together Time (PACT)

The final component of the programme is implemented directly in the public schools. Parents are encouraged to visit their child's classroom at least one hour a week to work with his/her child. This helps the Even Start parents to become familiar with their child's teacher and the topics being studied in the school. There are also several Parent and Children Together Time activities each month, such as Read Aloud Day or Storytelling Sessions.

Research on the Effectiveness of Even Start Programmes

The national evaluation of Even Start programmes found that adult participants gained in literacy skills and more earned their high school equivalency diploma than control group subjects. Even Start preschool children learned school readiness skills faster than expected and sustained those rates over one year later. Parenting outcomes were that Even Start parents had a greater variety of reading materials. They also demonstrated gains in providing cognitive stimulation and emotional support for their children (Wasik, Herrmann, Dobbins, & Roberts, 2000).

Locally, Even Start parents in New York State read two-three more books per week than the previous year. The average family in Even Start also decreased television viewing from 2.8 to 2.5 hours per day. Lastly, only four percent of Even Start children in New York State were retained in their grade (Henry, 2000).

In summary, collaboration between academia and local boards of education can offer families at risk visible support to help them empower their children. Fluency in literacy is the gateway to higher education and improved earning power. Early intervention which integrates the home and school, provides a systems approach to a complex socio-economic issue. Working together, higher education and local boards of education can change the future, one family at a time.

REFERENCES

Bloom, B. (1964). *Stability and change in human characteristics.* New York: Wiley.

Ferguson, R.F. (1998). Can schools narrow the black-white test score gap? In C.Jencks & M.Phillips (Eds.). *The black-white test score gap* (pp. 318-374). Washington, D.C.: Brookings Institute Press.

Frede, E. C. (1998). Preschool program quality in programmes for children in poverty. In W.S. Barnett & S.S. Boocock(Eds.). *Early care and education for children in poverty: Promises, programs and long term outcomes* (pp. 77-98). Buffalo, NY: SUNY Press.

Frede, E. C., Austin, A. B, Lindauer, & S. K. (1993). The relationship of specific developmentally appropriate teaching practices to children's skills in first grade. *Advances in Early Education and Child Care, 5*, 95-111.

Henry, S. (2000). (September 25-27). New York State Even Start Evaluation. Paper presented at biannual New York State Even Start Conference. Saratoga Springs, New York.

Kamerman, S. B. (1999). *Early childhood education and care: Preschool policies and programs in the OECD countries.* Paper presented at the Early Childhood Education Workshop, Columbia University New York.

Lee, V., & Loeb, S. (1995). Where do Head Start attendees end up? One reason why preschool effects fade out. *Educational Evaluation and Policy Analysis, 17(1),* 62-82.

National Center for Family Literacy. (1997). *Even Start: Effective literacy programs help families grow towards independence.* Louisville, KY: National Center for Family Literacy.

National Research Council. (2001). *Eager to learn: Educating our preschoolers.* Washington, DC: National Academy Press.

St.Pierre, R.G., Layzer, J.I., Barnes, H.V. (1998). Regenerating two generation programs. In W.S. Barnett & S.S. Boocock (Eds.), *Early care and education for children in poverty: Promises, programs and long term outcomes.* Buffalo, NY: SUNY Press.

United States Bureau of Labor Statistics. (1999). Labor force participation of fathers and mothers varies with children's ages. *Monthly Labor Review, (June 3).* Washington, DC: US Department of Labor.

Wasik, B. H., Herrmann, S., Dobbins, D. R., Roberts, J. E. (2000). *Family literacy: A promising practice for the twenty-first century.* North Carolina Association for Supervison in Curriculum Development.

White, K. R., Casto, G. (1985). An integrative review of early inervention efficacy studies with at risk children: Implications for the handicapped. *Analysis and Intervention in Developmental Disabilities, 5,* 7-31.

13 Continuity and Discontinuity in Early Literacy Development in Slovakia

Ol'ga Zápotoèná, Branislav Pupala and L'ubica Hošková, Slovakia

This paper reports on an ongoing research project focusing on early literacy intervention. The project was conducted by the Department of Social and Biological Communication in collaboration with the Department of Pre-school and Elementary School Education at Comenius University, Bratislava and was supported by the Scientific Grant Agency (VEGA), Slovakia. The Department prepares future pre-school and elementary school teachers. They participate in our project as part of their work towards a diploma. The main objective of the project is to offer theoretical and empirical support for the development of an Early Literacy Intervention Programme for kindergarten children (5-6 years of age). This programme aspires to reflect current educational trends and needs and to offer an alternative to the traditional pre-school educational programme.

Traditional Early Literacy Instruction

What is the traditional approach to teaching literacy in Slovakia? In pre-school educational programmes, the focus is mainly on the development of spoken language – spoken vocabulary and verbal communication. The main goal is to achieve excellent articulation, grammar and syntax in standard Slovak.

The traditional approach to preparing children for reading and writing has focused on teaching basic pre-reading and pre-writing skills, i.e., perceptual-visual, perceptual-motor and phonological skills. The approach can be described as primarily code-oriented. However, this does not offer enough experience in and knowledge about more important aspects of the written language connected with meaning including the functions of writing and self-expression. Language education and literature represent separate elements of the pre-school curriculum.

The precise nature of pre-literacy programmes may vary, depending on the particular kindergarten class, and on teachers themselves. Some teachers offer different perspectives and pay more attention than others to literacy and the written language. However, additions and modifications often lack a unifying theoretical and conceptual framework for early literacy intervention. Some teachers are doing very well, but more or less intuitively, or without any clearly set objectives and goals.

Theoretical Background

Our programme has been particularly influenced by the conceptual framework outlined by Anne van Kleeck (1998). She derived her model of 'pre-literacy domains' from the four-component model of reading process outlined by Adams (1990). According to this model, reading is cognitively controlled by four hypothetical processors. Two of them are connected with the MEANING aspects of print: *context processor* and *meaning processor*, and two are connected with FORM: the *orthographic* processor and *phonological processor.*

The model assumes the natural sequence of stages in literacy development, beginning with understanding the contextual and meaning components of print (initial stage), progressing to the natural and spontaneous discovery of meaning-to-form correspondences, and concluding with the gradual improvement in understanding of form – i.e. the orthography and phonology of the written language. Van Kleeck recommends the presentation of tasks and activities specific to particular aspects of the framework. Her model served as a meaningful and purposive framework for organising educational activities in early literacy intervention.

The Research Project

In our research, several pilot training studies have been implemented. In agreement with the natural developmental stages described by van Kleeck's model, the initial programmes were related to the pre-literacy domains connected with the meaning and function of reading – i.e., the context and meaning processors. They included the following elements:

- A children's literature programme with a strong meaning orientation (reading books of different genres, group discussions, speaking about contextual clues, etc.)
- A development programme that focused on understanding the functions of language and print (selecting books for different aims, journal editing, writing letters and messages, etc.)
- A rich literacy environment designed to promote interest in reading and writing.

In this paper we present some preliminary results describing children's pre-reading and pre-writing skills as they naturally emerged in highly stimulating literacy settings, and compare them with the results for children in a traditional pre-school educational programme. Furthermore, we show that first graders did not perform as well as children in our experiment on some of these tasks, several weeks after school entry. This analysis is concerned with examining continuities between pre-school and formal (school-based) instruction in reading and writing, and the effects of different forms of instruction on children's initial acquisition of literacy.

Two groups of pre-school age children (5 to 6 yrs.) participated in the study described here. Our research looked at their phonological awareness, and their pre-reading and pre-writing strategies.

A literacy group consisted of 30 children who received pre-school education in a highly stimulating literacy environment. The literacy intervention consisted of complex activities and literacy events emphasising the meaning and function of printed materials. This instruction enabled the children to develop hypotheses about literacy by exploiting their experiences with books, journals, literary texts representing different genres, and other sources of printed information. The programme elements described above were implemented.

A control group consisted of 25 children enrolled in a traditional kindergarten programme (see above).

Following the intervention, data were gathered from the two groups. The data included the outcomes of:

- a series of phonological tasks, including rhyme detection and production, syllable segmentation, syllable blending, initial phoneme identification and phoneme segmentation
- letter-knowledge tasks including letter identification
- writing tasks including writing letters, messages, shopping-lists and other lists of objects
- reading tasks including reading written texts and books
- measures of reading behaviour, including choice of library books from the school library, and ability to manipulate books.

In addition to these measures, teachers were asked to complete questionnaires that included questions about each child's home literacy environment, their socio-economic status, and their parents' educational attainment.

Results

Family Background

The data on family background showed that more children from the literacy group originated from lower SES families than children in the traditional kindergarten (control) group. In addition the parents' educational level was higher among children from the control group. This was not surprising, as the control kindergarten group was located in the centre of Bratislava, while the literacy group school was located in a suburb of the city.

Phonological Awareness

Despite their lower SES, children in the literacy group outperformed their counterparts in the kindergarten group on several of the pre-literacy/literacy measures. No significant differences between the groups were observed on the phonological awareness tasks. This result might be interpreted as favouring the literacy group, since children in the control group had not been given explicit training on phonological tasks. Indeed, as indicated earlier, tasks such as blending phonemes, and segmenting words into their sounds, are a regular part of the traditional kindergarten curriculum. Since children in the literacy group did not receive explicit training, it can be inferred that they their phonological skills were developed through their participation in natural literacy activities in a print-rich environment.

Letter Knowledge

The children's knowledge of letters was assessed by three different tasks: letter identification, recognition of letters, and writing known letters. The literacy group performed somewhat better on all three tasks. In addition, several children in this group wrote their letters in correct alphabetical order.

Meaningful Text Writings

The children in both groups were also asked to write some meaningful text such as a shopping-list, a message or a letter to a friend or parent. The children's writings were scored using a scale adapted from Sulzby, Barnart and Hieshima (1989). The scale included four levels of conventional writing (invented-conventional mix, conventional words, sentences, and meaningful texts). A fifth level, representing pre-conventional writings (e.g., drawings, letter-like forms, random letters) was added to accommodate the full range of writing samples produced by the two groups. Children in the literacy group had fewer category 5 pre-conventional writings (35%) than the kindergarten group (64%). On the other hand, children in the literacy group had more conventional writing and demonstrated more advanced strategies. Sixty-five percent of children from the literacy group used some form of conventional writing in comparison with 39% of the control group.

Reading Strategies

The children's reading strategies were evaluated using the *Forms of Reading Scale*, also developed by Sulzby, Barnart and Hieshima (1989). This scale assigns a score between 1 and 7 to reading forms exhibited by the children. The literacy group were found to perform more frequently at the higher levels of the scale (see Table 1).

TABLE 1: PERCENTAGES OF CHILDREN IN THE LITERACY AND KINDERGARTEN (CONTROL) GROUPS DEMONSTRATING SPECIFIED READING BEHAVIOURS

Strategy	Percentages of Children	
	Literacy Group	Control Group
Labelling and Describing	20	24
Dialogue	5	12
Oral Monologue	10	18
Written Monologue	15	12
Naming Letters	10	10
Strategic Reading	5	4
Conventional Reading	35	19

Other differences between the groups were also apparent. Most children from the literacy group performed better when using conventional reading strategy (scale level 7). On a signature task, the surname was used by 15% of literacy group and 4.3% of controls; literate behaviour was more mature in some children from the literacy group (e.g., using the contents or book register, book choice from the library, etc.).

Literacy in Early Elementary School

The focus of a related study was on the literacy competencies of children in the early stages of formal schooling. The performance of first-grade children (at the beginning of school year – 6 weeks after school entry) on the same reading and writing tasks described above was compared with that of the literacy intervention group (i.e., pre-schoolers). The comparison showed that 41% of first-graders failed to write meaningful text. They found the task impossible to accomplish or simply refused to do it. In a follow-up attempt, in which it was explained to them that any form of writing was acceptable, 14% still failed. Furthermore, the proportion of conventional strategies used by first-graders (37% at the second time of asking) was lower than the proportion used by children in the literacy intervention group (65%).

In the task of writing alphabet letters, the performance of the first-graders was again lower. They wrote about 7 letters on average (in comparison to 14 letters written by pre-schoolers). In addition, some letter-number confusions and repeated letters appeared frequently, while no child demonstrated knowledge of alphabetical order.

The above findings suggest that, under the influence of formal reading/writing instruction – perhaps in their efforts to avoid failure – children may abandon their previously developed literacy competencies, and are limited to the skills in which they are formally trained at school.

Conclusion

The results of the our studies confirm the considerable literacy potential of pre-school age children in general, in both educational settings. The comparison of the two groups of children from different pre-school educational programmes has shown the higher the rate of the more advanced reading-writing strategies among children from kindergarten with the Early Literacy Intervention Programme. This meaning- and function-oriented intervention resulted in spontaneous discoveries of meaning-to-print relations as well as in the general improvement of orthographic and phonological skills, as manifested in children's writings.

The literacy competencies of pre-school age children could be significantly enhanced by the intervention, and the provision of a rich literacy environment across all curriculum areas.

On the other hand, the analysis of the performance of first-graders on a similar set of reading/writing tasks suggests that school practices in traditional Slovak schools may not be tied up with and may not allow for continuity in the development of pre-school literacy achievements. On the contrary, they seem to ignore or even suppress the literacy competencies acquired by the child before formal schooling begins.

REFERENCES

Adams, M. (1990). *Beginning to read: Thinking and learning about print.* Cambridge, MA: MIT Press.

Sulzby, E., Barnart, J., & Hieshima, J. (1989). Forms of writing and rereading from writing: A preliminary report. In J. Mason (Ed.), *Reading-writing connections* (pp. 31-63). Boston, MA: Allyn & Bacon.

van Kleeck, A. (1998). Preliteracy domains and stages: Laying the foundation for beginning reading. *Journal of Childhood Communication Development, 20*(1), 33-51.

14 Issues in Family Literacy Programmes in Inner City Communities

Jim Anderson, Suzanne Smith, John Shapiro and Fiona Morrison, Canada

Nearly two decades after the publication of Denny Taylor's *Family Literacy* that called attention to the family as a rich context for early literacy development, much has changed. Our understanding of family life has shifted, as has our understanding of literacy. In this article, we describe emerging issues in a family literacy programme (Parents As Literacy Supporters-PALS) currently running in two inner city areas in Western Canada. We are learning the importance of seeing literacy as a social practice that is linked to families' languages, cultures and daily lives. We are also learning to see schools as contexts for social literacies that interact in complex and interesting ways with families and communities.

Accompanying the interest in family literacy engendered by the publication of Taylor's (1983) research has come a proliferation of family literacy programmes. However, there has been considerable criticism of such programmes in that many are aimed at immigrant or poor families and are based on deficit notions of families (e.g., Auerbach, 1995; Tett & Crowther, 1998). Implicit in many family literacy programmes, critics argue, are assumptions that such families don't engage their children in literacy or they don't engage them in enough literacy or they don't engage them in the 'right kinds' of literacy. These assumptions exist even though ethnographic research (e.g., Heath, 1983; Hirst, 1998; Taylor & Dorsey-Gaines, 1988) has clearly shown that literacy events and practices are embedded in the lived experiences of non-mainstream families, though they often differ from the literacy occurring in middle class homes. Furthermore, literacy is increasingly seen not just as a set of linguistic and cognitive skills but as complex social practice (Barton, Hamilton & Ivanic, 2000). That is, there is considerable variation in literacy practices, the meanings ascribed to literacy and the way in which literacy is mediated across and within cultural groups (Clay, 1993).

The PALS Programme

Thus it is a challenge for those working in family literacy programmes to design programmes that respect and build on the literacy already occurring in the homes of families in ways that are contextually appropriate. One such programme is Parents As Literacy Supporters (PALS), developed by Anderson & Morrison (2000) whose major aim is to support parents of kindergarteners (4 and 5 year olds) as they work with their children at home. As a starting point, the developers of PALS met with parents and had them identify that which they wanted to learn. Sessions focus on topics such as learning the alphabet, early mathematics development, learning to write, environmental print and reading with children. Each session begins with the families, facilitators and teachers sharing a meal together. Then, the facilitator and the parents spend about one-half hour discussing the topic (e.g. early writing) that is the focus of the session while the children go to their classroom(s). Parents, children and teachers then spend an hour in the classroom(s) at a number of literacy centres, each containing a different activity reflecting the topic of the day. Each session concludes with the parents debriefing what they have observed about their children. They are presented with a book, and sometimes other materials and resources. About a third of the 15 biweekly, two-hour sessions are kept 'open' so that topics and issues that parents identify can be addressed. For example, the parents in one school wanted to learn more about computers and learning to read and write, while in another school parents wanted a session devoted to children and television. Books, art materials such as crayons, glue and scissors, and writing materials such as pencils, paper and markers are provided. Different possibilities for using these materials are discussed; however, great care is taken to honour and value that which parents do with their children and for example, no effort is made to teach parents to read to their children in particular or prescribed ways.

PALS has been in operation for two years in four inner city schools in two school districts – one urban, the other suburban. In the schools in the urban area, nearly all the parents are new immigrants. Most are not proficient in English, many are underemployed, working in minimum-wage service jobs that severely restrict their budgets and the time they have to participate in school and community activities. Most of the suburban school parents are native English speakers, many are single parents and again, many are unemployed, underemployed or work in minimum-wage jobs.

Within this context then, we have been documenting through field notes, journals and interviews, the issues that arise as we have implemented PALS. Several themes have emerged, including attendance and patterns of participation, child-care and support, language and translation, and availability of appropriate storybooks in the families' home languages. Although these themes intersect, each is described separately below.

Attendance and Participation

To ensure that as many parents as possible are able to attend sessions, we invite parents and teachers to suggest the most practical time to schedule them. We then develop a schedule keeping meeting time consistent (e.g. 9-11:00 Thursday morning, bi-weekly) and distribute it at the initial meeting. An underlying assumption is that if the programme is meeting the needs of the parents, they will attend when they can but that circumstances will sometimes prevent them from attending. It is here that attendance is linked to people's home and work lives and the unstable nature of low-income work.

Thus if parents are registered in PALS, we continue to provide them with materials for sessions that they were unable to attend. This can lead to tensions in that some parents and teachers have argued that parents do not derive the full benefits of the programme if they are not in attendance and they should not receive the books and other resources we provide. On the other hand, other parents have argued that some parents are unable to attend any of the sessions because they are working and that these parents (and their children) are being penalised. One suggestion (from one group of parents) that we are exploring is that parents from the different linguistic groups who are able to attend sessions assume responsibility for providing the materials and resources and the information from the various sessions to parents who are unable to attend.

Childcare and Support

Many of the parents with whom we work have younger children, including infants. Since many of them are new immigrants, they do not have extended family or a social network to call upon for support. Because of funding limitations, the degree of childcare we have been able to provide has varied from school to school. However, it has become apparent that providing adequate childcare is important for the success of the programme. One possibility that was tried in one school, with considerable success, was to have older students who need practice reading easier material read storybooks with younger children (with appropriate supervision and support). However, there are legal issues here and it seems to us that funding for quality childcare needs to be an integral part of family literacy programmes, as this issue also relates to attendance. One idea that has been brought forward is to hire and train parents or older youth in the community, providing extra income and opportunities for networking for underemployed people. In this way, programmes such as PALS can contribute to community development by developing relationships between parents and teachers, responding to local needs and promoting a sustainable project that parents and teachers can take over, which is a long term goal.

Language and Translation

In one of the schools in which we work, parents represent more than a dozen linguistic groups and most of them are only beginning to learn English. Fortunately, through the collaboration of the school district, we were able to provide simultaneous translation at most of the sessions in Mandarin and Vietnamese, two of the larger linguistic groups. In another school, one of the teachers was able to provide translation in Cantonese. However, speakers of other languages were often left with no support and their struggle (and frustration) to make sense of what was happening around them was palpable. Furthermore, because of funding limitations, very little of the print material we provided could be translated from English. While we have attempted to have parent volunteers help in this regard, it should be remembered that many of these parents work full-time or attend ESL classes while raising several children and simply do not have the time to volunteer for this task. Furthermore, many do not have sufficient facility in English to be able to translate into another language. In one school where teachers spoke Cantonese and other languages shared by the families, there was more active participation, indicating the importance of recruiting teachers who know the languages and cultures of the school community. However, teachers' attitudes towards parents, and their willingness to engage with them, to share their stories, and to see their own roles in literacy development as extending beyond the classroom walls, are equally important to the success of the programme.

Appropriate Books/Texts

As we indicated earlier, at the end of each PALS session, parents are provided a storybook to bring home and share with their children. Because of budget limitations, the prohibitive costs of bilingual books, and the fact that children's books are simply unattainable in many of the home languages of the parents, we have only been able to provide books written in English, despite the fact that many parents do not feel confident reading in that language. While we are sensitive to the cultural appropriateness of the books we select, and brainstorm with parents various ways that they might share the books with their children (e.g., telling a story based on the illustrations, etc.), we still see this as problematic. For example, Janes and Kermani (2001) found that the parents in their family literacy project – recent immigrants to the United States from Central America – had great difficulty sharing popular children's books with their children and the shared reading was a tension-filled affair. However, when the parents were provided with texts written in Spanish and reflecting the moralistic, didactic genre with which they were familiar, the shared reading became a pleasurable event. Such ideas are an impetus for us to learn ways to support diverse languages and literacies in school and in this regard, we are beginning to work with a variety of strategies.

Conclusion

In this article, we have raised a number of issues with which we contend as we work with families in quite diverse contexts. While we have experienced considerable success with PALS and it has been extremely well received by parents and educators (Anderson, Morrison, Shapiro & Smythe, 2001), we are convinced that it is important for those who work in family literacy programmes to raise and share with others, the issues with which we grapple.

We recognise that the issues we raise in this article might be specific to the particular contexts in which we work. We see family literacy within a larger, community development framework and thus, we believe that many issues and problems must be addressed at the local level. However, we sense that policy-makers and those responsible for funding, see family literacy programmes as inexpensive ways to improve literacy-learning and thus are prone to download responsibilities that communities simply cannot meet. Some of the issues that we have raised (e.g., translation, appropriate books) could be resolved if we could access additional financial resources. While we believe that all family literacy programmes need adequate funding, some contexts will require additional support because of unique circumstances. Furthermore, we sense that some policy-makers and funding agencies believe that generic family literacy programmes can be imported into communities without regard for the makeup of these communities. However, we see communities as each presenting particular issues and believe that family literacy programmes must be organic and flexible to meet their needs.

While family literacy programmes have often been oversold in terms of helping people develop their literacy potential, we believe our work demonstrates that culturally-sensitive programmes can make a difference. However, this potential will not be realized unless all of us involved in family literacy own up to and deal with issues, no matter how challenging, or disturbing, these are.

REFERENCES

Anderson, J., Morrison, F., Shapiro, J. & Smythe, S. (2001, May). *Multiple perspectives on a collaborative family literacy programme: Parents, practitioners, and researchers* . Paper presented at the annual conference of the Canadian Society for the Study of Education, Quebec City, Canada.

Anderson, J. & Morrison, F. (2000). *Parents As Literacy Supporters (PALS): A culturally responsive family literacy programme*. Langley, BC: Langley School District.

Auerbach, E. (1995). Deconstructing the discourse of strengths in family literacy. *Journal of Reading Behaviour, 27,* 643-61.

Barton, D., Hamilton, M., & Ivanic, R. (2000). *Situated literacies: Reading and writing in context.* London: Routledge.

Clay, M. (1993) Always a learner: A fable. *Reading Today, 3* (10), 3

Heath, S. B. (1983). *Ways with words.* New York: Cambridge University Press.

Hirst, K. (1998). Pre-school literacy experiences of children in Punjabi-, Urdu- and Gujerati-speaking families in England. *British Educational Research Journal, 24,* 415-429.

Janes, H. & Kermani, H. (2001). Caregivers' story-reading to young children in family literacy programmes: Pleasure or punishment? *Journal of Adolescent and Adult Literacy, 44,* 458-446.

Taylor, D. (1983). *Family literacy: Young children learning to read and write.* Exeter, NH: Heinemann.

Taylor, D. & Dorsey-Gaines, C. (1988). *Growing up literate: Learning from inner city families.* Portsmouth, NH: Heinemann.

Tett, L., & Crowther, J. (1998). Families at a disadvantage: Class, culture and literacies. *British Educational Research Journal, 24,* 449-460.

15 Family Literacy Programmes: The Whole is More than the Sum of its Parts

William T. Fagan, Canada

The two main components in understanding a family literacy programme are content/format and participants. Both of these suggest that a programme is more than the sum of its parts. Content is not bits and pieces but must be interwoven in some way into an integrated whole. Likewise, participants include a range of people: the child, the parent, the facilitator of the parent, and the author/source which provided the necessary expertise for the facilitator. Evaluating the success of a family literacy programme must take into account each of these components.

Content and Format

PRINTS (Parents' Roles Interacting with Teacher Support) (Fagan & Cronin, 1998), a family literacy programme, is based on a model that was developed by Hannon and Nutbrown (1996). It is comprehensive or holistic in nature and is based around five STEPS or contexts in which parents can take advantage of literacy opportunities to foster their children's literacy development: talk/oral language, play, books and book sharing, environmental print, and scribbling, drawing, writing. Within each of these STEPS, a parent/caregiver may take five ROLES: providing opportunity for sharing with children, providing recognition or positive feedback, interacting in effective ways, modelling literacy, and setting guidelines. Parent input helps the facilitator develop the concepts or meaning for each STEP. The parents may learn 40 activities across the different STEPS, many of them through hands-on or direct learning. These activities cover a wide range of social and cognitive skills – from exposing children to nursery rhymes and rhythm, to providing a structure for storytelling, to observing literacy in action, to modelling concepts, to providing support for writing. The programme is structured yet flexible. There is a set format for each session but there is provision for parent input. Parents help develop the key concept underlying each step; they share the literacy experiences of their children. They have opportunities to discuss how activities may be best implemented with their children and may suggest modifications in light of their children's age and maturity. There is time for input and checkpoints on one's learning. The programme was first developed for low-income parents and many of the activities are cost-effective, being constructed from bristol board, sales flyers, magazines, and newspapers. At the start of the programme, parents are given a kit of items such as glue, crayons, scissors, etc. At the end of each session a small child's book is given to each parent for the child. The training sessions are conducted with the parents, who in turn engage their children in the literacy activities and practices with which they become familiar. Support for the programme/content is inferred through the responses of parents as reported below.

Transfer of Learning

The second component in family literacy programmes that must be considered in determining their success includes the various participants. The impact of a parent interacting with a child in various activities cannot be isolated from the training which the parent received from a family literacy facilitator. Transfer of learning across different participants can be likened to a chain, and in the case of the old adage about chains, the chain is only as strong as its weakest link. Therefore, if by chance, parents had received less than adequate preparation in how to best facilitate literacy activities with their children, it is unlikely they would provide their children with the best literacy development experiences. The parents of children who had very high or low scores on literacy tasks were the subjects of a study to determine how these parents differed.

Response Categories

The parents' responses were grouped into categories and are described below.

Experiencing a Change in Attitude/Insight

Parents realised that their insights and attitudes towards early literacy development had changed, or had been reinforced. Now they knew what they knew about fostering early literacy development. For some parents, it was an 'eye-opener'; they had just never thought in this way, but once introduced to information and possibilities, they immediately saw that it made sense, that it was 'common sense'. Some couldn't believe that they had not 'figured this out' on their own. The single biggest impact was that parents became aware that children were never too young to engage in learning activities. Many parents had been under the impression that age 4 was too young to engage children in literacy learning activities, even in a fun or play-like manner. They became aware that a lot of learning can occur in fun and play activities. 'Children learn more quickly and learn more if they enjoy what they do'. 'I had bought these alphabet cards and tried to teach Karla the letters. But she wouldn't pay attention. Then when I made the Alphabet House (A PRINTS activity), all she wanted was to learn her letters – and she did'. They learned how important it was not to push children but 'to be patient and let the child take the lead'. They became more observant of what children did, for example turning the pages of a book in the right direction.

Awareness of Conditions for Use

Many of the school-driven family literacy programmes consist of the school sending home books to be read which are then accounted for by keeping a tally of some sort. Parents often see this as 'something to get done' and try and do it as soon as they can, or wait until the last minute and are then reminded by the child who is aware of the deadline for getting information back to the teacher. Influenced by the PRINTS Programme, parents came to realise that 'all times are learning times'. What they did was not driven by the expectations of someone else, nor their being required to report to someone else, but on their understanding that sharing and interaction times were good for the child and, depending on the activity, there was a variety of venues in which learning could take place. Perhaps the most poignant statement exemplifying this from one parent was, 'I never realised that outside my door was a learning field'. Parents talked about such activities as putting a carton/tin on the counter that may be used as part of supper and using this as a learning experience for recognising labels, or walking down the street with their child and talking about the print on the bus stop or other display, or of playing a guessing game such as 'I Spy' or reciting a nursery rhyme as they rode on the bus. The child's life space became the focus for learning, not a particular activity, such as reading a book or playing a word game. The latter took their meaning from the former and not vice versa.

Developing a Sense of Ownership

Much has been written about participants having a sense of ownership of the activities they participate in. Developing a sense of ownership is not always that easy, however. It involves a willingness and opportunity on the part of the initial owner to transfer that responsibility, and a willingness on the part of participants to accept it. Ownership was not used to mean 'possession' and 'control'. Instead, there was a sense of respect for oneself and a respect of others towards them. In other words, the parents were trusted; they were not told what to do and were not accountable to others for doing it. This, of course, led to positive self-concept development, self-esteem, and self-efficacy. Allied to this was a feeling of independence. When you are trusted, respected, feel good about yourself and what you are doing, there is a sense of independence – of 'yes, I can do it'.

Understanding the Organisation and Structure of the Programme

Parents who understood the larger framework of STEPS and ROLES, were much more likely to interact with their children in a more insightful, supportive way, were likely to draw on related materials and experiences in moving the experience to conclusion, and were in more control in monitoring what a successful literacy experience would look like. Parents without this greater understanding saw the programme not as a programme but as a 'lot of activities'. These were then used with the children in a hit or miss manner. Sometimes it just happened they provided a meaningful experience in which there was closure to the children's learning; other times, it was merely being involved without strategy.

Knowing How to Access and Utilise Materials and Resources

Many of the communities/centres in which the programme operated did not have access to school or public libraries. The participants were often on low-income (social assistance) and did not have much money to purchase literacy materials. In one sense their actions contradicted the silk purse-sow's ear expression. The programme focusses on utilising low-cost materials, so that many word games, activities, prompts, cues, models, came from sales flyers, magazines, newspaper, wrappers, etc. A lot depended on the parents' creativity and ingenuity. As one parent exclaimed on one occasion, 'I will never throw away a flyer again'. Supplied with a kit of bristol board, glue, scotch tape, etc., they were able to make a vast array of interesting literacy activities. Parents bringing home materials (books or self-constructed activities) from the programme became the connecting point between the programme and children. The word PRINTS became a household word with the young children, and almost all parents told of their children asking as soon as they got home, 'What did you bring from PRINTS?'

Developing Sensitivity to Children's Characteristics and Needs

The PRINTS Programme provides opportunity for parents to share experiences in their own and their children's lives. Many parents felt that they were alone in facing a particular problem or situation with regard to their children's learning. They felt that they were involved in a situation that was unique to them, and they felt they were not doing a very good job. Some children were developing slower than expected, were not interested in literacy-type activities, were inattentive, and did not seem to have very much knowledge about basic literacy/learning tasks. As parents later said, they felt ashamed that their children were not learning well. They had felt that they were inadequate as parents. Then as parents shared, the world of their children broadened. They saw their children not as isolates, but as members of a class exemplifying 'children-ness' characteristics. They were no longer ashamed, upset or frustrated. They had a broader perspective on children and learning and often benefited from suggestions that other parents made on how to approach this situation. They were more confident and empowered to address the situation.

Conclusion

The whole is more than the sum of its parts! Effective family literacy programmes are not gimmicks. They must be well planned and well thought-through frameworks of learning and experiences which change or reinforce positive attitudes about children and literacy learning, are applicable to all aspects of a child's life, provide parents with a sense of ownership, inform parents how to access and utilise materials and resources, and encourage sensitivity to children's characteristics and needs. Family literacy programmes are not just about one group of participants. They are about all the participants who are involved at different points along the chain of learning. To understand whether a family literacy programme works is to understand how one group of participants impacts on another. Knowing that the whole of a family literacy programme is more than the sum of its parts and knowing the participants and factors that make up the whole, gives coordinators and parent facilitators a better understanding of how to capitalise on a holistic approach in facilitating and evaluating family literacy programmes.

REFERENCES

Fagan, W.T., & Cronin, M. C. (1998). *Growing into literacy: PRINTS Programme (Parents' Roles Interacting with Teacher Support).* St. John's, NF: Memorial University Printing Services.

Hannon, P., & Nutbrown, C. (April, 1996). *Teachers' use of theoretical framework for preschool intervention with parents.* Paper presented at the American Education Research Association Annual Meeting, New York.

Thomas, A., & Skage, S. (1998). Overview of perspectives on family literacy: Research and practice. In A. Thomas (Ed.), *Family literacy in Canada: Profiles of effective practices* (pp. 5-24). Welland, ON: Soleil.

SECTION 5

Libraries and Literacy

16   The Classics of Literature and the Library

Jadwiga Kolodziejska, Poland

The Social Functions of Libraries

Public libraries are institutions born during the Enlightenment era. 'Enlightenment', Piotr S. Wandycz wrote, 'meant the spreading of intellectual and scientific achievements of the 17th century such as the attainments of Locke, Descartes, or Newton [...] the saying *sapere aude* (have the courage to be wise) became a motto, while the belief in progress became the foundation of that era [...]. For its advocates, spreading light and education was a kind of crusade against prejudice, irrational tradition, obscurantism, and suppression which they saw in the past.'[1] The individual's right to operate in the economic sphere, in politics and culture became one of the most prominent postulates of the time and it gave basis for the French and American revolutions and, to some extent, also for the 1794 Tadeusz Koœciuszko insurrection in Poland, whose leader, in his *Polaniec Proclamation*, promised personal freedom and liberation from drudgery to every peasant who joined his ranks. The Enlightenment-style model of public library is the closest to the Polish experience and it allows communication between generations to carry the humanistic and scientific message. In this model, the knowledge of the past was promoted by fiction, primarily the romantic literature of the uprisings. This was a source of hope for many people. It was what guided the development of minds over several generations. And little effort was needed to make fiction and basic science literature popular. The public library, having received a mandate to preserve continuity of awareness of the past and to maintain the patriotic spirit, could do so while using a minimum of material resources: modest rooms, bookshelves, a catalogue, and a lady-librarian working there as a volunteer or receiving a rather small salary.

The cultural elite which was opening education-oriented libraries in the second half of the 19th century tried to attract peasants, artisans, and workers to participation in the national culture. The structure of Polish society at that time, when the peasants were the largest group (70% of the population) did not make the task easier, among other reasons, because of the specific regime of farm work. One who wants to spend time on reading must have some free time. The Polish village did not know the concept of free time until World War I. Villagers kept working from sunrise to sunset.

Everyone, even five-year olds, had to work, grazing cattle, sheep, and geese. Labour was the foundation of upbringing in peasant families. Free time was part of the gentry culture. Only after Poland had gained independence in 1918, did the state introduce the obligation to go to primary school, which entailed doing homework and reading books. Although this changed the situation, it did not erase the differences between urban and rural life.[2] All the contemporary studies show that book-reading was part of the urban rather than rural culture. It was a continuation of the reading tradition dating back to the 19th century and associated mainly with the gentry and landowners. Reading at that time was a symbol of belonging to the higher culture. It carried, especially among women, an interest in French literature (romance, novels about upper class life) read in the original language or in translation, while Polish authors were preferred when reading about important national matters, tradition, memoirs, that is, subjects which educated people had to be versed in. It is certainly a historical paradox that the communist state, having imposed censorship, supported the readership of the classics of literature that used to belong to the higher culture. The school was the number one institution where this literature was considered as obligatory. The coming generations received the images of the Polish character, patriotism, history, national heroes, the value of work and social justice through literary texts. Publishers and libraries were taking part in this process. What the publishers produced ended up in the hands of school students and on library shelves. Since the school students and other young people used public libraries, their reading choice was usually convergent with the contents of the school curricula.

Obviously, children were also reading entertaining books, adventure stories, and travel reports, but the choice of these was not very rich. The school reading matter was the same as books offered by the libraries. So the most-popular titles belonged to Polish literature: Józef I. Kraszewski, Henryk Sienkiewicz, Boleslaw Prus, Eliza Orzeszkowa, Stefan Zeromski, Adam Mickiewicz, Juliusz Slowacki, Gabriela Zapolska, Wiktor Gasiorowski, Wladyslaw Orkan. Few books by foreign authors could compete with these in terms of popularity: those most frequently selected were written by Ernest Hemingway, John Steinbeck, Mikhail Sholokhov, and, among the older ones, Jack London, Alexander Dumas, and Joseph Conrad. Seventy percent of books borrowed from village libraries in 1969 were written by Polish authors, and 30% by foreign authors.[3]

The year 1989 opened a time of dramatic changes in Poland's political, economic, and cultural system. This change covered all that is related to the production and circulation of books. Censorship was abolished, the free market ruled the production of books, the system of purchasing new publications for public libraries was de-centralised. The reader was offered more choice of reading material – s/he could now buy or borrow from a library. But it soon became obvious that book prices posed a new barrier. This was a blow not only to individual readers, especially the now worse-off intelligentsia, but also to public libraries. The purchase rate in 1999 was 5.6 books per 100 population, the lowest figure during the last decade of the century. According to a standard adopted by the Ministry of Culture and Art in 1982, public libraries should buy 18 new books per 100 population. The standard recommended by the International Federation of Library Associations is 30 new books per 100 population.

After 1989, the book market was flooded with entertainment publications, all sorts of sensational materials, detective stories, science fiction, romance, etc., chiefly written by American authors. Books published by Harlequin became extremely popular in the early 1990s. As reading researchers suspected, the temporary fascination with popular (mass) literature which was unavailable to the Polish reader for five decades before, turned out to be a short-lived phenomenon, although it had an influence on publishing programmes designed to meet the readers' preferences. Under the competitive conditions of a free market, publishers must follow the preferences of potential book buyers, otherwise they could go out of business. The readers' choice has recently moved clearly towards non-fiction. As recently as 1994, 29% of Polish people declared an interest in buying reference books like encyclopaediae, educational and professional types of book; this rate grew to 44% by 2000. At the same time, the interest in romance-type fiction dropped from 31% to 12%.[4]

Little has remained of the above-mentioned classics of the 1960s and of the predominat interest in classical literature. Comparative studies in 1992, 1994, and 1996 show that only a few titles have kept their position, among them, *The Trilogy*, *Quo Vadis* and *The Teutonic Knights* by Henryk Sienkiewicz, *Pan Tadeusz* by Adam Mickiewicz, *On the Neman* by Eliza Orzeszkowa, and *The Doll* by Boleslaw Prus.[5] These are all school reading-matter which stood the test of time and kept a stable position in the school curricula. It is hard to predict now whether these titles will continue to enjoy the status of the inter-generation literary classics and whether the symbols they carry will be shared by all of society.

There is no doubt that movies, video tapes, all sorts of summarised novels called *bryk* in Poland, have replaced book reading by students these days. Movies based on famous classical novels, such as *Quo Vadis, With Fire and Sword, The Deluge*, and *The Teutonic Knights* by Henryk Sienkiewicz, *The Pharaoh* by Boleslaw Prus, and *Pan Tadeusz* by Adam Mickiewicz cause young people absorb the messages of these novels in a superficial way, involving no reflection. They memorise the main points of the plot, being unaware of the broad historical and social context, and of virtues presented in these books, such as justice, compassion, mercy, and sensitivity to those wronged – virtues so typical of the 19th century novel. The younger generation finds it increasingly difficult to understand the old customs, philanthropy, social and religious conflicts, medical treatment methods, attitudes towards labour, etc., not to mention the names of plants, animals, garments and legislation. Even school teachers sometimes have problems with these. So, there is little wonder that many writers and columnists say that book reading will never predominate again, and that we should accept the fact that it will be an activity practiced by a minority, just as it was in the 19th century.

Can public libraries play an inspiring role in raising interest in good, classical literature in these circumstances? There is no clear answer to this question. An important factor is that the public, which uses libraries, is also in a state of flux. Poland has 9,046 public libraries used by 7,332,0000 readers, that is, 19% of the Polish population. Nearly 60% of library users are students. Libraries provide for these readers a variety of literary and poetry competitions, exhibitions, concerts and theatrical performances. Young people take part in them. They write poems, try to write stories, paint, draw, and attend theatrical presentations. Libraries do a lot to maintain and strengthen this interest. They find sponsors to finance publishing of young writers' poetry, and organise concerts and exhibitions. About 250,000 such events were held across Poland in 1999. Considering the financial hardship troubling the libraries, this is a real success. The cultural activity of libraries is especially valuable in rural communities. In many villages a public library is the only institution which offers access to good literature and art.

The cultural differences between town and village are obvious. City dwellers have an incomparably easier access to cultural institutions: libraries, theatres, concert halls, art galleries, and museums. There is no way theatres or art galleries could be opened in villages. This is impossible even in the richest countries. But it is possible to spread the country's cultural values, including the classics of literature, by using public libraries as a resource. The main aim of this activity should be a bridging of the social and geographical gap, after which the fact that someone comes from a village or a small town is no longer the measure of participation in culture and the fact of being born to a farming or worker family no longer determines the destinies of an individual in a negative sense. Building a democratic and open society should lead to the elimination of differences in social status or, at least, it should prevent it from becoming hereditary. This is, however, one of the most difficult tasks to be accomplished by education and cultural policy on a local, nationwide and, perhaps also a European scale.

It is a truism to say that literature shows us the world with its problems, that it encourages us to intellectual effort, to ask questions about our own existence, and that, by referring to the past, it helps us to understand the destinies of the nation and the community we are living in. Television or the Internet cannot replace literature in producing this effect. The new information technologies help us to research; they increase the possibilities of accessing sources, thus changing the procedures involved in using library services. The reader increasingly pops into a library just to look something up on a map, to consult a dictionary or an encyclopaedia, to get something out of a database, or find a bibliography list. But even the most advanced technology will never help us answer the fundamental question about our goals and about the directions we are heading in. Do we want to be more tolerant in ourselves, more sensitive to the destiny of those wronged, ailing, and weak, or do we want to treat them as ones people have failed?

Let us be optimistic anyway. All is not lost. In 2000, 50% of Poles reached for a book, 41% bought one or more than one. Reading is not disappearing from the cultural landscape of my country and, although it is not a prestigious distinctive factor, as Grazyna Straus puts it, the book continues to represent some value for many Polish people.[6]

Architects of the Classics of Literature

What are the classics of literature and why are they important? In simple words, classics are works about which members of some specific social group should know something. Andrzej Szpociński contends that this knowledge epitomises the ideas, values, and behavioural patterns of the group, and is the symbol of the group itself.[7] This applies not only to the symbols associated with national culture but also to the cultural classics-based standard of the better-educated social groups, at least at the level of secondary general education schools. In Europe, these classics include certain literary masterpieces and phrases by William Shakespeare ('To be or not to be'), Moliére ('Give him a big glass of clean water') and others. The Polish classic pieces, for instance, include some writings and sayings by Stanislaw Wyspiañski (How is politics? Do the Chinese fight well?) and others by Juliusz Slowacki, Cyprian Kamil Norwid and, above all, Adam Mickiewicz. The fact that people often say 'a box with Pandora' instead of 'Pandora's box' definitely reveals their poor general education and little knowledge of ancient Greek culture. As few as a dozen years ago, such a slip of the tongue would have raised strong comments but today hardly anyone even notices it. No one in a 60-strong group of students in an arts department could tell why saying 'a box with Pandora' was wrong.

This situation results from the fact that knowledge of classical literature is no longer a distinguishing factor proving membership of an elite group. It has become a private and personal matter. And this certainly results from the changes that have taken place in the structure of the Polish nation. Throughout the 19th century, it was the intelligentsia who evaluated literary works: teachers, educators and social activists, literary reviewers working for various magazines, Roman Catholic and Protestant clergy. Their opinions were often geared to didactic ends and were supposed to convince the peasant, worker, and artisan readers about benefits they could get from reading the classics. A high illiteracy rate (in some Polish regions reaching 70%) was a natural barrier to their efforts. But there is no doubt that the architects of the literary canon were convinced about their patron-like mission among the uneducated social layers and about their ability to make a value judgement of literary work.

The widespread provision of primary and secondary education and the opening of Polish universities after re-gaining independence in 1918 changed the principles of building the classics of literature. Although the intelligentsia continued to play the leading role, now the institutions such as universities, Polish philological departments, literary periodicals, writers' associations, book sellers and publishers, and librarians began to have a decisive voice concerning the selection of books. Back in the 1930s, the catalogue *Library Books* was published on the initiative of the Association of Polish Librarians. The catalogue comprised a selection of the most valuable Polish and foreign fiction, which was recommended to libraries. It was an attempt made by book professionals to promote top-class literature.

Such literature, which we can call classical literature, was and continues to be considered as a tool helping to achieve educational, patriotic, religious, and moral goals. It influences the collective memory through the contents of the individual titles and, consequently, it influences the symbols which are common in the national identity. This is why various institutions are trying to influence or co-decide access to the classics. From 1945 to 1989, the Polish state and its agencies had a monopoly in making decisions concerning the production and distribution of books. This system involved the relevant organs of the communist party (The Polish United Worker's Party) and state administration (ministries of education and culture), with the Main Office for the Control of Press and Shows playing a key role, publishing houses (most of them state-owned), schools, libraries, clubs, cultural centres, etc. The aim of this publishing policy, which promoted some titles and banned others, was to indoctrinate people with the spirit of Marxist ideology.

This system also fluctuated during its five decades according to the intensity of political presence in the sphere of education and culture.[8] The authorities used to design school curricula, with sections addressing the knowledge of literature, in a way that served the idea of education in the spirit of scientific world outlook, particularly the attainments of the dialectic and historic materialism, and the programme of building 'socialist morality.' In her studies on the different phases of shaping the 'desired' attitudes, Zofia Zasacka analysed four patterns of patriotism present in literary texts included in the textbooks for Polish language classes. In line with the intensity of totalitarianism in public life, the list of titles included in the literary canon was also changing together with changes in the list of national heroes presented in those books and promoted by the school.[9]

This publishing policy and corresponding school curricula were substantially supported by the physical environment, especially in towns, which were getting a new appearance, severed from that of pre-war Poland. This included new names of streets, squares, parks, schools, and universities. Ceremonies marking national anniversaries and holidays were changed too. The national day of May 3, which was particularly cherished by the Polish people, was erased from the calendar.

In fact, the only national hero who survived all the communist era was Tadeusz Koœciuszko. His contributions to the nation (and also to the liberty of the United States) in relation to progress and social democratisation could by no means be challenged even by communists.

This elaborate system, whose intention was to re-arrange the national sense of identity, especially in relation to the past, had one important deficiency: it overlooked the message and knowledge passed within the family with the support of the Roman Catholic Church. The removal of all literature about the 1944 Warsaw Uprising from school curricula stood in glaring contradiction to the direct experience of a whole generation of Varsovians who had fought on barricades and then told their children not only about their battles but also about the related books, songs, poems, etc. (some published in the early post-war years), and showed them photographs and other memorabilia (white-and-red ribbons, helmets, parts of the uniforms, etc.). This was, of course, taking place only within certain social groups, mostly within the intelligentsia and those who were lucky to preserve their memorabilia from the destruction of war. But most home libraries, family photo albums, pieces of art, paintings, sculptures, correspondence, and all that could serve as a source of historical knowledge, which is normally absorbed during the natural contacts between generations, were lost for ever. And so were good manners, and with the good manners the specific Polish lifestyle was gone too.

The classics of literature were a factor shaping the Polish language. The world 'Polish' is often used nowadays to describe the literary language as opposed to the colloquial language or regional dialects. A glance is enough to notice that major changes have also taken place in the Polish language spoken today by school and university students, politicians, and representatives of various occupational groups. Their accent, intonation, and grammar are all permanently changing. Vocabulary and the pool of concepts are shrinking, the place of the abundant variety of adjectives is now taken by just two words describing all things as 'fine' or 'super'. This newspeak is most strongly promoted by TV ads, according to which ice-cream is no longer delightful; it is 'super'. And children love to watch TV advertisements. Politicians dominating newspaper front-pages often find it difficult to construct one correct Polish sentence. Sometimes they begin with the words which belong to the middle of the sentence, then confuse subject with predicate, and all of them desperately try to speak as fast as possible, which results in a chaotic noise hardly similar to correct Polish pronunciation.

Correct Polish language was always an indicator of the success of a school. A school developed the literary language in its students, using the classics of literature as a tool. Today, the school seems to be close to surrender in the face of the students' reluctance to read classical books, which are somewhat more difficult than other literature. By its tolerance for movies, summaries and abstracts being used by students instead of reading the novels, the school gives up its influence on building the cultural community and on developing the Polish language. It may well turn out in the near future, that the nation will no longer be able to communicate and this may lead to irreversible consequences. Studies on the range of books read, reading frequency, organisation of libraries, and the effectiveness of school education allow an insight into the social trends going on today and suggest prevention measures which can be undertaken according to our resources, to counteract the cultural disintegration, not only in Poland, but in many other counbtries as well.

NOTES

1. P. S. Wandycz, *The price of freedom. The history of central and eastern Europe from middle ages to present day'.* (*Cena wolnoœci. Historia Europy œrodkowo-wschodniej od œredniowiecza do wspólczesnoœci*). Cracow 1995, p. 161.
2. Stanislaw Siekierski, *Polish reader of the 20th century* (*Czytania Polaków w XX wieku*), Warsaw 2000.
3. *Rural Youth Reading.* (*Czytelnictwo mlodziezy wiejskiej*) Warsaw 1971, pp. 187-188.
4. Grazyna Straus, *A stable non-reading* (*Stabilne nieczytanie*) Notes Wydawniczy 2001 No. 3/4.
5. Grazyna Straus, Katarzyna Wolff. *The interest in books among Polish people in 1996* (*Zainteresowanie ksiqzkq w spoleczeñstwie polskim w 1996 r.*) Warsaw 1998, p. 54.
6. Grazyna Straus, *Stable non-reading* (*Stabilne nieczytanie*) Notes Wydawniczy 2001, no. 3/4.
7. Andrzej Szpociñski, *The classics of culture today,* (*Kanon kultury w dobie wspólczesneij*) In: Kultura popularna-literatura-ksiqzkq-rynek. Forum Czytelnicze II, Warsaw 1995, p. 36.
8. Stanislaw Adam Kondek, *Paper revolution* (*Papierowa rewolucja*) Warsaw 1999.
9. Zofia Zasacka, *The image of motherland and the image of patriotism in Polish textbooks for primary school, 1945-1990* (*Wyobrazenia ojczyzny i oblicza patriotyzmu w podrêcznikach do jêzyka polskiego dla szkoly podstawowej w latach 1945-1990*) Warsaw 2000.

17 Demonstration in Reading Instruction in Hungary: A Historical Analysis

Anna Adamik-Jászó, Hungary

Demonstration is the realisation of the principle of descriptiveness in practice; it is a procedure applied in process of teaching and relates to the activities of both teacher and pupils. Demonstration creates a connection between sensation and abstract thinking in order to facilitate the understanding of abstract knowledge. Demonstration is more effective if it is concerned with several sense organs at the same time, because pupils can process more information, and cognition will be stronger.

While written language is an abstraction, human beings live in the visible, audible and tangible world. Hence, demonstration is extremely important in reading instruction. However, Comenius himself draws attention to the fact that one cannot know the essence of things only through experience, through sensory perception. Demonstration is merely a tool which helps the complicated process of cognition; it only completes the explanation of the teacher and the learning of pupils.

During the process of language acquisition, the child develops language awareness – an access to language – whose final stage is phonemic awareness, which is a prerequisite for learning to read. There are two critical points of beginning reading instruction: teaching and confirming letter-sound correspondences and blending sounds into syllables and words. The teachers of the past understood the challenges these presented, and used visual and other aids to facilitate instruction. This type of demonstration could be called *demonstration for decoding.* Where illustrations are used to facilitate instruction in comprehension, we can have *demonstration for comprehension.*

Classification of Demonstration

Demonstration can be classified on the basis of five senses. We can distinguish visual, auditory, tactile, tasting-smelling and kinetic aids. It is interesting that the history of reading instruction provides examples of instruction centred on all five. This idea can be supported with reference to Johannes Amos Comenius' (1685) classic work, *Orbis Sensualium Pictus,* which means 'The World Depicted by the Senses.' Examples of demonstration in reading associated with the five senses are:

- an illustration (visual)
- a song, sounds (hearing)
- concave letters (touching)
- dried letter pasta (taste)
- ginger-bread letters (smelling)

The grouping above can be supplemented by *kinetic* demonstration which employs *motion* (e.g., motion by hand). It is interesting that the history of reading instruction produces examples for all these possibilities. Comenius himself used not only vision (pictures) but hearing in *Alphabetum Vivum*; i.e., the Living ABC attached to the beginning of *Orbis Pictus*. In his school drama entitled *Schola Ludus* (1656), Comenius introduces the sounding method of teaching reading. Comenius wrote *Schola Ludus* in Sárospatak, Hungary between 1651 and 1653, at the invitation of Zsuzsanna Lorántffy.

From another point of view we can distinguish between *artificial* and *natural solutions* in demonstration. Artificial aids are constructed by the teacher and might include columns of syllables, diagrams, models of sentences, virtual demonstration by the computer; natural aids are simply examples from the environment such as a portrait, a landscape, an object which demonstrates the shape of a letter, expressive reading aloud of the teacher.

The methods of demonstration can be classified according to their location in the teaching process or lesson plan. On this basis, we can establish *demonstration for explanation* and *demonstration for generalisation* (see in New Pedagogigal Lexicon, Budapest, 1997).

Finally, we can observe demonstration and *lack of demonstration* in the history of reading instruction. The lack of demonstration deserves attention. It is interesting to examine the reasons for protests against demonstration. The opposite solution is interesting, also: the abundance of demonstration.

A Brief Historical Survey

Studying the history of demonstration, we can observe the pedagogical sensitivities of a period or an educator and obtain data on the cultural history of a period. It is interesting that similar solutions could be found in different periods.

Demonstration has a long history. One can think about the illuminated codices, the statues and painted windows of the cathedrals, etc. The printing of books and the development of national languages gave an impetus to the establishment of schools. Gradually, it became recognised and widely accepted that the child was not a small adult; consequently, more child-centred approaches to teaching reading had to be developed. In 1829, the first illustrated ABC-book in Hungary – *Pali and Minka Learn to Read* by Gábor Döbrentei – appeared, and was followed by others.

The Hungarian Public Education Act of 1868 was a milestone in the history of Hungarian education. It ordered compulsory school attendance (before most other European countries), and prescribed the teaching of reading and writing to all children. The number of textbooks grew immensely, and several books on the methodology of teaching were produced. It was the most prosperous era of Hungarian education, at every level of the school system. It is interesting that the educators of the era deleted the pictures from the ABC books. First, they wanted to produce cheap books. Second, there was the philosophy of Pál Gönczy, the under-secretary of the Ministry of Religion and Education and an author himself: he was against the pictures in the ABC books, arguing that children must decode the words without guessing. In addition to producing a carefully-organised ABC book, he produced 12 wall-tables for teaching and practising reading, which were sent to every school, and suggested the use of movable letters. On the other hand, he ordered beautiful, colour wall-pictures for the demonstration of object lessons (in our terminology: speech and thought development exercises). The object lessons focused on the development of children's vocabulary in preparation for meeting the same vocabulary in the ABC books. The ideas of Gönczy were undoubtedly logical. Eventually, however, the pictures returned to the ABC books and other readers. Indeed, it could be argued that, by the beginning of the 20th century, there were too many of them.

The pedagogy of the 1930s created a healthy balance which remained until 1950 when the communist era began. During the 40 years of communist era, education was subjected to daily politics and ideology, which had an impact on demonstration. After 1989, a more varied situation arose with continued emphasis on demonstration by textbook authors.

Demonstration in Practice

Let us look at demonstration in the Hungarian ABC books used during the past 500 years. The first of these was published in 1553 in Kolozsvár (which now belongs to Romania).

Visual Aids

This type of demonstration is very common, suggesting that educators find it to be particularly effective. Very often, visual aids consist of *columns of syllables*. These columns are presented in order of difficulty with respect the acquisition of blending skills. They were used in the ABC books until the middle of the 19th century, and were similar to those found in other countries. Such columns may still be found in a small number of publications, such as the recently-published ABC book by Ildikó Meixner (Játékház, 1992), which was originally written for dyslexic children, but is used in regular classrooms also. Undoubtedly, the approach to teaching and learning syllabification implied by columns of syllables is monotonous since syllables are themselves meaningless. One teacher, Gyuláné Tolnai, tried to solve this problem by creating series of shapes – zigzags, flowers, wheels, robots – and locating the syllables in them.

From the middle of the 19th century, the authors of the ABC books gradually replaced the columns of syllables, and applied meaningful words. The perennial problem is that the beginning reader's eye can span only a few letters, but the words – especially in the Hungarian language, which is agglutinative – are much longer. Resourceful educators found different solutions. In 1853, one of them – Péter Erdélyi Indali – edited lessons containing words of increasing length and structural difficulty. He even edited a lesson which contained only words with one syllable (entitled *The Sad Girl*). This solution has not died out completely. For example, the Adamik-Gósy-Lénárd programme (*Wonders of Tales*, 1996) uses reading lists in which the arrangement of the words is based on modern research in speech perception. It puts the open syllables on the first lists, then uses gradually more and more difficult structures. Word lists are also edited for the second, third and fourth grades.

Syllabification is very important in Hungarian reading instruction. The ABC books give the words broken into syllables at least during the first six months of instruction, and often during the whole first year. In 1978, the syllabification approach was set aside by curriculum developers, causing tremendous problems in early reading acquisition. After 1989, syllabification was re-introduced but some bad habits or routines persisted.

The sounding-analytic-synthetic method, introduced by Pál Gönczy in 1869, has several prescribed steps. Consequently, the pages of his ABC book are structured according to those steps. The teacher starts the lesson with a story. S/he draws the attention of the children to a word which contains the sound/letter to be taught. This is the key-word. The letter, taken out of the beginning of the key word, stands at the beginning of the lesson. The words, sentences and stories (i.e., the reading material) follow. Gönczy taught first the written (cursive) forms of the letters and then the printed ones. Hence, his approach is called the reading-through-writing method.

In 1910, László Nagy put the picture for the story at the top of every page, giving the arrangement of the page used even now.

The size and thickness of the letter is important for an unskilled reader. Gönczy and his contemporaries used different letter-sizes in written (cursive) and printed forms, even within the same lesson, arguing that the reader must be trained in reading every type of letter. Later, the ABC books used larger print sizes for teaching lower-case letters, with a gradual reduction in size. In the Adamik-Gósy-Lénárd ABC book and reader, published in 1996, we introduced a unique solution: at the very beginning of the teaching process, we used large print. We reduced print size in the middle of the teaching sequence. At the stage of instruction at which syllabication was set aside, print size was again increased, on the basis that it is more difficult to read whole words than words broken into syllables. Then print (letter) size gradually decreased again.

Pictures for Decoding

Among the more natural aids for reading are pictures for decoding and pictures for comprehension. It is an old and nowadays well-known and used technique to compare the shape of a letter with an object whose word (label) starts with the letter to be taught. For example, the lower case *a* brings to mind a goose on the water, *b* is like a child with a wide frock behind, *c* is like an open mouth or a crescent moon or the tail of a cat. In Hungary, correspondences of this nature appeared in the ABC book of Gábor Döbrentei published in 1829, and in several other books afterwards. This thechnique is perennial, and used in the present ABC books also. The authors usually use nouns to represent letter shapes because they are easily depicted.

These little pictures disappeared from the ABC books after 1868, due to the objections of Pál Gönczy, but they re-appear towards the end of the 19th century. A small picture demonstrating a letter is seen at the beginning of every lesson, even though there may be no other pictures in the book. *The Book of Little Peoples* by Áron Kiss and Lajos Pósa is a little bit different: next to the printed lower-case and capital letters is a picture and a nursery rhyme. This large and beautiful book was published for the public;

therefore it does not contain the prescribed steps of the sounding-analytic-synthetic method. Similarly popular books were published in every period; they were generally called *Golden ABC Books* because they contained wise sayings. Later, the wise sayings were replaced by nursery rhymes. A current example is the *Ringing ABC* by Ferenc Móra.

In the old ABC books, the authors wrote the key word next to the picture if the child already knew every letter of the word so s/he was able to decode it. The primers after 1978 are exceptional: the authors used words containing unknown letters so the child was encouraged to guess the word. We are against this guessing strategy; in our ABC book, we published only the picture and not the key word if it had unknown letters. We published the key word only in cases where all of its letters were familiar to the child.

The authors of the past knew well that they must draw the child's attention only to one thing; therefore they used only one picture to represent one letter. József Gööz who worked at the beginning of the 20th century brought out a whole series of texts. His ABC book of 1903 is a good example of overdoing demonstration.

There are some unique ABC books. One of them – the Sófalvy-Pataki ABC Book published in Arad in 1904 – shows the transformation of letters; i.e., it shows the transitional steps between the thing and the letter.

The ABC books of the 1930s depict both the rural and city environment. Later, between 1950 and 1989, during the communist era, it was much the same. Nowadays, we can see television, missiles, robots, and other technological objects among the pictures. These pictures are generally simplified and emphasised by sharp contours.

Pictures for Comprehension

Pictures are particularly prominent in object lessons (designed to develop speech and thought) and literary-historical texts. Pictures may also serve to bring readers close to the spirit and atmosphere of a particular period. Sometimes, such illustration may serve to shape children's moral upbringing – a shepherd boy running in front of a wolf, a disobedient boy sinking in a frozen lake as the thin ice gives way under him, a punishment for an idle boy or a vain girl. In every ABC book and reader, we can see pictures of the beggar and the donor (an adult or a child). There are pictures about the everyday life of the family: kitchen-work, dinner around the table, praying and asking for blessings. In the 20th century, pictures designed to deter children from behaving in particular ways disappeared from the schoolbooks.

After 1868, the readers were written in patriotic spirit. The year 1868 is an important date in Hungarian history; the compromise with Austria came into being and Hungary gained back her independence. According to the patriotic spirit, we can see the Hungarian hussar in every book, and the wish of every boy was to become a hussar and to defend the homeland. After the Trianon or Versailles peace treaty in 1920, the Hungarian credo about the resurrection of Hungary came into being. (Under the treaty, the country lost 71 percent of her territory.) Apart from this, the ABC books were not under the influence of politics, especially after 1925; instead they were child-centred. However, the influence of politics can be observed again in the ABC books of the communist era; we can see in them the pictures of the political leaders, the scenes of political movements and child organisations, the military parades, the pine holiday instead of Christmas, the Winter-Dad instead of Santa Claus. Recently, politics has again disappeared from the ABC books. They are child-centred again, but the religious spirit of the pre-war period has not come back.

Another recent development is the use of the global method (rather than the sounding-analytic-synthetic method) to teach reading. The global method focuses on the whole word or whole language instruction. It requires children to read words without previous instruction in letter-sound correspondences. In this type of primer – it cannot be called an ABC book – we can see words with pictures. The child tries to comprehend the word with the help of the pictures. Therefore this primer has many pictures. Indeed, these pictures may cover whole pages. In Hungary, educators wanted to introduce the global method several times, first in 1862, last in 1978, but these experiments failed. This method does not match the agglutinative character and special orthography of the Hungarian language.

Auditory Aids

The old school-masters let the children read syllables aloud, but they read the names of the letters first, then pronounced the syllables according to their sounds. It was relatively late when they first taught the sound corresponding to each letter. It was Comenius – in the *Living ABC* (*Alphabetum Vivum*, 1658) – who first used the sounding method; i.e., he first taught the sound and then its letter. He demonstrated the sound with a natural sound from the environment of the child, for example the *a* is the sound of a crow, the *z* is the sound of a horse-fly, the *r* is the bark of the dog, etc. The teachers still use similarities nowadays, but the *n* is the sound of the vacuum-cleaner, or the *s* is the sound of a leaking tyre.

Comenius suggested sounds be taught first, but the principle of sounding became widely accepted much later – at the beginning of the 19th century after the initiative of the German educators. Now sounding is a basic principle of teaching reading. It means that we start teaching reading with development of speech (especially phonemic awareness). We start each reading lesson by teaching first the sound and then the corresponding letter. We teach and practice reading aloud during the first year. Silent reading is developed later.

Tactile Aids
The movable letters can be mentioned here. They stimulate the creativity of the child because s/he can create words from the letters. Besides, it is important that the child can touch the letters, can perceive their shape. The movable letters were suggested in the 19th century when they were sold as toys. In Hungary, the so-called letter-rail is very popular; the child puts the letters in order to form a given word. At the beginning of the 20th century, when creative methods became popular, educators suggested that letters be produced from wire, clay, dough, paper, etc. Nowadays children produce letters from plasticine or modelling paste. Sometimes the letters are cut out from sandpaper and glued on cardboard, so the child can touch them. In our programme, a workbook was edited with concave letters on its front and back covers.

Olfactory/Taste Aids
Surprisingly there were and are such aids. We need only go to the supermarket and take the box with letter-pasta. The Hungarian children like to discover them in their soup. Niala Banton Smith, in her book, *American Reading Instruction* (1934) refers to the 'gingerbread-method' in which children eat gingerbread letters as they learn them.

The famous German educator, Basedow (18th century) suggested baking gingerbread letters, and hiring a baker at least for the first three weeks of the school-year. He was convinced that the child, having eaten the gingerbread-letters for three weeks, would learn to read. The scent of the gingerbread was pleasant, no doubt.

Kinetic Aids
It is well known that demonstration is the more effective if it uses more than one sense; the child can see, hear, say the letter, and memorise it better if s/he can show it. A woman-teacher, Róza Czukrász Tomcsányiné,

devised an ingenious method: she introduced movement into the teaching of letter-sound correspondences and blending, especially in the beginning reading period. She named her method phonomimics (in Hungarian: fonomimika), and published her ABC book in 1903. Until 1950, phonomimics was the officially-recommended method in Hungary, and, to the best of my knowledge, Hungary was the only country in which the method was used in public education.

In 1910, László Nagy, founder of child psychology in Hungary, published an ABC book and manual using phonomimics. In the manual he explains that the main purpose of the signs made by the hand is to facilitate blending. The effectiveness of the signs is based on the law according to which our inner associations of ideas are facilitated as a result of extraneous movements. These movements are called synchronic movements. In the small child, psychological processes are not isolated as they are in the adult. The child is more likely to follow ideas with extraneous movements. That is why the phonomimical signs make the difficult work of blending easier. Furthermore, the phonomimical signs have an influence on the memory, which is why it is important to make the signs and to pronounce the sounds simultaneously and continuously.

Let us put phonomimics into historical perspective. Until the 20th century, teaching reading was the same everywhere; methodological differences in European countries were few. Teaching reading was under the influence of German education in the 19th century. Education in the beginning of the 20th century was defined by the reform pedagogy or child study. At this point, the methods of teaching reading separated: in the English-speaking countries the whole-word method was introduced; in most of the European countries, the traditional analytic-synthetic method was retained. In Hungary, it was combined with phonomimics.

Naturally, it was not only phonomimics which used play and movement in education. The old school-masters knew that it was useful for children to perceive the lines with their whole body. Therefore the games children played during breaktime were important. They formed straight lines, parallels, circles, S-lines, etc. The teachers demonstrated the written letter-elements and letters with their whole arms, then with the hand, and finally with fingers; the children imitated these movements, and this helped them to eventually write letters.

At the very beginning of reading instruction, the children were asked to put their index finger under the letters. This helped with blending. An interesting invention was the letter-wheel: we can see it in the synthetic reader written by the American Rebecca Pollard in 1880, in the reader by Gyula Gabel in 1904, and in the ABC book Gyuláné Tolnia in 1990. The child was asked to put his/her index finger on the spokes of the wheel and blend a vowel with consonants. Mrs. Tolnia devised a unique demonstration tool which is the programmed wall. It is used for developing of phonemic awareness, and teaching sound-letter correspondences and blending.

Conclusion

The study of demonstration is a central issue in the area of language arts. In every era, teachers are confronted with the problem of linking the abstract to their students' interests. Studying the history of demonstration can help to establish the pedagogical sensitivities of a certain period or person. It is clear that current approaches to demonstration reflect accumulated experience at the historical, psychological and practical levels. An important consequence is that historical material helps us to distinguish between useful and unnecessary and rather harmful demonstration. A historical study is useful if it connects the old achievements to the present.

BIBLIOGRAPHY

Adamik-Jászó, A. (1999). *A magyar olvasástanítás története.* (History of Hungarian reading instruction) Budapest: Tankönyvkiadó, , 1990.

Adamik-Jászó, A. (2000). *Az írás és az olvasás története képekben.* (History of reading and writing in pictures). Budapest: OPKM.

Kotkaheimo, L. (1989). *Suomalaisen aapisen viisi vuosisataa* (Five hundred years of Finnish ABC books). Joensuu: Joensuun Yliopisto.

Mathews, M. (1996). Teaching to read: Historically considered. Chicago: University of Chicago Press.

Smith, N. B. (1986; First edition, 1934). *American reading instruction.* Newark, DE: International Reading Association.

SECTION 6

Literacy and Democracy

18   Censorship and Reading in the New Poland

Janusz Dunin, Poland

What is read by the public is to a large extent dependent on what publications are available. This in turn is conditional on whether everything is published freely or is subject to censorship.

Censorship has been a common practice for centuries. Texts have been destroyed and their authors punished since ancient times. After the invention of print, control over the written word became more organised and structured. Since the 16th century, more or less organised forms of church and state censorship have been continuously operating in Europe. It was both preventive (prior restraint) and repressive (ex-post-facto punishment) censorship, which destroyed publications. The history of censorship in the past was complicated and only partly reported. It was exercised by state authorities or delegated to the church and universities. The objective of censorship was to protect the person in power, his religion and the social system. Additionally, censorship focused on the danger of disseminating what was considered improper or offensive – publications about sex or even those which only contained obscene words or illustrations. The situation in Poland in the past was complex and we do not have a complete record or the final version of the history yet. In multi-national Poland, besides Catholicism, other religions like Protestantism, the Orthodox Church, the Mosaic Law and Mohammedanism were also tolerated. This complicated the issue of censorship in Poland even further.

At the end of the 18th century Poland lost its independence and control of its territory was taken over by three superpowers: Russia, Germany and Austria. Their influence and the systems of internal censorship shaped the situation in Central and Eastern Europe for more than a century. Various more or less democratic national states of Central Europe, which regained independence after 1918, had diverse types of censorship. In Poland at that time, censorship laws were relatively liberal and the repressions were directed primarily at communist and pornographic publications. In contrast, the period of Nazism and occupation were times of extremely strict policy of control over publications.

Generally speaking, censorship agencies have been operating in Europe since the 16th century. After uprisings and upheavals, if new authorities appeared, they tried to introduce their own new system of control over publications. Society considered the existence of censorship as natural. If it was criticised, it was mainly because it was viewed as imperfect, for example too rigid, or vested in incompetent people, and often exercised by the enemy. The general sentiment was that censorship should be practised by 'our own' people. At the same time, throughout the 19th and the 20th centuries, different national, political and religious groups were trying to get around legal rules in order to print and disseminate publications without the intervention of censorship. They were creating publications called 'alternative' or 'underground'. Attempts were also made to publish some materials abroad, in more liberal countries and to smuggle forbidden books into Poland. During Nazi occupation, the most active conspiratorial publishing organisations in Europe existed in Poland.

After the World War II the tendencies as far as censorship was concerned became very diversified. In democratic countries, censorship began to disappear. Even in West Germany where the occupiers – the victorious Allies – introduced a rigorous control of publications after the war, censorship was practically lifted, leaving behind only those few rules and regulations whose aim was to eradicate the remains of Nazi racism. Western countries followed the example of the Constitution of the United States and introduced freedom of speech, which practically rendered censorship illegal. Even the Catholic Church abolished in 1966 the *Index librorum prohibitorum* or index of banned books, which had existed in different forms since 1559.

The history of censorship evolved quite differently in socialist or communist countries. From China and North Korea, throughout the German Democratic Republic, all the way to Cuba, the written word was subject to strict control. Usually the word 'censorship' was avoided as such; in the German Democratic Republic its existence was even denied and something called the 'collective will of the nation' was invoked. In Poland, the new speak required commentators to talk about, and especially write about censorship as 'Control of Publications', probably because totalitarian regimes often invoked Karl Marx, who openly opposed censorship. In Poland, the main censorship agency was called The Office for the Control of the Press, Publications and Public Performances'. In various countries of the Soviet bloc, different solutions were applied, but they were all aimed at subordinating publications and cultural events to the control of the ruling party and the state. In the USSR there was a secret agency called 'Glavlit', which placed its agents in all organizations responsible for editing, printing and disseminating the written word. The existence of censorship in a country can be easily tested by checking whether any publications are controlled and seized at the borders. The strength of censorship was that it was a secret service not subject to any judicial or civil control. Whenever a section of a text was considered suspect by the preventive censorship, the publisher was obliged to edit it in such a way as to remove any signs of censorial intervention. There was a central system of 'entries'; the censors in regional offices were given detailed instructions on which information, opinions and names could not even be mentioned and which people or issues could not be described approvingly. The readers did not always realise that they were often reading texts which were inconsistent with the original intention of the authors. Even translations differed considerably from the original. One of the censors in Cracow, Tomasz Strzyzewski, smuggled well-protected secrets of the Office for the Control of Press, Publications and Public Performances out of Poland and published them in Sweden as 'The Black Book of Censorship'. The publication stirred up a lot of controversy and served to compromise the authoritarian rule once again. Even the more intelligent communists were aware that control over the written word stripped it completely of its credibility.

One of the aims of opposition and revisionist movements has long been the limitation of censorship. However, many people got used to this institution, and the idea that it might vanish completely seemed unrealistic and even shocking. Originally, the objective was to make the activities of censorship agencies public and to subject them to judicial control, which would allow the publishers to appeal against their decisions. In the latter years of the 20th century, the opposition movements became stronger and underground publications became more popular in different countries of Europe. They were often called publications 'without censorship' or 'second circulation'. The Russian name 'samizdat' became known worldwide. The attempt to maintain the monopoly of the state on information led to a strict control of all information channels; at the borders, imported books and newspapers were confiscated, all duplicating machines were controlled, even photocopying machines and typewriters had to be sealed for the night, foreign radio stations' programmes were jammed. Control over the written word was strengthened by concentrating the printing houses in state hands and by introducing state and ruling party monopoly on the trade in paper.

One of the first successes of the opposition movements and a disclosure of 'entries', which compromised the state authorities, was 'the Law of 31 July 1981 concerning the control of publications and performances', which introduced a more liberal censorship law and which declared at the beginning that the Polish People's Republic guaranteed freedom of speech and print, and only later specified 10 exceptions to this rule. These were theses which prohibited activities such as expressing opinions against the alliances formed by the Polish state or calling for a change in the political system. The law permitted indicating points of censorial intervention in publications and enabled the publishers who did not accept the censor's decision to appeal against it before the courts. After six months, the law was rescinded and the government imposed martial law against the trade union 'Solidarity' (*Solidarnoœœæ*). When, in 1990, thanks to the agreement called 'The Round Table', power was transferred bloodlessly to non-communists and Poland severed its ties with the Soviet bloc, our country started preparations to join the European Union. Censorship was completely lifted and state control over allocations of paper and printing houses was also abolished.

In many instances attempts were made to harmonise Polish law with western standards. The example to be followed in this case was the Constitution of the United States, which prohibits censorship. However, neither in the USA nor in other countries did censorship vanish by itself, automatically. It was a long-term, evolutionary process and, in the meantime, there were many attempts to limit freedom of speech. Societies tried to adapt to the changing situation, as even the Catholic Church abolished in 1966 its *Index Librorum Prohibitorum*. In Poland, events gained momentum very quickly: censorship was abolished in 1990 and in 1997 the constitution of the Republic of Poland was passed. Paragraph 54 of the Constitution declares, among other things, that 'everyone is guaranteed freedom of expression and the right to gather and disseminate information' and that 'preventive censorship of mass media and licensing of the press is prohibited'. What is left is a legal possibility of taking action against texts before courts, which may then issue an injunction. However, this is only an illusory possibility, which has many qualifications and reservations to it; moreover, the trials are long and costly. The vanishing from social life of restrictive publishing policy was caused not only by political changes, but also by the progress in the field of information technology. Easy availability of duplicating machines, for example photocopying machines, satellite dishes and computer networks makes effective control of information possible only in countries with very strict regimes, like in Northern Korea or Iran. It should be remembered, however, that even in authoritarian regimes a significant proportion of people, despite rigid censorship, managed to find their way to good literature. The news about a book which was worth reading spread by word of mouth. Many people turned to older or illegal publications.

Complete abolition of censorship in a country such as Poland, in which it had existed continuously for centuries, changed the situation for books and the press. The number of new books published annually has almost doubled. However, the lack of control bodies means that a large, and yet unspecified proportion of books is not bibliographically registered. Many publishers do not submit obligatory copies. Books have to compete with other media. The situation of many publishers is becoming difficult; with more titles on the market editions become limited, which in turn leads to an increase in the prices of publications and difficulties in selling them.

The Poles know from experience that censorship agencies always tend to increase their authority and do not allow criticism or appeal. Additionally censorship drives a wedge into society, dividing it into two categories – those who have access to all media and have the power to decide what will be made available and to whom, and the masses which are denied the right to decide for themselves. Respect for freedom of speech does not mean that all texts which are published are equally good and that there are no stupid, harmful or even criminal works among them. In pluralist societies, the evaluation of particular publications may differ. Works appreciated by some people are rejected as valueless by others. It is also difficult to establish a valid hierarchy of literary values. There are some kinds of information or theses which are rejected by all responsible citizens; examples are information contradicting logic or science; texts promoting crime, like manuals teaching people how to produce explosives or drugs at home; publications which advance alternative methods of treatment which contradict medical knowledge and which discourage consultations with doctors; materials advocating anti-Semitism and xenophobia or other harmful and ugly ideologies are also universally condemned. However, such texts are sometimes published and find their way to the public and there is no way of eliminating them. In Opole, which is close to Auschwitz, a historian working at the university published a book which propounded a view that information on the Holocaust was grossly exaggerated if not completely false. After a trial, the propounder of the Holocaust-denial was removed from the university, but the book managed to get published.

Some Poles experience shock in the new democratic society, in which the rigid state policy of control over publications suddenly disappeared. In the year 2000, the Polish Parliament called Sejm, in which Catholics constituted the majority, passed a law prohibiting all kinds of pornography. It was not signed by the President, however, and failed to come into force. It was unclear what the precise definition of pornography should be and thus what was pornography and what was not, and who would be competent to take decisions in this matter, whether a separate office would be necessary etc. If the law had been enforced, it would have been in fact tantamount to introducing censorship.

The freedom of the decentralised publishing market influences the situation of libraries, which do not have enough funds to buy the whole rich array of new titles and have to make a selection. Librarians, especially the older ones, were used for years to being instructed in detail by the authorities about what should be promoted; moreover, they knew that every title found in a bookshop had already been checked and approved by censors. Now the duty to choose from what is on offer on the publishing market has become more difficult and it is not clear what criteria should be applied when making a selection. The state authorities do subsidise libraries (though very modestly), but they do not pursue an active cultural policy any longer. Some people criticise public libraries for continuing in the new situation the practice to which they got accustomed in the former period – i.e., promoting leftist opinions both as far as general outlook and political affiliations are concerned.

The reading public is criticised for making wrong choices and preferring sensational, often brutal or erotic literature, mawkish romances and second-rate new titles. It is true but, at the same time, it is also true that valuable publications can defend themselves. The problem is how to show tolerance, which is due to citizens of a democratic world, and simultaneously support higher culture, which may be more difficult; how to promote real values, which may be diverse, and not the mediocre works of transient fashion.

Yet, for me the opportunity offered by a rich book market in our country is worth taking. I am convinced that even a less sophisticated publication helps a person maintain his or her reading ability and makes the readers able to use a very important medium – writing, which is a backbone of our culture. Reading is a cure for many ailments – it is not a neutral placebo; the saying 'he who reads, sins not' cannot be applied here. We know that those who read a lot can cope better in modern society and can use modern media more effectively. The fate of reading culture in Poland is a concern for all those people whose lives are linked to books.

Abolition of censorship in Poland coincided with a period of increased availability of many leisure activities and methods of communication besides reading. Travelling, including travelling abroad has become easier, the range of new TV channels has become wider, it is possible to watch videos at home; computers offer not only games but also an easy way of communicating with the whole world. These are all competitors for the time which might be spent on reading. Thus we face the challenge of defending the tradition of reading against competition, because we believe that it is an indispensable element of our European culture.

19 Literacies, Contexts and Practices

Maria de Lourdes Dionísio, Portugal

Literacy is a fairly new term in the Portuguese lexicon. Already used at the level of research and by those dealing with reading and writing in the educational and social systems, the term 'literacy' acquired public importance in October 1995, with the publication of the report on the First National Literacy Assessment.

For a while, together with a strong reaction against the term itself – closely associated with basic reading skills and 'foreign trends' – several voices in the media claimed a 'decline in culture'. This 'decline', it was alleged, was found in the low levels of literacy attained by the population and in the poor performance of individuals on 'basic' reading tasks or 'skills for written information processing in everyday life' (Benavente, 1996; CNE, 1996: 111).

At the level of the public Discourse[1], despite so many curricular and social questions raised by this first literacy report, the explanations for such literacy rates were easily and quickly found in low levels of reading habits (easier to see and measure) that a previous national study had already identified and characterised (Freitas & Santos, 1992). Considered by many 'socially relevant voices' – politicians, public figures, journalists and experts – as an 'obscure concept' (CNE, 1996: 78) and very difficult to characterise and assess, the immediate and unique association of literacy with reading habits is almost understandable. Therefore, more than the discussion of literacy practices, or even the assumed skills, their nature or the conditions for their improvement, for instance, it was 'reading habits' that became most visibly the central issue in the public debate. In the last few years, 'reading habits' and not 'literacy' became a privileged object for research, both at academic and governmental levels (Master and Ph. D. theses have been written; a Foundation for the Study of Cultural Practices has been created).

Since the mid 1990s, the amount and kind of reading engaged in by young people has been measured, with the results interpreted in the same way as measures of literacy.

Surveys of Reading Habits – Status and Roles

One possible way to understand what literacy really is and why, when and how people engage with written texts, is by beginning to pay attention to 'the institutional processes whereby 'truths' about literacy become translated into policy and practice' (Hamilton, 1999). Thus, my aim here is to discuss how surveys of reading habits may contribute to preventing an understanding of literacy in terms of its links with a range of broader social, economic and ideological issues; how they may be contributing to the maintenance of a narrow, strict definition of reading and a specific and very particular version of the reader. In doing this, I am trying to challenge some public perceptions, some 'social visions and ideologies' made possible through devices such as these surveys, which by means of the facts they 'create', the way they create them and the kind of the relationships they privilege and allow, produce and reproduce meanings and their values.

The high status I am giving here to surveys of reading habits comes from the influence that some of them – and some of their claims – have at the level of public and institutional discourse (almost all of them are sponsored and sometimes published by state agencies – the Ministry of Culture, for instance). At this level, they integrate with other objects, texts and practices[2] to shape and legitimise views of literacy and of the literate person. The fact that they are sustained by statistics adds to this privileged institutional position the power of 'objective evidence' that easily 'feeds' the 'moral panic' that periodically invades all societies (Luke & Freebody, 1999).

Functioning as a part of a 'cultural model' which defines 'what counts as normal and natural and what counts as inappropriate and deviant' (Gee, 2001), the surveys have the power to influence the way people see specific problems, putting pressure on schools, and teachers for instance, and leading them to practices that may be more in accordance with the point of view of this particular stance.

The possibility that surveys of reading habits might inform 'social practices' and might support cultural and educational policies is not just a mere hypothesis. This role is explicitly stated in their goals, particularly when they claim that 'information about reading habits is necessary for teachers and for developing a grounded educational policy' (Fortuna & Fontes, 1999). Even if some of these surveys assume their 'descriptive nature' with 'practical objectives', which don't justify, according to the authors, 'theoretical considerations about reading' (Conde & Antunes, 2000), they also see their contribution as 'a response to the general problem of literacy that has been growing as a national concern, as a relevant object of analysis and political intervention, namely through projects whose investigation about this problem may illuminate the measures needed to minimise illiteracy and social exclusion' (Conde & Antunes, 2000: 13-14). Attempting to contribute to an understanding of literacy problems, which 'nowadays endanger citizenship' (Fortuna & Fontes, 1999), these studies not only propose 'to discover what students read and if they read' but also 'to travel beyond the present into the future of the reading habits of people as far as it is possible to anticipate them from the present habits and practices' (Monteiro, 1999, p. 13). Although recognising some of them (for example, Conde and Antunes (2000) refer to 'social nature of reading [...] that it is structured by different processes' (p. 13), the belief that the future will be a mirror of the present deletes some of the relevant dimensions of reading and literacy, particularly the fact that 'literacy is historically situated' being 'as fluid, dynamic and changing as the lives and societies of which they are a part' (Barton & Hamilton, 2000, p. 13).

Ways and Words for Defining THE Literacy

In order to understand how these studies structure practices and their correlate values and then influence and pattern models of behaviour, defining what is significant reading, who is entitled to be considered a reader, therefore who is entitled to enter and to belong to a social group which is recognised as being distinctive, I scrutinised four reading habits surveys[3], conducted in 1999 and in 2000, in four different Portuguese cities. The data from these four surveys have been collected using a questionnaire to which students in the 14 to 24 years age range provided responses.

The first thing that must be said about the four instruments used in the inquiry is that they are almost exactly the same and very much like the national survey of 1992[4]. Hence, they integrate a broader process of reproduction and of power relations[5]. With small variation, all questionnaires, together with questions about the primary socialising contexts of the students, give privilege to the same dimensions through questions and items such as the following examples:

- Do you read regularly?
- What's the main motive for not reading regularly?
  Processing difficulties; Prefers to do other things; Doesn't like reading; Doesn't have time; Other motive.
- At this moment are you reading any book not for school?
- How many books other than those for school did you read last year?
- Do you like reading?

- How much time approximately do you spend each week reading books not for school?
- What kind of books do you prefer? Put a mark on the following list//
- What type of non-school books do you usually read?[6]
- How long ago did you read your last book?
- Mark no more than three possibilities concerning your reading purposes.

When the questions are the same over time and place, although they are intended for different persons, living and studying in different contexts, the role of relevant dimensions such as social conditions – particularly pedagogical ones – that structure literacy events is not taken into account. Reading and ultimately literacy is conveyed here as a set of fixed practices (which don't depend on the contexts), acquired once forever, and highly dependent on the individual's will.

The French sociologist Pierre Bourdieu teaches us that if we want to understand reading we have to inquire, above all else, about how readers are formed, in what places, under which circumstances (particularly discursive ones). Accordingly we have to ask: what kind of relation is established between reading practices and, for instance, curricular changes? Are there differences between the school libraries of those four cities? Do these students have access to libraries? What are the characteristics of the libraries? How many hours of free time are those students allowed? What are the patterns of classroom reading practices? The answers to questions like these will allow understanding that literacy changes as contexts change, that literacy practices have broader social meanings and that they are 'supported, sustained, learned and impeded in people's lives and relationships' (Barton & Hamilton, 2000: 12), that they aren't an individual matter but a community issue.

If the questionnaire through its questions may be taken as a discursive device that, from the very beginning, positions readers in relation to a specific version of reading, the description and interpretation of the data, more than anything else, contribute to the (re)production of that specific version.

Consider for a moment some of the survey conclusions synthesised in Table 1 according to the following general categories: purposes, characteristics of the reading practices and readers, objects, libraries, and general comments.

In the judgements of value – disguised as facts – that run through almost all of the comments, reading for learning, for knowledge is not valued, on the grounds that this puts 'future reading' in danger. We can conclude that, in this 'cultural model', the kind of reading one will have to do after leaving school will be only the 'aesthetic one', reading to occupy leisure time and for personal development. The legitimate reading – the good one – is that which is done for pleasure, as an end in itself. But people, as David Barton (1994) says, 'do things for a reason. In general, people do not read in order to read; rather, people read and write in order to do other things' (p. 49). And these comments and the data that gave them origin show clearly that students read to update knowledge, to learn, to acquire information – which seems quite understandable: they are students after all.

Obviously many of us read for pleasure, sometimes also as an end, not as a means, to occupy leisure time, just to enjoy ourselves. However we have to be aware that this is only one possibility of practice involving written texts, but it may be the smallest one in the totality of our lives. 'In varied communities, literary reading and writing are a relatively minor part of people's everyday lives', Luke, O'Brien and Comber (2001, p. 112) remind us, calling attention to the works researchers such as Heath (1986). Seeing this separation between reading for knowledge and for pleasure from another angle, it must be said that the underlying assumption is also very strange, as it isn't necessarily true that reading for personal purposes and needs has to be a boring task.

In this context, if reading for pleasure is the valued practice, the one that is appropriate, the standard according to which all reading activity is to be measured, then negative results in relation to other purposes of reading are almost natural and expected. As can be seen in Table 1, as far as reading practices are concerned, 'they aren't regular among half of the students'. They are 'parcelled' and 'fragmented', words that are by no means free of negative connotations.

At this point, it is almost inevitable to ask about the kind of reading those conclusions are referring to. The answer is obvious if we consider the questions exemplified above and the synthesised conclusions. In the first place, they are referring to reading books. As the students read for learning and the preferred reading materials are said to be 'magazines, newspapers, computer…' or books for 'specialised/curricular readings', books 'for research', the only book that seems to allow pleasure is a very special one. Not the one for school purposes, not the one to become a computer/ sports/electronics … expert – these are for information – but the Book or literature (although never 'said aloud' and moreover, never 'said why'). Looking at things this way, the real meaning of 'Reading is not a regular practice…' is 'Reading of literature is not a regular practice…'.

TABLE 1: SYNTHESIS OF THE MAIN CONCLUSIONS OF THE FOUR SURVEYS

Personal reading: views and purposes	• Reading is for learning, not for pleasure • Reading is viewed as learning, formation and knowledge • Reading is for updating knowledge • It's a kind of 'applied reading' … endangering future reading • Among older students, an instrumental view of reading prevails • Reading for exams … this means that the end of school will be the end of reading • This growing use of reading for school purposes constrains the desire for more uncommitted reading practices
Characteristics of reading practices and of readers	• Reading is not a regular practice among half of the students • Low levels of reading of books • *Fast* reading – preference for newspapers and magazines • Parcelled reading – therefore inattentive readers • Specialised readings; curricular readings • Very low levels of reading of books other than those for school purposes • Day-by-day, fragmented reading • Very low levels of time for reading … not sufficient to become a reader • Using the computer doesn't mean 'a solid' reading competence
Reading materials	• Books as tools • Prevalence of magazines, newspapers, computer… endanger the book • A great number of the books mentioned belong to the school curriculum
Libraries	• Use of libraries mostly for research or study • Very low levels of those who use library for pleasure • Very low levels of requisition of books other than those for school
General comments	• Contradiction between what is said and what is really done – reading is recognised as important but… • Students don't develop reading for pleasure… future of reading is in danger • The possibility of exercising citizenship is at risk • School doesn't motivate for reading • School provides students with a limited set of reading values • The quality of future citizenship is won or lost during this phase of life

What is implied by these surveys is that the 'normal' reading is the literary one. To read a book to get some kind of information is to use it as a tool, which is a deviant behaviour in the 'cultural model' that these surveys convey and, ultimately, inform. If we took the hermeneutics a little further, it would be possible to see how literature is being emptied of functions other than to occupy leisure time and merely reduced to a symbolic role, while readers are being defined almost only as 'consumers of stories' (Lankshear & Knobel, 1998, pp. 162-163).

Reading for information among these students is almost natural, particularly if we take into account the social contexts to which they belong, even when literature is the issue. At this particular time of their life, the literary canon is a curricular object and students have to read it for several purposes. Literature is for these students strongly tied to hard work, which might explain the preferences for other kinds of reading and for other cultural pastimes during leisure time.

To view reading from such a perspective subtly leads to the consideration of readers as 'strong – weak' and 'attentive – inattentive' – words that are thoroughly value-laden and contribute to the constitution of the reader's identity. But it is not only the reader that sees his/her identity being constituted. Seen from this narrow perspective, libraries, for instance, are committed to purposes that reduce their perceived importance. According to students, they go to the library to 'research' and 'study' (Table 1).

These surveys claim the importance of reading and literacy for the exercise of citizenship. However, when the students show that they read to be in the world, to know things, that they somehow participate in society, these facts are undervalued and the students' identities as readers are denied because they read the way they choose, the way they need: mostly for information.

Looked at this way the 'contradiction' that is said to exist between what students say concerning their reading and what is really done (from the researchers' point of view) is indeed only apparent. Students read for their own purposes, thereby identifying themselves as readers. However, when they are asked about what books they read, how much time they spend reading books not for information, the answers they could give don't fit the questionnaire items, nor are their answers valued. Students and researchers are not speaking the same language. They are actually speaking of different realities. They are using different discourses.

Conclusion

Four recent Portuguese surveys of reading habits have been scrutinised under the assumption that, on the one hand, the way literacy practices are assessed, judged or even spoken of is another device of a broader process where economics, politics and ideologies play a relevant role. In the words produced by means of such surveys, a version of the world is being shaped and reshaped. Particularly in a historical moment where the issue of literacy is growing both at the level of its conceptualisation and of political and educational concern, it seems crucial to analyse such surveys according to the version of literacy they are supporting, and at the same time, are supported by.

Without aiming at a quantitative analysis, it was possible to identify some constant features that contribute to recovering the meanings and values that structure and sustain a narrow definition of reading and literacy as well as who can be considered a reader or literate. Integrating the continuous 'recycling' process of prevalent ideas, everything in these surveys conveys a 'literary discourse' (cf. Barton, 1994, p. 168) about reading. Book literacy is afforded a higher status than other forms of literacy, pushing into marginal places literacies associated with other domains of life. Pushing these literacies to these marginal places, individuals are being pushed as well and conflicting positions on the issue of reading are being created.

The practices that are characterised in these studies let us perceive the nature of the social context to which these students belong at this particular moment of their lives as well as the kind of literacy demands this context requires from them: to learn, to acquire information, to research, to study. Students in these questionnaires speak about reading as a situated practice while these studies speak about an autonomous one. Although all four surveys take into consideration the socialising contexts of these students and their specificities, the facts these surveys produce and give relevance to do not value the particular uses of literacy people need and use in certain roles (cf., Barton, 1994).

As I tried to show here, confining discussions on literacy and reading to the number of books that students read reinforces a prevalent Discourse, and supplements its particular model of literacy and of literacy education. In a way that the researchers didn't necessarily and objectively aim for, the model that they present is the one that doesn't value the plural and significant practices that link school and the broader community and world outside school, and, by implication, students' school lives and their lives outside school. To deny these plural practices is a way to condemn significant practices and significant people to oblivion; it is also to participate a process of restricting the access and participation in civic life to a great part of the population.

NOTES

* This text has been developed in the context of a research project – Literacies. Contexts. Practices. Discourses (FCT-POCTI 33888/99) funded by Fundação para a Ciência e Tecnologia and it has been sponsored by Fundação Calouste Gulbenkian.

[1] Discourse with a capital D, as in Gee (1999; 2001) in order to distinguish from the meaning of discourse, 'language in use'.

[2] Among these objects, texts and practices, the media and the school textbooks are particularly relevant (cf. Castro, 2000, Dionísio, 2000a, 2000b).

[3] The four surveys used for this analysis are the following: Fortuna & Fontes (1999); Conde & Antunes (2000); Marques (2000); Monteiro (1999).

[4] It must be noted that the comparison of the results was not among the survey's goals, although sometimes comparisons are made both to stress the conclusions and to legitimatise the comments on those conclusions.

[5] Some of these surveys are conducted in the context of post-graduation courses where the teachers, in some cases, include the authors of the previous national studies, and persons holding positions in the Foundation that sponsors the students' research.

[6] The list of items for this question in Survey 2, for instance, is the following: Art/ Theatre/Poetry; Comics; Technical/Scientific; Short Stories/Novels/Romance; Cooking/Bricolage; Encyclopaedias/Dictionaries; Erotic; Scientific fiction; Historical/Biographies; Adolescent; Thrillers/Espionage; Political/ Philosophical; Religion; Terror/Mystery; Travelling/Adventures.

REFERENCES

Austad, I. & Lyssand, T. (Eds.). (2000). *Literacy. Challenges for the new millennium. Selected papers. 11th European Conference on Reading.* Stavanger: Center for Reading Research/Norwegian Reading Association.

Barton, D. (1994). *Literacy. An introduction to the ecology of written language.* Oxford: Blackwell.

Barton, D. & Hamilton, M. (2000). Literacy practices. In D. Barton, M. Hamilton & R. Ivanic (Eds.). *Situated literacies. Reading and writing in context.* London: Routledge.

Benavente, A. (Coord). (1996). *A literacia em Portugal. Resultados de uma pesquisa extensiva e monográfica.* Lisboa: Fundação Calouste Gulbenkian.

Castro, Rui V. (2000). Ways and factors of adolescent reading: discourses about reading. In I. Austad & T. Lyssand (eds.), *Literac: Challenges for the new millennium* (pp. 241-248). Stavenger: Center for Study of Reading/ Norwegian Reading Association.

Conde, I. & Antunes, L. (2000). *Hábitos e práticas de leitura de uma população juvenil. Caracterização dos concelhos de Almada e Seixal. Sobre a Leitura, IV.* Lisboa: IPLB/Observatório das Actividades Culturais.

Conselho Nacional de Educação (1996). *Situação Nacional da Literacia.* Lisboa: CNE.

Dionísio (de Sousa), Mª de Lourdes (2000a). Reading pedagogic discourse. Social linguistic features of school teaching practices of reading. In I. Austad & T. Lyssand (Eds.), *Literacy: Challenges for the new millennium* (pp. 241-257). Stavenger: Center for Study of Reading / Norwegian Reading Association.

Dionísio, Mª de Lourdes (2000b). *A construção escolar de comunidades de leitores.* Coimbra: Almedina

Freitas, E. & Santos, M. Lurdes (1992). *Hábitos de leitura em Portugal.* Lisboa: D. Quixote.

Fortuna, C.& Fontes, F. (1999). *Leitura juvenil: hábitos e práticas no distrito de Coimbra. Sobre a Leitura, I.* Lisboa: IPLB/OBS.

Gee, J.P. (1999). *Social linguistics and literacies. Ideology in discourses,* 2nd ed. London: Falmer Press.

Gee, J.P. (2001). Reading as situated language: A sociocognitive perspective. *Journal of Adolescent and Adult Literacy, 44* (8), 714-725.

Hamilton, M. (1999). Framing Literacy: emergent issues for research. *http://www.education.uts.edu.au/AILA/Symposiumhamilton* (accessed 25th Oct. 1999)

Lankshear, C. & Knobel, M. (1998). New times! Old ways?. In F. Christie & R. Misson (eds.). *Literacy and schooling.* London: Routledge

Luke, A. & Freebody, P. (1999). Further notes on the Four Resources Model. *Reading Online.http://www.readingonline.org/research/lukefreebody.htm* (accessed September, 1999).

Luke, A., O'Brien, J. & Comber, B. (2001). Making community texts objects of study. In H. Fehring & P. Green (Eds). *Critical literacy.* Newark, DE: International Reading Association/Australian Literacy Educators' Association

Marques, R. M. (2000). *Hábitos de leitura juvenil – Évora e concelhos limítrofes. Sobre a Leitura, vol. II.* Lisboa: IPLB/OBS.

Monteiro, A. (1999). *A Biblioteca Pública de Beja como espaço de inter-acção. Sobre a Leitura, vol. II.* Lisboa: IPLB/OBS.

20 Levels of Literacy

Keith Nettle, England

I begin with a quote from the distinguished Central American educationalist Emilia Ferreiro (2000):

Democracy, that form of government that we are all staking our hopes on, demands, needs and requires literate individuals. Full democracy is impossible without levels of literacy that surpass the minimum of spelling and signing. It is impossible to continue to support democracy without making the necessary efforts to increase the number of readers – complete readers, not spellers. (1)

Democracy now in western countries depends on literacy at every level: censuses by which governments can plan for the future; elections which are the cornerstone of democratic choice; local meetings which have agendas and minutes – the whole apparatus of social living is organised and recorded through literacy.

At one stage a generation ago, it seemed to some that computers might do away with much traditional literacy and numeracy, bypassing language altogether in many contexts, and number crunching all the sums. But the reality was quite different.

Banks of computers can run whole industrial processes, but it is the PC in the home or school which has had the greatest social effect on individuals. Whereas forecasters twenty years ago thought personal computers would take over tasks from people, reducing their linguistic and mathematical skills, almost the reverse has in fact happened. This is partly because of the enormous growth of emailing, with millions of messages now crossing the world each day. Emailing obviously demands good reading and writing skills to be carried on effectively and fast. Another aspect of PCs is the vast amount of material available for reference, but demanding high literacy skills to access and use.

The early predictions mistook the developing course of electronic communication. There was a mistaken belief that electronically-published content would develop much quicker than it has, rather than personal e-mailing, whose rapid progress was not so widely predicted. While electronic publishing has been strong in some areas – encyclopaedias, for example – it has hardly shifted consumer publishing away from book format. This is despite enormous research and experimentation by

Microsoft and other big firms who have consistently – yet wrongly – predicted the death of the book.

There seems over the past year, in fact, to have been the first real setback to technological progress in communications. The e-Book has shown little sign of replacing the paper book. Sweden has announced a drop in the income of electronic publishers. The dot.com companies have collapsed. The next generation of mobile phones have not attracted enough interest in, for example, surfing the Net on a mobile. A recent survey by the UK Publishers Association has shown that learning from books is more effective than learning from multimedia screens (2). These are perhaps setbacks in the general progress of the electronic medium. But at a recent conference on the e-Book, Mark McCallum of Random House made the intelligent comment that 'just because technology can produce something, it won't necessarily have a market' (3).

Literacy and Democracy

This brings us back to Ferreiro's connection between literacy and democracy. For modern western economies, the problem is getting populations to engage with democratic obligations so that governments can justify their actions and remain in office. Modern governments work through language to win votes and sometimes to manage referenda on the constitutional issues of the day.

Ireland's recent referendum on the enlargement of the EC, or Britain's assumed future referendum on the Euro, are examples of the EU's fitful progress towards uniformity of purpose and policies. European government is highly complex, and as it further expands it makes big demands of understanding of the governments and peoples of the member countries. That is one of the problems of contemporary administration: we live in a regulatory era with multiple levels of government and subsidiarity, in which many of the issues are relatively technical, leading to over-simplification in referenda and elections. So what is the function and value of literacy in such a setting?

This brings us back to the literacy needed for democratic obligations. Traditionally, loyalty to party, whether left or right, was almost automatic for many voters, and neither election literature nor voting forms presented much difficulty. As we have seen, however, we now live in consumer societies where party loyalties are probably not as significant as the statements and perceived qualities of the candidates.

When referenda are called on issues beyond national ones, additional problems are raised. These questions are often technical ones where the arguments are complex. In one sense the Euro issue is economic: would Britain be financially better off if it adopted the Euro? Economists simply don't agree on this, probably because of the second issue, which is more an emotional matter, or, perhaps, a traditional one. People associate the national currency with the country itself. They feel that something British would be lost along with the pound. Can this sort of issue be meaningfully treated in pre-referendum literature, and in classrooms?

In the 1970s, the British Schools Council Humanities Project, a set of loose-leaf packs of printed material covering a series of social issues of the time, was published for use by older secondary pupils. The project topics included Housing, Relations between the Sexes, and Race. In the end, the project foundered owing to the racial issue. The material in the pack, which included illiberal posters and handbills of the time, was thought potentially inflammatory in its loose-leaf form: in a sense literacy could not cope with the democratic effort to address contentious issues of the day.

Thirty years later the British Government has tried a different approach. A new curriculum subject, Citizenship, is being introduced next year in State schools, following a build-up period of several years. The aim of the newly-formed Department for Education and Skills is to produce a literate and numerate population which is also aware of citizens' rights and obligations – education for democracy. The subject will be treated dispassionately.

This leaves the question of pupils' feelings of identity and loyalty to their family, group, or wider community, which will still be the subject matter of English, specifically literature. This in turn brings us to a distinction which has to be made between literacy and reading, between the vocational and the academic, between politics and life. Literacy as a concept is only about a hundred years old. It came in late in the 19th century, as universal education in western countries was demanding a new type of basic language, which the newly-educated could learn as a basis for their work in the large industries or offices of the period.

Boundaries of the New Literacy

The higher order literacy skills arise from the changes we have noted in employment and society. They have raised the concept of literacy to the point that bodies such as the International Reading Association and its affiliates now use it regularly in their publications and conferences.

Britain's curricular programme is called the National Literacy Strategy, though it extends beyond the traditional boundaries of literacy. What are the boundaries of the new literacy? If it demands higher order skills, does it also encompass a substantial part of the old subject of 'English', or the range implied by the old term, 'reading'?

The distinction between functional and imaginative language remains an important one. It is best defined, in my experience, by the Swiss child psychologist Bruno Bettelheim, in these words from his book, with Karen Zelan, *On Learning to Read* (4):

> There are two radically different ways in which reading (and the learning of it) can be experienced: either as something of great practical value, important if one wants to get on in life; or as the source of unlimited knowledge and the most moving aesthetic experiences...

> Consciously, most of us take pride in our rationality, and are correctly convinced that more than anything else it is our literacy that lifts us out of irrationality into rationality. That an earlier, childish idea of literacy's magic power may still be at work in us is suggested by what we experience when we are deeply affected by art, poetry, music, literature, for then we feel touched by magic. (p. 51)

This reminds us that imaginative reading is different from functional reading. It touches deeper parts of our minds and satisfies us in ways that aren't normally attainable from rational reading. For many of us, the satisfactions of imaginative reading are among the chief benefits of a good education.

Yet is this an outdated view? We live in an information age and computers are particularly good at storing and making available chunks of information. Some dons consider that the day of reading whole books has largely passed for students. Rather than reading whole books, many students now locate sections, papers, paragraphs even and print these out from the PC, to be organised into an essay. What may be the outcome is the change in many non-fiction texts, from whole paper books to electronic summaries and anthologies.

The term 'literacy' was coined in the late 19th century to cover the supposedly limited language needs of universal primary education. It has expanded over the past century to include features we once associated with traditional reading or language: what would be really exciting would be for the enlargement of literacy to take in imaginative literature. Those who write and legislate for literacy programmes in school would need to fully subscribe to Einstein's assertion that 'imagination is more important than knowledge'.

This possible outcome is not entirely far-fetched. Britain's National Literacy Strategy already includes references to children's books: reading comprehension is provided at each level for fiction, as are poetry and non-fiction. In a sense literacy has been substituted for most of the language and literature work formerly done in primary schools. But something is held back. What Bettelheim calls the magic is missing. The gap is the space between the functional/vocational on the one side, and the imaginative/pleasurable on the other. Is this gap bridgeable?

This brings us back to education, because it is in the early years that children learn to read, and establish the habits that will generally stay with them in adult life. One defence of basic literacy has been the view that reading and writing at a basic level have to be mastered before the learner can go on to more interesting aspects of language. This argument was used a good deal as the British National Literacy Strategy was introduced a few years ago. But underlying the Literacy Strategy and its admirable aim of raising standards across the school population, lies the continuing issue of imagination.

It is difficult to find research backing for the beneficial effects of leisure reading. The words used in the imaginative context suggest why this may be so. For Bettelheim, 'magic' is adduced to explain the aesthetic effect of literature and art; Margaret Meek Spencer writes of 'a dimension of feeling' (5); UNESCO's Charter for the Reader (6) used the adjective 'spiritual' for the effect of good books.

If imaginative fiction and poetry appeals to a different part of our mind from more functional writing, can we expect it to be part of a literacy system designed for other purposes? Yet young children love stories and rhymes, and contact made with books at an early age is clearly of great benefit to children fortunate enough to experience it.

With education changing its focus towards the individual (increasingly served by electronic resources); with society shifting from monolithic classes to individual consumers; and with imagination valued as never before (for scientific as much as for artistic purposes), the time is ripe for idealism and positive change. I have shown how literacy has grown as a concept over its 110 year history. It can grow further, encompassing the missing quality of imagination.

REFERENCES

(1) Emilia Ferreiro, 'Reading and Writing in a Changing World', paper delivered at International Publishers Association World Congress, Buenos Aires, May 2000.

(2) Publishers Association 'Spending in Schools' survey, March 2001.

(3) Worshipful Company of Stationers and Newspaper Makers, Summer Colloquium on e-Books, Stationers' Hall, London, June 2001.

(4) Bruno Bettelheim & Karen Zelan, *On Learning to Read*, Thames & Hudson, London, 1982.

(5) Margaret Meek Spencer, 'Fantasy to Fiction' in *The Times Literary Supplement*, July 1978.

(6) 'Charter for the Reader', International Publishers Association, Geneva, 1982.

21 Contemporary Discourse on Literacy: Reading in the Media

Rui Vieira de Castro, Portugal

In our contemporary and complex societies, demands concerning literacy are increasing everyday. If people fail to give the adequate responses to such demands, fundamental dimensions of their citizenship will be put in danger. In this sense, an orientation that must be ethically assumed is to support the idea that every single person has the right to access and exert the benefits of literacy.

Although literacy is but one variable among others involved in the development of life conditions, it can play a very important role. Hence, it is reasonable to analyse how literacy is shaped through discourse.

In this paper, I hold one general assumption: in a given society, at a certain moment, what literacy *is*, for instance what counts as 'good' or 'bad literacy', is shaped, to a certain extent, by discourses, potentially competing, which therefore constitute 'literacy practices' (Barton & Hamilton, 2000: 7-9). Such discourses give expression to deep structures and relations constituted on the basis of economic, social, ideological and political factors; in this sense, concepts such as 'literate person', 'literate society', 'levels of literacy' or 'literacy standards' are strongly embedded in history.

This makes the study of discourses most relevant, especially if the analytic task should have as its ultimate goal to reveal the connections between text and context. In doing so, one can go beyond the surface of the 'rhetoric masks' that most often obscure the real foundations of those discourses. In the course of this movement, one may hope to contribute to a better understanding of why in a specific moment and place certain discourses are available or why we can find certain discourses as dominant while others become dominated. Actually, if some literacies can be seen as more 'legitimate' than others, in practice and/or theoretically, it is because in contemporary societies 'particular literacies have been created by and are structured and sustained by (certain) institutions' (Barton & Hamilton, 2000, p. 12).

In this respect, mass media, which is a relevant arena for the construction of representations of the world, of social relations and identities (Fairclough, 1995), play a crucial role. Media discourse is structured upon the confluence of two kinds of sources: i) it conveys what is said in other fields through means of 'discourse representation' (Fairclough, 1995a, p.54), in the form of news, reports, and interviews; ii) it gives voice to what is regarded as proper in mass media communication through editorial frames. These sources are usually articulated in such a way that the former is always regulated by the latter, through operations of recontextualisation.

It is true that not all perspectives concerning literacy can be found in the media; however, it is also true that newspapers, magazines, radio and television are plausible contexts in which to find 'alternative views of the world' (Clark & Ivanic, 1997, p. 31). Thus, media analysis appears to be a very significant means to identify, characterise and situate some of the most relevant discourses on literacy that are produced and reproduced in society.

Reading in the Printed Press

Discourses on literacy in the media constitute a subject that is very large and diverse in nature. For the purposes of this paper some restrictions were placed both on the subject of study and on the materials to be analysed. It was decided to privilege one domain of literacy – reading – and one element of media – the press. The first of these options is based upon the fact that, in the common sense, reading very often equates with literacy, and when people are arguing about literacy they nearly always have reading in mind. The reason for selecting the press was of a different, methodological, order – discourses conveyed by the press can easily be made available to scrutiny; however, this option by no means implies that one should distinguish between the power of the press and of other media.

In this context, the following objectives for research were defined:

(i) to identify the relevance of the production of discourses on literacy, namely on reading, in the press, the status of their producers and the contexts of their production;

(ii) to identify and characterise the main structure of the argumentative frames concerning reading;

(iii) to establish the *loci* of consensus and divergence among the different positions.

As the universe of press is a very large and hardly manageable one, I selected one newspaper and one magazine for the this study – the *Jornal de Letras, Artes e Ideias* ('Journal of Humanities, Arts and Ideas') and *Ler* ('Reading'); these are two of the most influential media in the Portuguese cultural arena.

Jornal de Letras, a fortnightly newspaper, is presented by their editors as 'the only cultural newspaper in the Portuguese language'; founded by Portuguese journalists in 1980, it is now the property of a multinational press group. *Ler* is a three-monthly magazine published by Círculo de Leitores, a publishing house owned by the Bertelsmann group; it is 'a journal exclusively concerned with the world of books', as its editor puts it. *Jornal de Letras* does not give any indication of its sales per issue; *Ler* indicates around 20,000 copies per number.

Jornal de Letras has a recognisable organisation, with sections covering News (including 'books of the fortnight'), People, Interviews, Unpublished Work, Themes, Arts, Essays, Pre-publication, and Debate. The different sections in *Ler* are not so easily identifiable, but the following sections are evident: Editorial, Letters to the Editor, News, Chronicles, Essay, Theme, Interview, Poetry/Literature, and Literary Criticism.

These publications deal largely with questions of reading and, to a certain extent, reading literature, though this is more evident in the case of *Ler*. In order to make the research task more manageable, a decision was made to consider only those texts that addressed reading habits, reading attitudes and contexts of reading. In addition, if a particular text – a commentary on a work of literature, for instance – said something about these topics, it was also included in the corpus.

We studied the selected media over a period of three years, starting in 1996. In that year, a national study on literacy based on a representative sample of the Portuguese population was published (Benavente *et al.*, 1996). The middle of the nineties also gave rise to extensive studies in the area of reading habits and practices. These facts seemed to be relevant enough to establish the second half of the decade as the period to be studied; at that time, literacy issues emerged with a certain visibility in political, academic and social fields.

In this study, the unit of analysis is defined as the text fragment which, in a larger textual unit (news, interview, editorial, letters to the editor, chronicle), gives a perspective on reading. These fragments are analysed according to a particular set of dimensions – type of text; status of the producer; selected topic; arguments produced. Taking these dimensions into consideration, my purpose, at a further stage, is to establish different types of discourse concerning reading. In consequence, I will try to proceed from frequency of texts, to types of text, topics and argumentative frames corresponding to different kinds of discourse.

Rui Vieira de Castro 181

Results

The analysis of the *corpus* established the frequency of those texts which in both publications deal with topics on reading. The results are presented in Table 1.

TABLE 1: FREQUENCY OF TEXTS DEALING WITH THE TOPIC 'READING'

Publication	Number of Issues	Texts with Content on Reading	Percentage of Issues with Texts on Reading
Jornal de Letras	78	38	49%
Ler	12	11	92%

In almost all the issues of *Ler* and in half of the issues of *Jornal de Letras* we can find commentaries, opinions, or facts concerning reading (as defined above). However it must be stressed that the nature of the references to reading in the analysed texts varies significantly: it is possible to find texts that deal extensively with the topic, but we can also find other texts where reading appears as a minor subject, texts where some piece of information on reading habits, for instance, is made available. Besides, both media usually have a large number of articles and this fact also serves to present a scenario where topics on reading do not appear to be of major importance; this is particularly the case for *Jornal de Letras*, a newspaper that includes general cultural information.

Regarding who produces statements on reading and where those statements occur, the analysis proved the existence of a great variety of authors as well as a great diversity of texts. The contexts where statements on reading occur are described in Table 2.

TABLE 2: CONTEXTS OF STATEMENTS ON 'READING'

	Jornal de Letras	*Ler*
Editorial	3%	22%
Newsreport/interview/inquiry	36%	15%
News	24%	–
Essay/opinion texts	36%	62%

The data suggest two different strategies: i) in the case of *Jornal de Letras* reading is a topic mainly generated or conveyed in the context of news and interviews; the editor considers the topic very occasionally; ii) as far as *Ler* is concerned, the topic is mainly introduced directly, through 'internal voices' and, the editor frequently expounds on the topic. This suggests the existence of two perspectives: on the one hand, *Journal de Letras* appears to provide a forum for the expression of external voices, even if those voices are 'framed' by internal ones, being filtered by the point of view of the *medium*; on the other hand, and this is clearly the case with *Ler*, the publication plays a constitutive role in the field; it acts much more as a producer than a reproducer of what was said elsewhere. However, it must be noticed that, overall, only very few texts select literacy and reading as their main or structural topic.

If one takes into account the status of those whose voices emerge in the context of interviews, reports or inquiries, one can have a better understanding of the legitimate voices.

TABLE 3: VOICES IN INTERVIEWS AND REPORTS

Media Voices	*Jornal de Letras*	*Ler*
Journalists	14%	10%
Researchers	14%	-
Publishers	23%	-
Writers	14%	54%
Politicians	32%	-
Others	3%	36%

Again, we find significant differences between the two media. In accordance with its status, *Ler* privileges the voice of writers. In *Jornal de Letras*, the production of statements on reading has two main sources, politicians and publishers, but others are also given an opportunity to state their positions. A vision of the whole shows that, in this context, the dominant voices are from the field of politics, from the market and from the places of production; in this context, positions originating in the field of research have little relevance.

TABLE 4: PERSPECTIVES ON READING

Topics	Sample Statements
Selling Books • the crisis in bookshops • the crisis in publishing • the claim for fixed prices for books • the claim for cultural diversity	'There are great difficulties as far as bookshops are concerned, as a consequence of the amount of books sold in supermarkets [...] there are distortions at the level of the edition.' Politician, *Jornal de Letras*, 1996(661) 'Portuguese publishing houses [...] in the context of the 'crisis of reading', are doing in very positive work.' Editor, *Ler*, 1996 (36)
Reading habits and choices • the dissatisfaction with reading habits • the crisis in reading • the need to identify the causes of low levels of reading	'There are no readers for the books that are written.'Journalist, *Ler*, 1997 (38) 'I am not mentioning reading for employment. Here what matters is reading for pleasure.' Journalist, *Ler*, 1997 (37)
Libraries • positive results in public libraries • problems in school libraries	'In the cultural field, the creation of a public library network was probably one of the greatest achievements since 1974.' Editor, *Ler*, 1997 (40)
Reading and book promotion • political measures to be taken • rising of standards of living • good and bad practices in reading promotion	'We started a programme to promote reading, a programme whose slogan is 'To make the whole country read'. We need to read more.' Politician, *Jornal de Letras*, 1997 (686)
Functions of reading and of books • reading to promote citizenship • reading as a measure of freedom • books as testimonies of our creative capacity	'The destiny of the book can hardly be separate from the human destiny [books are the place where] the alliance or the confrontation between people and the times they live in takes place.' Politician, *Jornal de Letras*, 1997 (705)
Reading and school • the inadequacy of school practices concerning reading • school as a foundation for a politics of reading • the correlation between reading habits and school success	'Teachers and educators do not motivate for the pleasure of reading.' Teacher and writer, *Jornal de Letras*, 1997(686)

When we analysed the texts from the point of view of what is said about reading, we found that: (i) in the case of *Jornal de Letras*, more than 25% of all texts discuss aspects of the market for books, such as book-selling rates, distribution of books, etc.; topics on reading habits and choices, and on school libraries and public libraries can be found in between 20% and 25% of the texts; functions of reading and reading in school are topics that only very occasionally emerge; (ii) in the case of *Ler*, the market for books, reading habits and choices are the major themes; at a second level of relevance one can find information concerning libraries and discussion of the functions of reading and of books.

If the selection of certain topics, and the consequent deletion of others topics, can give us important information about how reading is conceived in these media, additional and significant information can be made available if we take into consideration not only the subjects that are chosen but also the commentaries made on them. Thus, the analysis proceeded by considering the main features of discourses on reading. To present the data, I used a set of general categories, detailed in subcategories; paradigmatic statements are used to illustrate the main discourse frames.

The analysis of the categories in the table (here represented through paradigmatic statements) revealed two main argumentative lines: on the one hand, the emphasis is on the potential of reading and on the relevance of books as cultural devices; on the other hand, the word used to describe many of the dimensions of reading is *crisis*. What is interesting to notice is that most of the arguments have as background what we may call the conventional reading of the legitimate texts – as one journalist says 'what matters is reading for pleasure'.

Conclusion

My goal in this paper was to contribute to the characterisation of certain dimensions of media discourse on literacy, namely those aspects concerning *who* speaks *where* and in *what terms* about *reading*. The study was conducted over one newspaper and one magazine, which are of great relevance in the Portuguese cultural field.

The analysis revealed that, in general terms, reading as social or individual practice does not have great visibility in what I called internal or external voices, which means that in the cultural field, including its representation in the media, reading, as defined in this text, is not a central subject.

A more detailed analysis made clear some similarities and some differences between two media – while *Jornal de Letras* gives voice to a larger group of contributors, acting as a mediator, in the case of *Ler*, the newspaper itself is most predominant, including a very significant presence of the editor; this fact reveals the existence of different discourse strategies which make visible the function of these media in the cultural field: one – *Jornal de Letras* – more dependent on immediate factual information; the other – *Ler* – is oriented to a stronger intervention in the field itself.

These media produce *a* narrative on reading[2]; like other narratives this one selects and rejects certain characters and themes. When characters are given such an opportunity, the voices one can hear first are from the producers (writers), from the market (publishers) and from politics; joining journalists' voices, they all speak, in close accord, about the market and about reading habits and the word that is commonly used to qualify reading in its different dimensions is *crisis*. It is as if relevant meanings were limited and have become established [3]; in this sense, these texts appear to have a major function – to fix a certain image of reading and to reproduce that same image. Actually, the *discourse of crisis* is the dominant one, although it co-exists with the *discourse of promise*. However, both of these discourses are characterised by the deletion of relevant dimensions of reading, namely those that are concerned with readers' purposes, diversity of texts, and significant contexts of reading. Because they forget these dimensions, deliberately or not, these discourses act as rhetoric masks and, certainly, they do not make it as clear as possible, in what terms reading is a relevant practice.

NOTES

1. This text has been developed in the context of the research project – *Literacies. Contexts. Practices. Discourses* (FCT-POCTI 33888/99) funded by the Portuguese *Fundação para a Ciência e Tecnologia*.
2. Barton & Hamilton (1998) suggest this representation of literacy in media as a narrative, explaining its principles, characters and themes (see especially pages 20-22).
3. For the analysis of similar processes in the representation of illiteracy in media discourse, see Matencio (1999).

BIBLIOGRAPHY

Barton, D. & Hamilton, M. (1998). *Local literacies. Reading and writing in one community*. London: Routledge.

Barton, D. & Hamilton, M. (2000). Literacy practices. In David Barton, Mary Hamilton & Roz Ivanic, Eds., *Situated literacies. Reading and writing in context*. London: Routledge.

Benavente, A., Rosa, A., Costa, A.F., & Ávila, P. (1996). *A literacia em Portugal. Resultados de uma pesquisa extensiva e monográfica*. Lisboa: Fundação Calouste Gulbenkian.

Clark, R. & Ivanic, R. (1997). *The politics of writing*. London: Routledge.

Fairclough, N. (1995). *Media discourse*. London: Edward Arnold.

Fairclough, N. (1995a). *Critical discourse analysis. The critical study of language*. London: Longman.

Matencio, M. de Lourdes (1999). Analfabetismo na mídia: Conceitos e imagens sobre o letramento. In Angela B. Kleiman, Org., *Os significados do letramento*. Campinas: Mercado de Letras.

SECTION 7

Reading Comprehension

22 Strategic Habits for Struggling Middle Grades Readers

Leslie W. Crawford, Margaret M. Philbin and Charles E. Martin, U.S.A.

Many students, who were apparently capable readers in early grades, struggle to comprehend content material in the middle grades. Accustomed to heavy guidance and support from their teachers, they are suddenly expected to read subject-area materials independently. This is a formidable task for which many students are not prepared. They simply have not developed the strategic habits necessary to independently meet the new demands of content-area reading. The purpose of this paper is to describe those habits that struggling readers need and to propose an instructional model to guide their development.

Over the past three decades, our conceptions of reading have changed dramatically. We no longer view reading as a set of discrete skills taught to students to get the author's meaning. Reading is now seen as an interactive process between the reader and the text. Meaning is constructed and is affected by the purpose and the setting for reading (Bloom and Green, 1984; Anderson and Pearson, 1984). Marinak and Henk (1999) emphasised that we must identify strategies used by good readers and teach those strategies in a developmentally-appropriate manner. When these strategies are learned, they improve reading comprehension (Pressley, 2000).

Nine Good Habits

We, too, were interested in identifying the essential things that good readers do and in creating a format that allows them to be easily learned and used. This effort resulted in a list of nine habits (three for each of the cognitive reading processes- *before, while,* and *after* reading) and a set of strategies that help struggling readers develop these habits. The following sections describe each of the Nine Good Habits and provide an explanation of how the strategies help readers develop good comprehension habits.

Before I Read Habits

The *Before I Read* habits are routines that readers should employ before they read a selection. Developing these habits helps students prepare to read by previewing what the selection will be about, activating background knowledge, and creating purposes for reading.

Check it out. The first Good Habit students should develop is to check out a selection before they read. Checking a passage out before you read helps to develop a mind set or a framework for understanding and develop a plan for reading. Strategies like looking at titles, previewing headings and subheadings, examining illustrations and graphics, and identifying the kind of writing (genre) help students develop this habit. (Henk, Moore, Marinak & Tomasetti, 2000; Pressley & Wharton-McDonald, 1997; Stein, 1978)

Think about what I already know about the subject. We need to think about what we already know so that we can use that information to make connections with what we read (Anderson, 1994). Strategies such as listing what you know about the topic before you read help readers activate prior knowledge and get ready to make connections when they read. (Readence, Moore & Rickelman, 2000; Ollman, 1996; Cunningham, Moore, Cunningham & Moore, 1995; Pressley, Wood, Woloshyn, Martin, King & Menke, 1992; Ogle, 1986; Langer,1984)

Decide what I need to know. Strategies such as using titles, headings, or illustrations to create questions help provide a focus for comprehension. Students can use the teacher's questions or actual questions from the text to decide what they need to know. Students can even think about what they would like to know more about to guide their reading (Simpson & Nist, 2000; Ogle, 1986; Paris, Cross & Lipson, 1984; Manzo, 1969)

While I Read Habits

While I Read habits keep readers actively involved and help them make connections while they read. These connections may be within a selection, with something else they have read, or with their background knowledge. In addition, *While I Read* habits help students monitor their understanding and fix it when it's faulty. Being engaged focuses the reader's attention and improves comprehension.

How does it connect to what I know? To comprehend, readers must connect what they read to what they know (Ruddell & Ruddell, 1994). Strategies that help develop this habit include visualising while you read, thinking about similar things that have happened to you, making predictions while reading, or elaborating on what you read (van den Broek & Kremer, 2000; Keene & Zimmerman, 1997; Gambrell & Jawitz, 1993; Schumaker, Ally & Warner 1984; Levin, 1973)

Does it make sense? Good readers stop periodically and see if what they've read makes sense. They examine boldfaced vocabulary and summarise information to check their understanding of concepts. Learning these strategies and others can help developing readers get in the habit of monitoring their comprehension. (Baumann, Hooten, & White, 1999; Swanson & de la Paz, 1998; Palincsar & Brown, 1984)

If it doesn't make sense, what can I do? What separates proficient readers from those that struggle is the ability of good readers to draw on a variety of strategies to fix their understanding when it breaks down. Teaching students to reread, use context clues, refer to graphics, and look to summaries for clarification help to develop an independent 'fix-it' habit (Pearson et al, 1992; Nagy, 1988; Palincsar & Brown, 1986; Davey & Porter, 1982)

After I Read Habits

For good readers, reading doesn't end with the last word in a selection. They are in the habit of thinking about what they have just read: What do they remember? Do they like or dislike what they've read? Using such strategies helps them remember what they've read, make connections after reading, and see the relevance in the material.

React to what I've read. Good readers critically analyse and react personally to what they've read. This deeper level of processing leads to better comprehension. Strategies that encourage students to examine choices the author made and positions on issues help readers develop this habit. (Asselin, 2000; Karolides, 1999; Pressley, Wood, Woloshyn, Martin, King, & Menke, 1992)

Check to see what I remember. When good readers finish reading a selection, they use strategies such as summarising and listing important ideas to check what they remember. They go back and use headings, illustrations, and charts to create questions to test their understanding. (Oakhill, 1993; Rosenshine, Meister & Chapman, 1996; Armbruister, Anderson & Ostertag, 1987; Bean & Steenwyke, 1984).

Use what I've read. Using what we have read forces us make the internal and external connections that improves our understanding and helps us generalise what we learn (Mayer, 1989). It provides us with the kind of practice that Perkins and Salomon (1987) feel is necessary to apply what we have learned. Strategies such as thinking about how the information can be used, using what is read as a springboard for new ideas, or deciding what else you'd like to know help develop the habit of applying what you've read (Graves & Braaten, 1996; Ziegert, 1994; Simpson, 1994; Linden & Whittrock, 1981)

Model for Instruction

The instructional model for the nine habits is based on the four concepts: explicit instruction, modeling and think alouds, text scaffolding and teaching for transfer. These four concepts were synthesised into an instructional model that uses *modeling, guided practice*, and *application*. The strategies are modeled through 'think alouds,' and students have an opportunity to try out each new strategy guided by reminders and prompts concerning the strategy steps. Finally, students have an opportunity to independently use the strategies and reflect on their use. These reflections provide teachers and students with valuable information about how well the strategies are understood.

Why Use Explicit Instruction?

Explicit instruction lets all readers in on the secrets of good readers. Wilkinson (1995) captures this idea:

It's about making the hidden obvious; exposing and explaining what is taken for granted; demystifying mental processes; letting children in on the information and strategies which will enable them to become powerful literacy users.

Explicit instruction provides a way for teachers to develop students' metacognitive processes (Wilkinson, 1999) and helps students become strategic readers who can look at a reading task, decide the best way to approach it, monitor their understanding as they proceed, and decide which strategies to use when confronted with a problem.

The explicit instruction model provides a concrete framework for comprehension instruction. Dole (2000) states that 'Despite a significant body of research in the 1980s suggesting the effectiveness of strategy instruction, especially for lower-achieving readers, strategy instruction has not been implemented in many American classrooms' (p. 62). Explicitly teaching comprehension strategies has been effective in reading and writing (for example, Keene & Zimmerman, 1997) and gives teachers a framework in which to teach strategic thinking.

Why Use Modeling and Thinking Aloud?

Modeling, and peer modeling in particular, has been an important component in many social-learning approaches and has been shown to improve reading comprehension (Greenwood, Delquadri & Hall, 1989; Rosenshine & Meister, 1994; Stevens, Madden, Slavin & Farnish, 1987). Vygotsky theorised that children learn through expert guidance, provided by adults or by their peers (Vygotsky, 1962). One technique for modeling is using a think aloud (Duffy & Roehler, 1989). Thinking aloud, talking about what you are doing when you are doing it, reveals a good reader's internal processes and is an important component in successful strategy-teaching programs (Pressley, 2000). We also want to encourage struggling readers to think aloud. According to Barrell (1991) encouraging this kind of thinking aloud, or self-talk, is beneficial.

> Saying things to ourselves such as 'What is my problem? … What can I try? … Where have I been in a situation like this before? I can solve this problem if I really persist at it.' All these statements will eventually be internalized and part of a repertoire for confronting difficult situations. (p. 14).

Thinking aloud about reading also serves to enhance students' comprehension-monitoring abilities (Baumann & Jones, 1993) and can be a tool in encouraging readers to make connections with other things they've read (Lenski, 1998). These are the kinds of metacognitive behaviors necessary for reading independence.

What is the Importance of Text Scaffolding?

Scaffolding is that support or help that learners need to progress from where they are to the next level (Vygotsky 1978). It may come in many forms including prompts, reminders, modeling, and answers to questions; however, it is not limited to help provided by individuals. It may also include support provided by the text. Textual scaffolding may be found in the organisation of a text (e.g., a predictable children's book (Brown, 1999/2000) or by authors making inferences more explicit (Graves et al, 1988)). It also might include features such as bold-faced key vocabulary, and inclusion of headings, introductions, or summaries. These text-scaffolding techniques make the selection more reader-friendly by reducing the cognitive demands on the reader (van den Broek & Kremer, 2000).

How Do We Teach for Transfer?

Transfer depends on teaching both declarative knowledge (what the strategy is) and procedural knowledge (how to use the strategy). In addition, conditional knowledge (when and where a strategy may be successful) is needed for students to transfer what they have learned from the specific learning situation to novel situations (Winne & Butler, 1994). To teach declarative knowledge of strategies, the steps of the strategy are presented explicitly. Procedural and conditional information is presented through modeling and think alouds. Students are given opportunities to reflect on their understanding of the strategies and to draw on their declarative, procedural, and conditional knowledge to complete reading tasks, choose appropriate strategies, and reflect on which strategies they found most useful.

Conclusion

Research indicates that students can develop good reading habits when a model, practice, apply instructional approach is taken and that instruction is embedded in meaningful reading and good literature (Baumann, Hooten & White, 1999; Dowhower, 1999). These studies emphasize the value of informal as well as formal instruction in comprehension strategies and the importance of teachers developing a strategic stance, ready to seize opportunities to help their students learn strategies and develop good reading habits.

REFERENCES

Anderson, R.C., & Pearson, P.D. (1984). A schema theoretical view of basic processes in reading. In P.D. Pearson (Ed.), *Handbook of reading research* (pp 255-292). White Plains, NY: Longman.

Anderson, R.C. (1994). The role of the reader's schema in comprehension, learning and memory. In R.B. Ruddell, M.R. Ruddell, & H. Singer (Eds.), *Theoretical models and processes of reading* (pp. 469-482). Newark, DE: International Reading Association.

Armbruster, B. B., Anderson, T. H., & Ostertag, J. (1987). Does text structure/ summarization instruction facilitate learning from expository text? *Reading Research Quarterly, 22,* 331-346.

Asselin, M. (2000). Reader response in literature and reading instruction. *Teacher Librarian, 27 (4),* 62-64.

Barrell, J. (1991). *Teaching for thoughtfulness: Classroom strategies to enhance intellectual development.* NY: Longman.

Baumann, J.F., Hooten, H., & White, P. (1999). Teaching comprehension through literature: A teacher-research project to develop fifth graders' reading strategies and motivation. *Reading Teacher, 53,* 38-52.

Baumann, J.F., & Jones, L.A. (1993). Using think alouds to enhance children's comprehension monitoring abilities. *Reading Teacher, 47,* 184-193.

Bean, T. W., & Steenwyke, E L. (1984). The effect of three forms of summarization instruction on sixth graders summary writing and comprehension. *Journal of Reading Behavior, 16,* 297-306.

Bloome, D. & Green, J. (1984). Directions in the sociolinguistic study of reading. In P.D. Pearson (Ed.), *Handbook of reading research* (pp. 395-452). White Plains, NY: Longman.

Brown, K.J. (1999/2000). What kind of text- for whom and when? Textual scaffolding for beginning readers. *Reading Teacher, 53,* 292-307.

Cunningham, P.M., Moore, S.A., Cunningham, J.W., & Moore, D.W. (1995). *Reading and writing in elementary classrooms: Strategies and observations (3rd ed.).* NY: Longman.

Davey, B., & Porter, S. M. (1982). Comprehension-rating: A procedure to assist poor comprehenders. *Journal of Reading, 26,* 197-202.

Dole, J.A. (2000). Explicit and implicit instruction in comprehension. In B.M. Taylor, M.F. Graves, and P. van den Broek (Eds), *Reading for meaning: Fostering comprehension in the middle grades* (pp. 52-69). Newark, DE: International Reading Association.

Dowhower, S.L. (1999). Supporting a strategic stance in the classroom: A comprehension framework for helping teachers help students to be strategic. *Reading Teacher, 52,* 672-688.

Duffy, G.G., & Roehler, L.R. (1989). Why strategy instruction is so difficult and what we need to do about it. In C.B. McCormick, G. Miller, & M. Pressley (Eds.), *Cognitive strategy research: From basic research to educational applications* (pp. 133-154). New York: Springer-Verlag.

Gambrell, LB., & Jawitz, R B. (1993). Mental imagery, text illustrations, and children's comprehension and recall. *Reading Research Quarterly, 28,* 264-273.

Graves, M.F., & Braaten, S. (1996). Scaffolded reading experiences: Bridges to success. *Preventing School Failure, 40,* 169-173.

Graves, M., Slater, W.H., Roen, D., Redd-Boyd, T., Furniss, D.W., & Hazeltine, P. (1988). Some characteristics of memorable expository writing: Effects of revisions by writers with different backgrounds. *Research in the Teaching of English, 22,* 242-265.

Greenwood, C.R., Delquadri, J.C., & Hall, R.V. (1989). Longitudinal effects of classwide peer-assisted learning strategies. *Journal of Educational Psychology, 81,* 371-383.

Henk, W.A., Moore, J.C., Marinak, B.A.; Tomasetti, B.W. (2000). A reading lesson observation framework for elementary teachers, principals, and literacy supervisors. *Reading Teacher, 53,* 358-369.

Karolides, N. J. (1999). Theory and practice: An interview with Louise M. Rosenblatt. *Language Arts, 77,* 158-70.

Keene, E.O., & Zimmerman, S. (1997). *Mosaic of thought: Reading comprehension in reader's workshop.* Portsmouth, NH: Heinemann.

Langer, J.A. (1984). Examining background knowledge and text comprehension. *Reading Research Quarterly, 19,* 468-481.

Lenski, S.D. (1998). Intertextual intentions: Making connections across texts. *The Clearing House, 72,* 74-80.

Levin, J. (1973). Inducing comprehension in poor readers: A test of a recent model. *Journal of Educational Psychology, 65,* 19-24.

Linden, M., & Whittrock, M.C. (1981). The teaching of reading comprehension according to the model of generative learning. *Reading Research Quarterly, 17,* 44-57.

Manzo, A.V. (1969). *The ReQuest procedure. Journal of Reading, 13,* 123-126.

Marinak, B.A., & Henk, W.A. (1999). Balanced literacy instruction in the elementary school: The West Hanover story. In S.M. Blair-Larsen & K.A. Williams (Eds.), *The balanced reading program.* Newark, DE: International Reading Association.

Mayer, R. (1989). Models for understanding. *Review of Educational Research, 59,* 43-64.

Nagy, W. E. (1988). *Teaching vocabulary to improve reading comprehension.* Newark, DE: International Reading Association.

Oakhill, J.V. (1993). Children's difficulties in reading comprehension. *Educational Psychology Review, 5,* 223-237.

Ogle, D.M. (1986). K-W-L: A teaching model that develops active reading of expository text. *Reading Teacher, 39,* 564-570.

Ollman, H.E. (1996). Creating higher level thinking with reading response. Journal of *Adolescent and Adult Literacy, 39,* 576-581.

Palincsar, A.S., & Brown, A.L. (1984). Reciprocal teaching of comprehension-fostering and comprehension-monitoring activities. *Cognition and Instruction, 2,* 117-175.

Palincsar, A.S., & Brown, A.L. (1986). Interactive teaching to promote independent learning from text. *Reading Teacher, 39,* 771-777.

Paris, S.G., Cross, D.R., & Lipson, M.Y. (1984) Informed strategies for learning: A program to improve children's reading awareness and comprehension skills. *Journal of Educational Psychology, 76,* 1239-1252.

Pearson, P.D., Roehler, L.R., Dole, J.A., & Duffy, G.G. (1992). Developing expertise in reading comprehension. In S.J.Samuels & A.E. Farstrup (Eds.) *What research has to say about reading instruction?* Newark, DE: International Reading Association.

Perkins, D.N., & Salomon, G. (1987). Transfer and teaching thinking. In D.N. Perkins, J.C. Lockhead, and J.C. Bishop (Eds.), *Thinking: the second international conference.* Hillsdale, NJ: Erlbaum.

Pressley, M. (2000). Comprehension instruction in elementary school: A quarter-century of research progress. In B.M. Taylor, M.F. Graves, & P. van den Broek (Eds.). *Reading for meaning: Fostering comprehension in the middle grades* (pp. 32-51). Newark, DE: International Reading Association.

Pressley, M., & Wharton-McDonald, R. (1997). Skilled comprehension and its development through instruction. *School Psychology Review, 26,* 448-466.

Pressley, M., Wood, E., Woloshyn, V. E., Martin, V., King, A, & Menke, D. (1992). Encouraging mindful use of prior knowledge: Attempting to construct explanatory answers facilitates learning. *Educational Psychologist, 27,* 91-110.

Readence, J.E., Moore, D.W., & Rickelman, R.J. (2000). *Prereading activities for content area reading and learning* (3rd ed). Newark, DE: International Reading Association.

Rosenshine, B.,& Meiser, C. (1994). Reciprocal Teaching: A review of research. *Review of Educational Research, 64,* 479-530.

Rosenshine, B, Meister, C., & Chapman, S. (1996). Teaching students to generate questions: A review of the intervention studies. *Review of Educational Research, 66,* 181-221.

Ruddell, R.B. & Ruddell, M.R. (1994). Language acquisition and literacy process. In R.B. Ruddell, M.R. Ruddell, & H. Singer (Eds.), *Theoretical models and processes of reading* (4th ed., 448-468). Newark, DE: International Reading Association.

Schumaker, J.B., Ally, G.R., & Warner, M.M. (1984). Using visual imagery and self-questions to improve comprehension of written material. *Journal of Learning Disability, 17,* 145-149.

Simpson, M.L. (1994). Talk throughs: A strategy for encouraging active learning across the content areas. *Journal of Reading, 38,* 296-304.

Simpson, M.L., & Nist, S.L. (2000). An update on strategic learning: It's more than textbook reading strategies. *Journal of Adolescent and Adult Literacy, 43,* 528-541.

Stein, H. (1978). The visual reading guide (VRG). *Social Education, 42,* 534-535.

Stevens, R.J., Madden, N.A., Slavin, R.E.,& Farnish, A.M. (1987). Cooperative Integrated Reading and Composition: Two field experiments. *Reading Research Quarterly, 22,* 433-454.

Swanson, P.N. & de la Paz, S. (1998). Teaching effective comprehension to students with reading and learning disabilities. *Intervention in School & Clinic, 33,* 209-219.

van den Broek, P., & Kremer, K.E. (2000). The mind in action: What it means to comprehend during reading. In B. Taylor, P. van den Broek, & M. Graves (Eds.), *Reading for Meaning: Fostering Comprehension in the Middle Grades* (pp. 1-31). New York: Teacher's College Press.

Vygotsky, L.S. (1962). Mind and society: T*he development of higher psychological processes.* Cambridge, MA: MIT Press.

Vygotsky, L.S. (1978. Thought and language. Cambridge, MA: MIT Press.

Wilkinson, L. (1995) Explicit teaching. In *Cornerstones: Training and development program* (Modules 6 & 7, Appendix 1). Adelaide, SA: Department of Education and Children's Services, Curriculum Division.

Wilkinson, L. (1999). An introduction to the explicit teaching of reading. In J Hancock (Ed.), *The explicit teaching of reading*. Newark, DE: International Reading Association.

Winne, P. H., & Butler, D. L. (1994). Student cognition in learning from teaching. In T. Husen & T. Postlethwaite (Eds.), *International encyclopedia of education* (2nd ed., pp. 5738-5745). Oxford, England: Pergamon.

Ziegert, S. (1994). Reflection: A step beyond the reading of a chapter. *Journal of Reading, 38,* 132-134.

23 Integrating Children's Interests and Literature to Enhance Reading Comprehension

Gail Goss, U.S.A.

The world of today's children is more complicated than in the past. There is a larger volume of information available in a wider variety of forms and more text in non-fiction format. Teaching methods used in the past need to change to meet new needs. Children can no longer learn just facts as in prior times. Readers now need more skills and knowledge of how to find, use, and communicate information.

This presentation will discuss and demonstrate how to use children's interests combined with children's literature to make learning easier. The concept is to choose an area that excites children, one where they already have a developed schemata or knowledge base, and then use children's trade books about that topic to teach the skills and strategies that build stronger readers. I have always loved cats, and I know that many children do too, so I choose that theme as an example of an interdisciplinary approach to teach a variety of reading skills, strategies, and genres. This same approach is effective with any topic that interests children.

Background Information

Classroom practices have often divided the school day into compartmentalised subjects. Little was done to make connections for children between the various content areas or to demonstrate the use of the same skills across disciplines. The US National Council of Teachers of English (NCTE) recommends focusing instruction on integrated, inter-disciplinary activities revolving around a topic that interests children (NCTE, 1995).

What is an interdisciplinary approach? It is looking at a topic from various perspectives and subject areas, using fiction as well as non-fiction trade books and other sources of print information. It is building a large picture of the topic across content areas. Students read widely and use the information gathered to predict, retell, verify, question, and summarise as they pull their information together. Students learn to prepare ways to present or share the knowledge gained with others (Baumann, Hooten, & White, 1999). An interdisciplinary approach allows learners to connect new knowledge they are gaining with their prior knowledge about the topic. They have a variety of opportunities to build their competencies through meaningful writing, reading, listening and talking, all skills they will need throughout their lives.

Teachers identify areas or subjects that interest their children, collect materials, and build lessons and activities around those materials to make the many connections that enhance learning. Tevebaugh (2001) stated that ' . . . there is indeed much credence to the current theories surrounding cross-curricular instruction and providing student autonomy in learning. The methods we use might differ somewhat, depending on the students with whom we work, but the concepts remain the same. The time for separating language arts and skills instruction from academic subjects has passed. In today's increasingly integrated society, students must develop a sense of interdependence and an understanding of possible relationships between diverse endeavors and areas of study' (p. 346-347). Students taught using trade books with activities have significant gains in concept acquisition over students taught with textbooks and activities. They also acquire more concepts and a greater understanding of the concepts (Guzzetti, Kowalinski & McGowan, 1992).

Teachers should be striving to create lifelong readers and learners. To do this students need numerous opportunities to use authentic reading situations within the classroom environment to practice the skills they will use in their life outside of school (Hiebert & Colt, 1989). 'Juxtaposing fiction and non-fiction builds on the natural curiosity of students. The fictional accounts draw readers into the story world while the non-fiction texts add facts and depth to the students' understanding' (Gilles & Mitchell, 2001, p. 579).

The following are benefits of using an interdisciplinary teaching approach built on children's interests:

* Children's curiosity about a topic aids learning by capitalising on their interests, background knowledge, and strengths. Capitalising on their interests increases positive attitudes.
* Addressing multiple content areas helps students grasp the connections between subjects more easily than using a compartmentalized approach to instruction. Learning important concepts and ideas across curricular areas is simpler.
* Using real world or authentic activities such as researching, collecting and synthesizing data to statistical or narrative reports and sharing the information with others, unlike prepared materials which are not related

to students' needs, increases connections to real world situations. This also incorporates higher level math and language skills.

- Moving outside textbooks exposes readers to the variety of genre in trade books containing material about their interest. It makes it easier to recall pertinent information and helps teach the value of different opinions and sources of information. This allows for studying a topic in depth from various perspectives.

Accomplishing an Interdisciplinary Approach

The rest of this paper demonstrates materials and ways of using the theme of cats to implement an interdisciplinary approach. The activities can be adapted to any grade level.

Why cats? An interest in cats goes back centuries. Cats have been worshipped, thought to be magical, and also thought to be witches or from the devil; but they have always fascinated people. In Ireland in the 8th century, a monk wrote the poem *Pangur Bán* about his cat. Celts believed the eyes of a cat acted like windows to the palaces of fairy kings. The kings could look out and watch the world through the cat's eyes and people could look deeply into a cat's eyes and see the world of fairies.

The following are some examples and activities in each of the major genres of literature. These activities can easily be adapted to different grade levels by changing the materials and directions.

Fantasy

Two excellent books in the fantasy genre are *Cats of Myth* (Hausman & Hausman, 2000) and *Puss in Boots* (Perrault, 1990). Both books use wonderful, rich language to describe cats. Activities to use:

Step Grammar: The reader fills in each part of story grammar as they read the story. Using a graphic organiser helps children to organise the various parts of the story.

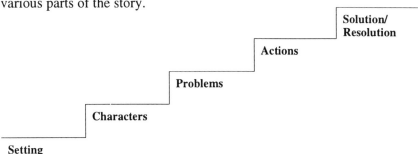

Story maps: (see an example of *Trait Maps* below under Developing Concepts and Vocabulary). This type of graphic organiser can be used for story grammar, too.

Realistic Fiction

Smoky Night (Bunting, 1994) is an American Caldecott winner. This story is an excellent one to use in a Venn Diagram to compare and contrast characters.

Daniel and   Mrs. Kim and
Jasmine   orange cat

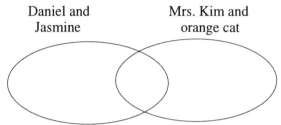

The readers lists all the points or ideas from the story that are about Daniel and Jasmine on the left and those about Mrs. Kim and the orange cat on the right. Items that tell about both characters are written in the middle of the diagram. This organiser helps readers determine the likenesses and differences between the characters. Discussion about the placement of items in a particular area helps develop more understanding.

Smoky Night is an excellent book to use for writing, too. The cats have no dialogue. The students could write what they believe the cats are saying during the crisis or how the two families interact after the riots.

Poetry

Introducing children to all types of poetry expands their appreciation of this art and provides another way to use words. In the lovely poem *I am the Cat* (Scheertle, 1990) the poet describes a typical cat action:

She flows around my ankles, lapping in soft gray waves against my legs.

Non-fiction

How to Talk to Your Cat (George, 2000) is an excellent book written in narrative non-fiction style. One section describes the 'vocabulary' a cat uses to communicate. One can check students' comprehension by having them read the descriptions of a cat's meows and then demonstrate the 'language' the cat is using.

Data sheets help students organize information they gain from their reading.

Data Chart for Summarising Information

Books	What is the best food to feed cats?	What kind of care does a cat need?	How do cats communicate?
Bonners, Susan (1998). *Why does the cat do that?*			
Gutman, Bill (1997). *Becoming your cat's best friend*			
Richards, James (1999). *Complete guide to cats*			
Taylor, David (1989). *The ultimate cat book*			
Summary			

A data chart can be used in several different ways. Children read several books on their own and write the answers to each question. Then the children meet in a group with the readers of other books and compare the information. Last, the group writes a summary of the information together.

This approach allows readers at different levels to gather the same information and to observe other readers' ways of obtaining and organising information. Another way to use a data sheet is to have each child read all the books and then do her own summary of the information.

Developing Concepts and Vocabulary

Word Banks
Have the children brainstorm all the words they know that tell about cats. When brainstorming, write the words as they come from the children. Later rewrite the words on tag board or chart paper. The children can re-arrange the words into categories such as:

alphabetizing

classifying phonologically – sounds, syllables, vowels, structural analysis

syntax – nouns, verbs, adverbs

antonyms/synonyms
categories – actions, colors, traits
The words make a bank to use for:
    writing using frame sentences (The cat is _____.)
    writing stories, poetry, presentations
    game activity

Trait Maps

Trait maps help readers pull together information they have been gathering. Any words or ideas can be used for the categories. The readers list all the words they have found that tell about each descriptor.

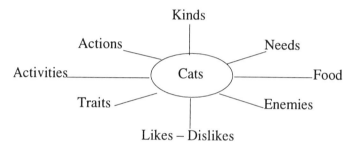

Developing Oral Language and Writing

Several activities can be used to develop oral language. These include interviewing a cat-owner or veterinarian and sharing the information; arranging a panel presentation on cats; making a video presentation; engaging in Readers' Theatre, using puppets, and using mime.

A number of activities can also be used to develop writing. These include creating a new ending for the story, changing the time and location of the story, writing/illustrating from the cat's point of view, and writing a biography of the child's own cat.

Summary

The following points are relevant in presenting an interdisciplinary approach to reading, using a topic such as cats:

- Comprehension is easier for the reader when new knowledge is connected to existing background knowledge.
- Over-plan resources and activities to accommodate students' interests. Attempt to have approximately 50-75 books and a variety of reading materials in all genres and include electronic materials.

- Have a variety of hands-on lessons, different ways of organizing information, graphs, charts, speeches, videos, paired activities, whole-class lessons, small-group work. Use mini-lessons to teach specific skills as they are needed.
- Use the topic as an outline to study research, organisation, and presentation activities that adapt to the needs and interests of students through meaningful content and authentic uses of summarising, retelling, predicting, verifying, and questioning.
- Highlight the importance of students developing knowledge and skills that derive from a variety of academic disciplines.

REFERENCES

Barton, K .C. & Smith, L. A. (2000). Themes or motifs? Aiming for coherence through interdisciplinary outlines. *The Reading Teacher, 54(1),* 54-63.

Baumann, J. F., Hooten, H. & White, P. (1999). Teaching comprehension through literature: A teacher-research project to develop fifth graders' reading strategies and motivation. *The Reading Teacher,* 53(*1*), 38-51.

Gilles, C. & Mitchell Pierce, K. (2001). Talking about books: Pairing fact and fiction for deep understanding. *Language Arts, 78(6),* 579-588.

Guzzetti, B. J., Kowalinski, B. J., & McGowan, T. (1992). Using literature-based approach to teaching social studies. *Journal of Reading, 36(2),* 113-122.

Hiebert E. H. & Colt, J. (1989). Patterns of literature-based reading instruction. *The Reading Teacher, 43(1),* 14-20.

National Council of Teachers of English (1995). *Position statement on interdisciplinary learning, preK-Grade 4.* Urbana, IL: National Council of Teachers of English.

Tevebaugh, T. (2001). Welcome to our web: Integrating subjects through entomology. *Language Arts, 78(4),* 343-347.

Children's Books

Bunting, Eve. (1994). *Smoky Night.* New York, NY: Harcourt Brace & Co.

George, Jean Craighead. (2000). *How to Talk to Your Cat.* New York, NY: Harper Collins Publisher.

Hausman, G., & Hausman, L. (2000). *Cats of Myth: Tales from Around the World.* London: Simon and Schuster.

Perrault, Charles. (Illus. Marcellino, Fred). (1990). *Puss in Boots.* New York, NY: Farrar Straus Girouxee

Scheertle, Alice. (1990). *I am the Cat.* New York, NY: Lothrop, Lee, & Shepard Books.

Gail Goss may be contacted at gossg@cwu.edu

Amélioration de la Lecture, pp. 206-215.

24 Quelle Durée Hebdomadaire d'Éntraînement Est Nécessaire à Une Amélioration de la Lecture chez des Collégiens ?

Denis Foucambert, France

Année après année, les évaluations menées en sixième montrent des résultats concordants: les compétences approfondies ne sont maîtrisées que par 15% des élèves et les compétences de base ne sont pas encore maîtrisées par 15% d'entre eux. Et pourtant, personne ne met en doute le rôle tout particulier de la maîtrise de la langue écrite dans la réussite des élèves tout au long de leur scolarité.

Pour tenter d'améliorer cette situation alarmante, le ministère de l'éducation nationale a engagé les collèges, depuis le mois de mai 1999, dans la mise en place d'importantes actions pour la maîtrise de la langue écrite. A été annoncée la 'mise en place d'ateliers lecture pour tous car l'incitation à la lecture est une priorité; il s'agit là d'inscrire à l'emploi du temps de tous les élèves une heure de lecture hebdomadaire' (Bulletin Officiel, juin 1999). Les mêmes propositions font référence à l'outil informatique tant dans les domaines de recherches d'informations (base de données, Internet, cédérom,...) que pour l'aide qu'il peut apporter à une meilleure utilisation du médium écrit.

Nous proposons ici une évaluation de l'utilisation d'un logiciel d'entraînement à la lecture dans des collèges de l'Académie de Loire-Atlantique[1]. L'organisation interne du collège est un point d'achoppement car, bien souvent, le découpage horaire freine l'introduction d'activités nouvelles. Aussi, avons-nous procédé à une évaluation de pratiques réellement à l'œuvre dans des établissements secondaires, impliquant l'usage de ce logiciel pendant l'horaire officiel de la classe de français. Nous partageons les propos de Jacqueline Levasseur[2], déclarant à propos des évaluations qu'il s'agissait aussi 'de trouver les démarches pédagogiques efficaces permettant d'atteindre la maîtrise des compétences nécessaires à la poursuite de la scolarité des élèves au collège et de les faire passer dans la réalité de la classe' (Levasseur,1995). Cette démarche renvoie également à la volonté affichée de «professionnaliser» les enseignants: la pédagogie n'est pas un art pour lequel seuls quelques-uns seraient doués.

Grâce à ces pratiques observées en collège, nous allons tenter de mieux comprendre l'effet d'un temps d'entraînement, défini comme la durée d'utilisation du logiciel, sur les résultats en lecture. En effet, les textes ministériels font référence à deux demi-heures consacrées à la lecture. Dans la mesure où cet horaire peut être utilisé à des fins d'entraînement à la lecture, il semble important de mesurer si ce temps est suffisant pour faire progresser de manière sensible le niveau de lecture des élèves de sixième.

Plan Expérimental

La Population Étudiée

Nous avons constitué une population de 85 élèves (36 garçons et 49 filles) de classe de sixième (12 ans) issus de cinq collèges de la région nantaise et participant à un entraînement à la lecture selon trois modalités différentes en fonction du temps et de la nature des activités consacrées à cet entraînement, pendant l'horaire normal de français (un quart des élèves ne participent à aucune action spécifique autour de la lecture).

TABLEAU 1: RÉCAPITULATION DES GROUPES

	Groupe A	Groupe B	Groupe C	Groupe D
Durée	Pas d'entraîne-ment	Une séance hebdomadaire pendant l'année scolaire	Une séance hebdomadaire pendant l'année scolaire	Deux séances hebdomadaires pendant l'année scolaire
Type d'activités	Pas d'activité	Elsa *avec* théorisation	Elsa *sans* théorisation	Elsa *avec* théorisation
Temps hebdomadaire de travail sur le logiciel	0 mn	41,25 mn	55 mn	73,33 mn

Le tableau 1 montre la répartition des temps d'activités en fonction des différents groupes. Pour chaque élève d'un groupe, on retrouve dans chacun des autres groupes un élève qui lui correspond au regard de l'âge, du sexe, de la performance en français (±5%) et enfin de la performance en mathématiques (±5%) aux épreuves de l'évaluation sixième, passé au début le l'année scolaire.

Le Logiciel d'Entraînement Utilisé

Les trois groupes qui s'entraînent en lecture à l'aide de l'informatique utilisent le logiciel ELSA, de l'Association française pour la Lecture, reconnu d'intérêt pédagogique par le ministère de l'éducation national. Pour ses

concepteurs (AFL, 1996), ELSA entraîne sept capacités techniques différentes qui participent à l'activité de lecture, à l'aide de sept séries d'exercices:
Trois séries portent sur les mots ou groupes de mots entraînent:
* l'élargissement de l'empan de lecture (et non de l'empan visuel) et la sureté de la prise d'information
* le fonctionnement et l'enchaînement des empans dans la lecture d'un texte
* les conduites de différenciation de formes proches (mots et groupes de mots).
Quatre autres séries exercent au niveau de la phrase ou du texte:
* les capacités d'anticipation des mots (closure),
* l'organisation progressive d'une représentation mentale du texte à travers une recherche sélective d'informations,
* l'organisation progressive d'une représentation mentale du texte à partir de l'examen de son matériau linguistique
* le développement d'une lecture efficace qui trouve le meilleur équilibre entre le temps de consultation et la compréhension.
Les séries sont constituées d'exercices de difficultés croissantes dont le franchissement est individualisé par le logiciel; l'élève revient à une série après avoir fait un passage sur chacune des autres, ce qui assure un travail simultané sur différentes composantes de l'acte lexique. Par ailleurs, ce logiciel ajuste ses exigences en fonction des comportements instantanés de l'utilisateur[3].

Les Épreuves d'Évaluation
Elles ont été passées en juin 1999 (fin de sixième). Elles couvrent des situations de lecture différentes et représentatives de ce qu'on attend d'un lecteur au collège (Foucambert, 1997).

Première Épreuve: Lecture de Textes Courts et Diversifiés
On précise à l'élève qu'on cherche à mesurer quelle est sa vitesse efficace de lecture, c'est-à-dire celle qui le fait aller le plus vite tout en lui assurant la meilleure issue, ici la réponse à une question posée après chaque lecture d'un texte. Les textes sont diversifiés entre presse, documentaire et fiction et sont d'une taille similaire d'environ 20 lignes et de même niveau de complexité aussi bien au niveau du lexique employé que de la complexité des phrases. L'épreuve se déroule sur ordinateur. Chacun des neufs textes s'affiche, l'élève indique qu'il en a terminé la lecture et répond alors à une question. Les questions portent sur des points explicitement

présents dans le texte et sont systématiquement exposées sous la forme « Le texte parle :» suivi de trois propositions parmi lesquelles une seule est correcte. Nous sommes ici dans une forme de lecture très courante, sans doute à l'œuvre dans plus de 60% des situations ordinaires, celles où il s'agit de travailler simplement sur l'explicite du texte, ce qui correspond à ce que l'ex Direction des Études et Prospective du Ministère (DEP) de l'Éducation Nationale décrivait comme une 'compétence approfondie'[4] (Vugdalic, 1995).

De cette épreuve, nous utiliserons deux variables primaires exprimant pour la première une vitesse de lecture de l'ensemble des textes lus (m = 14574 mots/heure; σ = 8164; minimum = 4994 m/h; maximum = 57295 m/h), et pour la seconde la qualité des réponses données (m = 32,98 points ; σ = 38 ; minimum = 0 ; maximum = 100).

Deuxième Épreuve: Lecture Experte d'Un Texte Long

Une seconde épreuve fait travailler l'implicite du texte, ce que l'ex DEP dénommait 'compétence remarquable' et dont semblerait disposer moins de 20% des élèves entrant en sixième. Il s'agit de franchir ce que dit le texte pour atteindre l'intention de l'auteur et apprécier les moyens qu'il emploie.

Un texte de fiction de Gianni Rodari, long de 1526 mots, est présenté sur un écran d'ordinateur; ce texte permet de nombreuses interprétations, en partie par l'usage que fait l'auteur de différents épilogues. L'élève peut parcourir à sa guise les 9 pages écran pendant le temps qu'il estime nécessaire. Ensuite, il répond à 12 questions par un système de QCM, le texte n'étant alors plus consultable. Un barème a été étalonné par un groupe d'enseignants et de bibliothécaires pour différencier des degrés d'interprétations et ne pas s'enfermer dans le tout ou rien. Ainsi, toutes les réponses proposées sont possibles mais certaines témoignent d'un niveau supérieur de compréhension.

Outre la vitesse de lecture (moyenne =14331 mots/heures ; σ = 7026; minimum = 4932 m/h; maximum = 45570 m/h), un niveau de compréhension est donc calculé à partir de la grille de réponses cochées par l'élève. Cette tentative pour évaluer la compréhension s'efforce de correspondre aux définitions de la lecture experte d'un texte littéraire, se rapprochant ainsi de ce qu'il est convenu d'attendre à partir des classes de premier cycle de l'enseignement secondaire. Ce score de compréhension (m = 57,41 points; σ = 10,67; minimum = 34; maximum = 84) peut théoriquement s'échelonner de 15 à 94 points.

Exploitations des Résultats

Construction d'Un Indice Composite de Lecture

Les deux épreuves utilisées pour construire la performance de lecture nous semblent révélatrices de ce qui attend un lecteur adolescent:
- parcourir des textes relativement simples pour en extraire de l'explicite
- conduire une lecture savante sur un texte.

Mais la double information, vitesse et compréhension, que chacune de ces épreuves révèle, n'est pas sans poser problème pour décrire la lecture. En quoi une grande vitesse est-elle positive si elle ne s'accompagne d'aucune compréhension? En quoi une bonne compréhension est-elle satisfaisante si c'est au prix d'un temps anormalement long de lecture? C'est pour tenter de résoudre ce problème que nous avons construit un indice composite de lecture qui tient compte à la fois de la vitesse et de la compréhension. Nous n'avons pas directement additionné les résultats que les élèves ont obtenus aux épreuves. Nous avons construit un indice de niveau général à partir des axes d'une Analyse en Composantes Principales. Les deux premiers axes de l'analyse rendent compte, à eux seuls, d'environ 75% de la variance totale ; on remarque (figure 1) que le premier axe est construit par les deux vitesses de lecture alors que le deuxième l'est par les points évaluant la compréhension, soit à partir du nombre de textes nécessaires pour que trois réponses successives soient correctes (épreuve 1), soit à partir d'un ensemble de questions posées après la lecture d'un texte (épreuve 2) . En conséquence, le plan proposé par ces deux axes représente bien la performance générale en lecture, en tenant compte de ces deux aspects. Pour représenter cette performance par une seule information, nous avons combiné les coordonnées des individus sur chacun des axes, en les pondérant par le pourcentage de la variance expliquée par les axes respectifs[5]. Cette variable sera ensuite transformée dans une distribution de moyenne 50 et d'écart-type 20.

Les Effets du Temps Effectif d'Entraînement

Pour étudier l'importance du temps d'entraînement sur les résultats en lecture, nous utilisons la régression multiple en y intégrant comme variables indépendantes catégorielles le sexe, la CSP et la possession d'un ordinateur à la maison, et comme variables indépendantes continues les notes de français et de mathématiques à l'entrée en sixième et, bien entendu, le temps passé sur le logiciel ELSA.

FIGURE 1: ANALYSE EN COMPOSANTE PRINCIPLE ENTRE LES 4
VARIABLES DE DÉPART

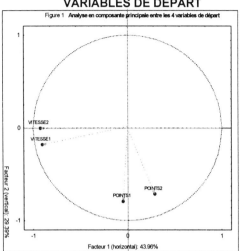

TABLEAU 2: RÉSULTAT DE LA RÉGRESSION: % DE LA VARIANCE DE LA
PERFORMANCE DE LECTURE, DE LA COMPRÉHENSION ET DE LA
VITESSE DE LECTURE EXPLIQUÉE PAR DIFFÉRENTS MODÈLES

Modèle	Modèle expliquant	Pourcentage de variance expliquée	Signifi-cativité
M1 : Modèle avec tous les élèves	La performance générale de lecture	29 %	0,006074
M2 : Modèle avec élimination des élèves à fort résidu	La performance générale de lecture	63 %	0,000000
M3 : Modèle avec tous les élèves	La vitesse	32 %	0,00135
M4 : Modèle avec élimination des élèves à fort résidu	La vitesse	54 %	0,000001
M5 : Modèle avec tous les élèves	La compréhension	19 %	0,1046

Les modèles M1 et M3, expliquant respectivement la performance de
lecture et la vitesse sont tout de suite significatifs, et expliquent le tiers de la
variance. A contrario, le modèle M5 ne parvient pas à expliquer la
compréhension de manière satisfaisante.

TABLEAU 3: MODÈLES M2 ET M4 VISANT À EXPLIQUER LA PERFORMANCE GÉNÉRALE DE LECTURE ET LA VITESSE DE LECTURE

VARIABLES	Modèle M2 Performance générale de lecture			Modèle M4 Vitesse de lecture		
	Coefficients Bêta	Coefficients	Significativité	Coefficients Bêta	Coefficients	Significativité
SEXE: femme	-0,29	-4,31	<0,0015	-0,35	-1680,9	<0,0007
homme	0,29	4,31	<0,0015	0,35	1680,9	<0,0007
CSP:						
Chômeurs, ss emploi	-0,16	-10,26	0,03	-0,18	-2521,76	0,07
Artisan commerçant chef d'entr.	-0.01	-0,62	0,90	-0,16	-2092,92	0,27
Cadres supérieurs, prof.intell.	0,36	11,15	<0,0015	0,10	990,05	0,44
Profession Intermédiaire	0,09	3,35	0,39	0,08	935,04	0,51
Employé	-0,25	-8,08	0,02	-0,13	-1258,37	0,27
Ouvrier	-0,23	-5,70	0,02	-0,28	-2121,26	0,02
Retraités	0,20	10,15	0,13	0,43	6069,21	0,01
Ordinateur à la maison: non	-0,04	-0,63	0,66	-0,08	381,63	0,45
oui	0,04	0,63	0,66	0,08	381,63	0,45
Temps d'entraînement sur ELSA	0,37	0,20	<0,0001	0,58	100,90	<0,00001
Note à l'évaluation 6ème en FRANÇAIS	0,43	0,50	<0,009	0,52	194,37	<0,008
Note à l'évaluation 6ème MATHS	-0.06	-0,06	0,72	-0,30	-92,60	0,16
Constante		10,81	0,17		2045,94	0,47

Note de lecture: Tous les effets décrits dans ce tableau sont nets, c'est-à-dire que les autres variables sont contrôlées. On voit par exemple dans la colonne « coefficients » du modèle M2 que le fait de disposer d'un ordinateur à la maison (variable qualitative) «contribue» à élever la performance de lecture de 0,63 points et que (variable quantitative) chaque point de la note de français de l'évaluation de sixième «contribue» à l'élever de 0,49 point ou que chaque minute d'entraînement l'élève de 0,198 points, etc...

Nous affinerons les deux modèles d'emblée significatifs en éliminant pour chacun d'eux les individus dont la différence entre la note attendue et la performance réelle excède un écart-type. L'élimination de 15 individus dans le modèle M2 et de 13 individus dans le modèle M4 provoque un gain explicatif de près de 34 points et de 25 points.

Le tableau 3 présente les contributions et significativités des différentes variables introduites dans les modèles M2 et M4.

On y note en premier lieu le poids prévisible du niveau initial en français (Bêta = 0,43) dans la performance finale de lecture. Pour autant le facteur temps d'utilisation du logiciel joue un rôle presque aussi important (Bêta = 0,37).

En revanche, dans le modèle M4 expliquant la vitesse, le temps d'entraînement sur ELSA est un facteur plus déterminant que le niveau initial en français (0,58 contre 0,52).

Il ressort de ces résultats que l'utilisation d'une partie de l'horaire de français pour renforcer les compétences techniques des processus de lecture a des conséquences incontestablement positives.

Discussion

Cette étude se proposait d'étudier le temps d'entraînement nécessaire à l'obtention de progrès en lecture, dans la perspective des modalités nouvelles proposées au collège pour améliorer les compétences transversales dont dépendent la réussite de tous les élèves.

Le groupe A qui n'a suivi aucun entraînement va servir de référence. La moyenne de sa performance en lecture en fin d'année est de 42,15 points dans une distribution, pour la population totale des 4 groupes, de moyenne 50 et d'écart-type 20. Les évaluations nationales montrent, nous l'avons signalé en introduction, que seulement 15% des élèves maîtrisent les compétences remarquables, au sens des évaluations ministérielles. La performance, dans le groupe A, au-dessus de laquelle se trouvent 15% des élèves se situe environ à 55.65 points, à mi chemin entre les moyennes des groupes C et D. Il s'agirait donc, pour le groupe A, sans doute représentatif de la population standard des élèves de sixième, d'élever sa performance moyenne de 13,5 points. On voit dans le tableau 4 à la colonne coefficient que chaque minute hebdomadaire d'entraînement élève la performance de lecture de 0.19 point. Il faut alors miser sur une utilisation hebdomadaire d'environ 68 minutes pour amener la moyenne générale au niveau des 15% actuellement les meilleurs, ce qui dépasse légèrement l'horaire proposé par les textes officiels dans le cadre d'une seule année d'utilisation.

Afin de contrôler les variables indépendantes et de rendre possible un groupe témoin, nous n'avons intégré que des élèves dont le temps d'entraînement était pris sur l'horaire normal de français. Mais rien n'empêche, comme cela se produit déjà dans certains collèges, de permettre aux élèves d'avoir un accès libre (par exemple par la présence d'ordinateurs au CDI[6]) à des outils d'entraînement à la lecture, ce qui offrirait le temps nécessaire, sans amputer excessivement les moments d'enseignement.

Enfin, on peut remarquer que l'amélioration de la performance générale de lecture est davantage liée à une vitesse de lecture plus importante qu'à une amélioration de la compréhension. L'effet d'un entraînement avec ce logiciel dans les conditions définies précédemment semble améliorer de manière significative la vitesse de lecture, donc le temps de traitement des textes susceptibles d'être rencontrés dans un cursus scolaire, et par voie de conséquence leur volume. La maîtrise de ces aspects techniques de la lecture n'est certes pas un but en soi, mais elle semble une condition indispensable à une véritable entrée dans le monde de l'écrit. 'On mesure, écrit Jean-Claude Passeron, à travers les vitesses de lecture, les divers seuils de cet accès à une lecture flexible qui est une condition sine qua non d'une utilisation réelle de l'écrit.' (Passeron, 1987).

Quant à la question initiale de décider si les temps alloués en sixième par les textes ministériels suffisent à l'amélioration des résultats en lecture, il semble, à partir de cette étude, qu'ils soient légèrement inférieurs à ce qui serait nécessaire, d'où la probable nécessité d'une mise à disposition complémentaire de ces outils pédagogiques grâce à des contrats passés avec les élèves et à l'accès plus individualisé aux équipements informatiques.

NOTES

1 Cette étude doit beaucoup à l'Antenne Maîtrise des langages de l'Académie de Nantes qui a organisé, avec les collèges pressentis, la passation des épreuves.
2 Alors chef du département de l'évaluation des élèves et des étudiants du ministère de l'éducation nationale.
3 Cette caractéristique a été retenue pour illustrer l'apport de l'informatique dans les processus d'évaluation, dans le cadre de l'exposition Désir d'apprendre de la Cité des Sciences.
4 Au niveau de la sixième, les grilles de nomenclature en trois postes sont:
• compétences de base: saisir l'explicite d'un texte
• compétences approfondies: reconstituer l'organisation de l'explicite

- compétences remarquables: découvrir l'implicite.
5 Performance$_{Individu}$ = ((43,96 * Axe1$_{Individu}$) + (23.39 * Axe2$_{Individu}$)) *(-1)
On multiplie par (-1) pour inverser les valeurs et faire que les bons résultats soient représenté par un score supérieur aux mauvais.
6 Centre de Documentation et d'Information.

BIBLIOGRAPHIE

AFL. (1996). *Guide d'utilisation du logiciel ELSA.* Paris, AFL.

Foucambert, D. (1997). *Conscience graphique et performance en lecture. Etude statistique sur un échantillon d'enfants de onze ans.* Mémoire de DEA de Sciences de l'Éducation. Université de Caen.

Levasseur, J. (1995). De la réalité des acquis et difficultés des élèves à l'entrée en 6ème. *Le français aujourd'hui, 111,* 10-20.

Ministère de l'éducation Nationale (10 juin 1999). Texte d'orientation: La Mutation Des Collégès: Un collège pour tous et pour chacun. *Bulletin Officiel de l'Éducation Nationale.*

Passeron, J.C. (1987). La notion de pacte, *Les Actes de Lecture, 17,* 55-59.

Vugalics, S. (1996). Les compétences en lecture, en calcul et en géométrie des élèves à l'entrée au CE2 et en sixième. *Note d'information, 96.22.* Ministère de l'éducation nationale, de l'enseignement supérieur et de la recherche.

25 Children's Metacognition as a Predictor of Reading Comprehension

Svjetlana Koliæ-Vehovec and Igor Bajšanski, Croatia

The developing relation between children's knowledge about the goals and processes of reading, their skills in applying metacognitive strategies, and their reading comprehension were examined. Participants were children in third, fifth, and eighth grades. A questionnaire of metacognitive reading knowledge, and measures of comprehension monitoring during reading were applied in addition to measures of reading fluency and comprehension. Students in the eighth grade manifested better metacognitive knowledge of reading than students in the third and fifth grades. Multiple regression showed that metacognitive self-monitoring during reading was a significant predictor of reading comprehension at all three developmental levels. Besides reading fluency, which explained about 17% of variance, the only significant metacognitive predictor in third-grade students was a cloze task, which explained an additional 17% of variance, suggesting that comprehension monitoring may operate at the local (sentence) processing level at that grade. In the fifth and eighth grades, self-monitoring played a more important role in students' reading comprehension than in the third-grade. The cloze task and an error detection task explained more than 25% of variance in reading comprehension.

Background

Reading can be regarded as a multidimensional activity including letter and word recognition, sentence processing and constructing meaning, but it also requires ongoing monitoring of comprehension and regulation of reading according to the goals of reading. Monitoring and regulation of reading are usually considered fundamental components of metacognition, in addition to metacognitive knowledge, which includes knowledge about one's self-thinking, about different types of tasks and about reading strategies (Flavell, 1979; Baker and Brown, 1984; Paris et al. 1984).

Acquisition of concepts about literacy and pre-reading skills emerges by age 3 with progressive improvement later (Hiebert, 1981; Bradley and Bryant, 1983; Lundberg, Frost and Peterson, 1988). Myers and Paris (1978) examined metacognitive knowledge of children between 8 and 12 years of age and also found that older children knew more about text structure, reading goals and reading strategies than younger children.

Knowledge about reading strategies is not a sufficient guarantee that readers will read strategically. Reading strategies are cognitive tools that can be used selectively and flexibly. Metacognition and strategic reading are manifested in various procedures that readers use to monitor comprehension. Differences in comprehension monitoring were consistently found between good and poor readers (Paris & Myers, 1981; Garner & Kraus, 1982; Grabe & Mann, 1984). Poor readers had difficulties identifying inconsistencies in the text.

There are also developmental differences in comprehension monitoring. Garner and Tylor (1982) asked second, fourth and sixth graders to find semantic inconsistencies in passages. Younger children did not find the errors in the passages spontaneously, and even older children had difficulty finding all inconsistencies.

Paris, Wasik and Turner (1991) summarised factors that contribute to the effects of age on comprehension monitoring. First, young children may not believe that there are mistakes in text. Second, attention capacity is engaged primarily in word understanding, and there are not enough cognitive resources left to construct meaning and monitor comprehension. Third, many young readers do not understand the standards that can be used to evaluate comprehension. Fourth, reporting comprehension failure is substituted for by making inferences in order to construct sensible text interpretation.

Pazzaglia, Beni and Caccio (1999) investigated the relationship between both aspects of metacognition and reading comprehension in a sample of children from 8 to 13 years. They have found a strong differentiation between declarative/procedural knowledge about text and strategies and on-line aspects of metacognition – comprehension monitoring and judgement on the importance of different parts of a text. On-line aspects of metacognition showed a continuous positive developmental trend, even in secondary school and later. Knowledge about goals and strategies showed different developmental trends, with striking improvements for the former between 8 and 9 years of age, and between 11 and 12 years, and for the latter between 8 and 9 years, 9 and 10 years and 11 and 12 years.

The first aim of the current study was to explore developmental differences in metacognitive knowledge of elementary school students from third to eighth grade. Measure of metacognitive knowledge includes examination of reading awareness and knowledge about strategies. The second aim was to explore the effects on reading comprehension of two on-line aspects of metacognition – metacognitive knowledge and comprehension monitoring – and of reading fluency at different developmental levels.

Method

Participants
The participants in the study were 93 third-graders (47 girls and 46 boys) from five classes, 105 fifth-graders (58 girls and 47 boys) from five classes, and 83 eighth-graders (44 girls and 39 boys) from four classes. The study was conducted in two primary schools in Rijeka, Croatia. All students were Croatian-speaking.

Measures
Reading fluency and reading comprehension. Assessment was made on three different stories, one story for each grade. The stories were chosen according to the curriculum for each grade. A measure of reading fluency was computed as the average number of words read in one minute. Stories were followed by the 15 questions. A measure of reading comprehension was the number of correct responses. Answers that were completely appropriate were awarded two points. Partially correct answers were awarded one point.

Metacognitive knowledge. A Croatian adaptation of the questionnaire constructed by Paris, Cross and Lipson (1984) was used for assessment of metacognitive knowledge about reading. The questions were about text structure, various goals of reading, and reading strategies. The original 20-item questionnaire was shortened to 15 multiple-choice questions. Internal consistency estimates the three components of the Croatian adaptation were $\alpha = .60$; $\alpha = .78$; $\alpha = .58$, respectively.

Comprehension monitoring. Cloze and sentence-detection tasks were used as measures of comprehension monitoring. Three different forms of cloze task were constructed, one for each grade. The passages used to construct the different versions were taken from readers for the corresponding grade levels. In passages for third and fifth grades, 13 words were missing, and for eighth grade 16 words. This created 13 or 16 blank spaces that children were required to fill in with single words. Children's close responses were scored according to the following procedure: (a) Responses that were both semantically and syntactically appropriate to the missing word were awarded 2 points; (b) responses that were either semantically or syntactically appropriate, but not both, were awarded one point; (c) blanks and responses that were neither semantically nor syntactically appropriate were not awarded any points.

In a sentence detection task, children read a story consisting of six passages. Each passage contained a sentence that was semantically inappropriate to the passage. Children were asked to underline the inappropriate sentence. The outcome measure was the number of errors detected correctly minus the number of incorrect detections.

All tasks were administered to children in their classrooms as intact groups during two school hours. The tasks were not time-constrained.

Results

Differences in metacognitive knowledge between students in third, fifth and eighth grades were tested by one-way ANOVA, which showed a significant effect of grade (F (2,278) = 12.95; p<.001). Post-hoc comparison using the Newman-Keuls test showed that eighth-grade students have better metacognitive knowledge of reading than third- and fifth-grade students.

Correlations between measures of metacognitive knowledge and measures of comprehension monitoring were computed for each grade. Significant correlations in third grade were found between metacognitive knowledge and the sentence detection task (r = .58), and in fifth and eight grades between metacognitive knowledge and both monitoring tasks. The correlation between metacognitive knowledge and cloze task was .53 for fifth-graders, and .35 for eighth graders. Reading fluency was related to metacognitive knowledge (r = .35) and sentence detection (r = .26) only in third grade.

Correlations of reading comprehension with reading fluency and the metacognitive variables were also computed separately for each grade (Table 1). Reading fluency was significantly related to reading comprehension only for the third graders. In general, correlations between measures of reading comprehension and measures of metacognition are moderately strong. Comprehension monitoring, especially performance on the cloze task, is more strongly related to reading comprehension than metacognitive knowledge.

TABLE 1: CORRELATIONS BETWEEN READING AND METACOGNIIVE MEASURES

	Reading Comprehension		
	3rd grade	5th grade	8th grade
Reading Fluency	.45**	.00	.05
Metacognitive Knowledge	.36**	.32**	.33**
Cloze Task	.51**	.54**	.49**
Sentence Detection	.38**	.56**	.36**

**p<.001

Multiple regression analysis was performed with reading comprehension as the dependent variable, and reading fluency, metacognitive knowledge and comprehension monitoring as the predictor variables, for each grade. Significant unique contributors for the third grade were reading fluency (9.6%) and cloze task (11.56%), but for the fifth and eighth grades both comprehension monitoring tasks made significant contributions. The cloze task explained 6.8% of the variance in reading comprehension in fifth grade, and 12.25% in the eighth grade. The contributions of the sentence detection task were 10.2% in the fifth and 4.8% in the eighth grade.

Discussion

Students in the eighth grade manifested better metacognitive knowledge of reading than students in the third and the fifth grades. Our results are similar to the results of Pazzaglia et al. (1999). Metacognitive knowledge showed improvement between fifth and eighth grades (11 and 14 years of age). Seemingly, both development and reading experience contribute to metacognitive knowledge about reading. Children's knowledge about reading develops concurrently with their understanding and control of strategies, and these factors become congruent with increasing age and skill (Cross & Paris, 1988).

Metacognitive knowledge is related to comprehension monitoring, but moderate correlations showed that this knowledge is not a sufficient guarantee that children will apply strategies. These results support Pazzaglia et al.'s (1999) multicomponent model of metacognition that differentiates between metacognitive knowledge and on-line aspects of metacognition.

Reading fluency is significantly related to reading comprehension only in third grade. Inter-individual variability in reading fluency in third grade is large enough to produce a significant correlation. Fluency is important because it enables readers to spend their cognitive resources on understanding the text rather than on attempting to encode individual words. At fifth and eighth grades almost all students read fast enough and there is no significant effect of fluency on reading comprehension. In fifth grade, comprehension monitoring becomes more important than reading fluency.

Results of regressions also support the hypothesis that metacognitive variables, especially comprehension monitoring, are considerably involved in reading comprehension (Paris & Myers, 1981; Vasniadou, Pearson & Rogers, 1988; Pazzaglia et al., 1999). Monitoring meaning in third grade students was not so important for text comprehension as in older students because their attention is directed at decoding and analysing the meaning of words. In the fifth and eighth grades, comprehension monitoring became a better predictor of reading comprehension than fluency.

Metacognitive knowledge is not a significant independent predictor of reading comprehension, because its effect is mediated by on-line metacognition. Active usage of metacognitive strategies is more important for reading comprehension than merely passive knowledge about strategies. Strategic reading reflects the interactive effects of metacognitive knowledge, sufficient practice, adequate instruction about strategies and motivational factors. There are different reasons why children don't use strategies efficiently. Children often believe that the strategies will not make a difference in their reading because they perceive the reading task as too difficult and out of their control. Proper instruction about reading strategies, ways and conditions of their usage (Palincsar & Brown, 1984; Cross & Paris, 1988) could stimulate students for strategy usage and improve reading comprehension.

REFERENCES

Baker, L., & Brown, A. L. (1984). Metacognitive skills and reading. In P. D. Pearson, M. Kamil, R. Barr & P. Mosenthal (Eds.), *Handbook of reading research* (vol. 1, pp. 353-394). White Plains, NY: Longman.

Bradley, L., & Bryant, P. (1983). Categorizing sounds and learning to read: A causal connection. *Nature*, 301, 491-521.

Cross, D. R., & Paris, S. G. (1988). Developmental and instructional analyses of children's metacognition and reading comprehension. *Journal of Educational Psychology, 80,* 2, 131-142.

Flavell, J. H., (1979). Metacognition and cognitive monitoring: A new area of cognitive-developmental inquiry. *American Psychologist, 34,* 10, 906-911.

Garner, R., & Kraus, C. (1982). Good and poor comprehenders' differences in knowing and regulating reading behaviours. *Educational Research Quarterly, 6,* 5-12.

Garner, R., & Tylor, N. (1982). Monitoring and understanding: An investigation of attentional assistance needs at different grade and reading proficiency levels. *Reading Psychology, 3,* 1-6.

Grabe, M., & Mann, S. (1984). A technique for the assessment and training of comprehension monitoring skills. *Journal of Reading Behaviour, 16,* 131-144.

Hiebert, E. H. (1981). Developmental patterns and interrelationships of preschool print awareness. *Reading Research Quarterly, 16,* 236-260.

Lundberg, I., Frost, J., & Peterson, O. (1988). Effects of an extensive program for stimulating phonological awareness in preschool children. *Reading Research Quarterly, 23,* 237-256.

Myers, M., & Paris, S. G. (1978). Children's metacognitive knowledge about reading. *Journal of Educational Psychology, 70,* 680-690.

Palincsar, A. S., & Brown, A. L. (1984). Reciprocal teaching of comprehension fostering and monitoring activities. *Cognition and Instruction, 1,* 117-175.

Paris, S. G., Cross, D. R., & Lipson, M. Y. (1984). Informed strategies for learning: A program to improve children's reading awareness and comprehension. *Journal of Educational Psychology, 76,* 1239-1252.

Paris, S. G., & Myers, M. (1981). Comprehension monitoring in good and poor readers. *Journal of Reading Behavior, 13,* 5-22.

Paris, S. G., Wasik, B. A., & Turner, J. C. (1991). The development of strategic readers. In R. Barr, M. L. Kamil, P. B. Mosenthal & P. D. Pearson (Eds.), *Handbook of reading research* (Vol. 2, pp. 609-640). Mahwah, NJ: LEA.

Pazzaglia, F., De Beni, R., & Caccio, L. (1999). The role of working memory and metacognition in reading comprehension difficulties. In T. E. Scruggs and M. A. Mastropieri (Eds.), *Advances in learning and behavioral disabilities.* (Vol. 13, pp. 115-134). JAI Press.

Vasniadou, S., Pearson, P. D., & Rogers, T. (1988). What causes children's failures to detect inconsistencies in text? Representation versus comparison difficulties. *Journal of Educational Psychology, 80,* 27-39.

The study is part of the project 'Developmental Aspects of Reading Comprehension' supported by Ministry of Science and Technology of Republic of Croatia. Svjetlana Kolic-Vehovec may be contacted at skolic@human.pefri.hr.

26 Middle-Grade Readers' Ability to Interpret Pragmatic Meaning

Linda M. Phillips and Stephen P. Norris, Canada

We propose to address the role of pragmatic meaning in reading and to present examples from our research on middle school students' understanding or lack of understanding of the pragmatic meaning of text. We will conclude with some remarks on the need to include pragmatic meaning as a consideration in reading instruction.

Pragmatics and Pragmatic Meaning

Pragmatics is the study of the relation between linguistic expressions and their contexts of use (Yule, 1996). Interpreting the meaning of text requires the interpretation of what is meant in a particular context through determining how the context influences the meaning of what is written (Stalnaker, 1999). Readers must make inferences about both what is written and not written in order to construct an interpretation of the intended meaning, because what is unsaid or not written is part of what is communicated. Determining the pragmatic meaning intended by text requires determining whether the text is an assertion, a suggestion, a question, a promise, and so on (e.g., Austin 1962; Searle 1969, 1979; Searle, Kiefer, & Bierwisch 1980). Such determinations can be made only through consideration of context, because the same words can be used in different contexts to mean quite different things.

Pragmatic theories of meaning focus less on the question, 'What do such-and-such statements mean?' and more on the question, 'What did so-and-so mean by uttering (writing) such-and-such sentence?' This focus transfers attention from an effort to grasp universal meanings to an effort to grasp the meanings of particular statements at particular times. Thus, in reading, the visual input (text) must be supplemented by the reader's knowledge of what the text might mean in the context. For instance, judging whether 'How are you?' is a question or a greeting depends upon a consideration of the context in which it is said.

Deciding what to believe, how information is structured, and how language is textured within a particular context influences greatly students' success in judging meaning and in understanding text (Phillips, 2001). Judgements about how statements are to be analysed, criticised, and interpreted in different contexts are at the heart of the readers' task of determining pragmatic meaning (Norris & Phillips, 1994a, 1994b). The study of the pragmatic aspects of reading a text addresses the fundamental role of students' beliefs and understandings in the construction of meaning. Just how middle-grade readers' interpretations of pragmatic meaning make a difference to the interpretative process is an empirical question concerning which preliminary evidence is discussed next.

Readers' Interpretations of Pragmatic Meaning: Empirical Investigations

The text used in the study reported here was a narrative from *The Test of Inference Ability in Reading Comprehension* (*TIA*) (Phillips, 1989). The text structure of *TIA* was analysed by a group of researchers and used as the normative, authoritative interpretation guiding the research. However, the focus of interest was not the text structure of *TIA,* but rather the middle-grade readers' interpretations of *TIA.*

TIA consists of three full-length stories in three genres: exposition (*UFOs*), description (*Money*), and narration (*The Wrong Newspapers*). Narrative text is taken to be the easiest for students to comprehend. We discuss in this chapter students' interpretations of the narrative, *The Wrong Newspapers* (Appendix).

There are twelve questions accompanying *The Wrong Newspapers.* The task for the students was threefold: to decide upon and to integrate the relevant information in the narrative and from their background knowledge; to interpret the request contained in each question; and to construct responses appropriate to those requests. Readers' responses to the questions about the passages read were examined to identify their interpretations of pragmatic meaning. Data were collected on 150 students from each of grades six, seven, and eight. Individual interviews were conducted that focussed on how students were using evidence and constructing meaning as they completed *TIA.* These interviews incorporated probes, clarification questions, and discussions where necessary in order to maximize completeness of information.

Pragmatic Meaning Inferred from Students' Interpretations

Students' responses were analysed on the basis of two criteria: the extent to which they interpreted successfully the intent of questions; and the extent to which they used information from the narrative to fulfil the requests in the questions.

The normal point of any question is to seek an answer. However, the pragmatic meaning of a question can be specified or particularised beyond this generality. The pragmatic meanings of the questions on *The Wrong Newspapers* were to elicit responses that provided hypotheses, conjectures, conclusions, justifications, or explanations.

Students' ability to interpret pragmatic meaning across the twelve questions on the narrative ranged from 23 to 78 percent correct and averaged 54 percent. Students demonstrated the highest percentage (78%) of understanding for question 1 and the lowest percentage on question 11 (23%). Both of these questions called for explanations that involved giving reasons. One common and dependable cue for interpreting the pragmatic meaning of a question requesting such an explanation is either the implicit or explicit use of the word, 'why'. Other cues include asking 'to account for', and 'to explain' (Ennis, 1969).

We might suspect that determining the pragmatic meaning of the question was not the challenge in this case, given the high scores on question 1 and the low scores on question 11. The difference may have been the amount of information to be integrated. Question 1, 'Why was the newspaper in a plastic bag?' asked about the setting and only one paragraph preceded the question (see Appendix). By the time students reached question 11, they had to analyse and synthesise information from the setting and exposition, complication, climax, and resolution. Furthermore, in order to answer question 1, a one-part explanation was required, whereas to answer question 11 a two-part explanation was needed. 'Why was it quicker for Skippy to get an old newspaper than the right one?' called for students to respond both that he could jump through a hole in the neighbour's fence in order to run to the house next door, and that the right newspapers were lying at the bottom of Mr. Jones's long driveway, which was further away than the hole in the neighbour's fence. Students most frequently replied, 'Because it was closer'. Such a response fails to provide a clear and complete answer to the question and raises the issue of whether students understood the pragmatic meaning of the question. This data forces us to reconsider the favourable interpretation of their good performance on question 1. We are uncertain whether students actually interpreted correctly the pragmatic meaning of question 1 or whether they merely gave a response that is an easy inference from the most salient information in the first paragraph.

Fewer than half of middle-grade students interpreted correctly the pragmatic meaning of questions 4 and 6, 'What mystery does Ann have to solve?' and 'Why did Ann want to hand-deliver Mr. Jones's newspaper?' These questions called for conjectures about another's perception of events and motives. These conjectures require that students identify with Ann in terms of her specific experiences as a newspaper-carrier puzzled by a series of events, and to interpret from Ann's perspective (rather than their own) those events of the story thus far. To answer question 4, students must recognise that the narrative is told from Ann's point of view: Ann knows where the right newspapers are, though she does not know why they are not picked up after she delivers them; and she understands that Mr. Jones is getting the wrong newspapers and that he does not understand why. Mr. Jones informs Ann of his displeasure about getting the wrong newspapers and she is puzzled. Students must interpret the pragmatic meaning of the question signalled by the words, 'mystery', 'does Ann' and other cues such as 'what', and 'to solve' based on the information available and make a conjecture about the nature of the mystery. That is, they are to focus on the link between why the right newspapers remain at the end of the driveway and why the wrong newspapers are coming into Mr. Jones's possession. Most students responded, 'The mystery Ann has to solve is to check why yesterday's paper is lying in a puddle'. Such a response reveals that students failed to attend to the context set by the question in order to surmise the nature of the mystery. Similarly for question 6, students misinterpreted the pragmatic meaning of the question. They failed to focus on Ann's motivation for wanting to hand deliver Mr. Jones's newspaper – to make sure he gets the right newspaper and to talk to him about the mix-up. Rather than make a conjecture about Ann's motivation, students tended to provide direct citations of text, where an answer to the question could not be found.

Questions calling for conclusions also were not well understood. To answer question 5, 'What was the first day Ann noticed the newspaper lying in the driveway?' students needed to attend to the time sequence of the narrative, to be cognisant of how pace is added to the story, and to place significant events along a time line. Four days are explicitly mentioned in the narrative: Sunday, Monday, Tuesday, and Wednesday. Students also must be alert to the word, 'noticed' in the question posed. To answer the question, students had to reflect upon the narrative information, to question their initial belief that the story started on Monday and to critically integrate the available information to determine Tuesday.

Students appeared to experience the most difficulty interpreting the pragmatic meaning of questions calling for explanations, conjectures from another's point of view (subjectification), and conclusions entailing time sequences. Students did not appear to attend to the function of particular words in the context of their use. Many students, for instance, appeared to pay no particular attention to the words, 'strange', 'mystery', and 'puzzled'. Consequently, they failed to foresee the unfolding events of the story, to capitalise upon the increasing pace of the story, to build a heightened sense of intrigue, and to interpret correctly the pragmatic meaning of questions posed in the context of the narrative.

Sixty to ninety-nine percent of the students experienced difficulty understanding the pragmatic meaning of information directly relevant to questions asked in the context of the narrative. By way of example, when students were asked to offer an explanation about what had happened to Mr. Jones's newspapers two days in a row, they most frequently replied, 'The papers were coming a day late'. This answer fails to take into account all elements of the complication: that Mr. Jones was getting a newspaper, that Ann was delivering the right day's paper, and Mr. Jones was not getting the right day's paper. Specifically, the pragmatic meaning of the question was not interpreted well and hence, relevant narrative information such as Mr. Jones saying, 'Tomorrow, I want tomorrow's paper delivered' was not applied. There was no evidence to support the students' interpretation that the papers were coming a day late. Moreover, their response does not explain what had happened to Mr. Jones's newspapers two days in a row.

Misinterpretations of the pragmatic meaning both of the questions and the story information were manifested in students' responses which provide evidence that they failed to focus on the specific context set by the question posed; failed to consider the texture of the language used in the narrative ('strange', 'mystery', 'puzzled') to inform their pragmatic interpretations; and tended to focus more on the narrative information to provide an answer, rather than on an answer to fulfil the request.

Conclusion

The premise of the present paper is that pragmatic understanding is necessary for interpretation and requires attention in its own right. The middle-grade students' responses afforded an extended series of signs of their understanding of the nature of reading. We are grateful for the insights made possible by their responses. Some of our insights include the confirmation that the views of reading enacted by teachers and the programmes used to teach reading influence students' responses to and understandings of the purposes and uses of language.

An implication of these preliminary results is that attention to pragmatic meaning in text understanding is a particular area of reading comprehension in need of specific instruction. We must teach that reading is as much about what is *not* on the page as what is, if we are going to be successful in educating students to consider the full weight of what it means to read.

REFERENCES

Austin, J.L. (1962). *How to do things with words* (J.O. Urmson, Ed.), Oxford: Clarendon Press.

Ennis, R.H. (1969). *Logic in teaching.* Englewood Cliffs, NJ: Prentice-Hall.

Norris, S.P., & Phillips, L.M. (1994a). Interpreting pragmatic meaning when reading popular reports of science. *Journal of Research in Science Teaching, 31,* 947-967.

Norris, S.P., & Phillips, L.M. (1994b). The relevance of a reader's knowledge within a perspectival view of reading. *Journal of Reading Behavior, 26,* 391-412.

Phillips, L.M. (1989). *Test of Inference Ability in Reading Comprehension* (Constructed-response format). St. John's, NF: Institute for Educational Research and Development, Memorial University of Newfoundland.

Phillips, L.M. (2001). Making new or making do: Epistemological, normative and pragmatic bases of literacy. In D.R. Olson, D. Kamawar, & J. Brockmeier (Eds). *Literacy and conceptions of language and mind* (pp. 283-300). Cambridge: Cambridge University Press.

Searle, J.R. (1969). *Speech acts.* Cambridge: Cambridge Univ. Press.

Searle, J.R. (1979). *Expression and meaning,* Cambridge: Cambridge University Press.

Searle, J.R., Kiefer, F., & Bierwisch, M. (Eds.). (1980). *Speech act theory and pragmatics.* Dordrecht: D. Reidel.

Stalnaker, R.C. (1999). *Context and content.* Oxford: Oxford University Press.

Yule, G. (1996). *Pragmatics.* Oxford: Oxford University Press.

Appendix

The Wrong Newspapers

Ann pedalled her bicycle faster as she headed up the hill to the last house on her paper route. The driveway was long, so she had been told that she could throw the paper from the road. 'Strange!', she thought. 'Yesterday's paper is still lying there.' The newspaper, in a plastic bag, lay in a puddle left from yesterday's storm. She knew that Mr. Jones wasn't away. Ann was late for dinner so she rode on. She could feel the rain starting again as she turned to look at the Whites' dog barking at her. The last two weeks had been sunny, until Monday.

1. Why was the newspaper in a plastic bag?
2. Why was yesterday's paper still lying in the puddle?

As Ann came in the front door, the phone was ringing. 'Ann, this is Mr. Jones. Yesterday I received a newspaper that wasn't the right copy. Tonight it has happened again. What's going on?'

'Mr. Jones, I just delivered your newspaper fifteen minutes ago. I saw yesterday's newspaper lying in a puddle at the end of your driveway. Haven't you been picking them up?' Ann asked.

'Of course I have a newspaper! Tomorrow, I want tomorrow's paper delivered,' Mr. Jones yelled, and slammed the phone.

Ann scratched her head, puzzled. The rain drummed down on the roof and the thunder roared. The mystery would have to wait until tomorrow.

3. What had happened to Mr. Jones's newspapers two days in a row?
4. What mystery does Ann have to solve?

The next day, Wednesday, Ann picked up her papers as usual and rode around her paper route. It was raining again. She skipped the Whites' house, as they had been away on vacation since Sunday, and headed up the Jones's driveway. She would hand-deliver Mr. Jones' newspaper. Ann saw Monday's and Tuesday's papers still lying in the driveway. As Ann rang the doorbell, she could see Mr. Jones sitting in the living-room. He waved at Ann to come in. Mr. Jones had a cast on his leg, and his crutches rested against a chair. Ann wondered how Mr. Jones had been getting a newspaper since he lived alone.

5. What was the first day Ann noticed the newspaper lying in the driveway?
6. Why did Ann want to hand-deliver Mr. Jones's newspaper?

Ann asked Mr. Jones what had happened to his leg. Mr. Jones responded that he had fallen from a ladder on Monday. Mr. Jones was upset by the weather since he could not get outside for a couple of days. Just then, Skippy, the White's dog, came trotting into the living-room. In his mouth was a newspaper, which he gave to Mr. Jones. Mr. Jones handed Skippy a cookie. Ann smiled and thought, part of the mystery is solved.

7. What part of the mystery was solved?
8. What part of the mystery remained to be solved?
9. How could Ann find out where the wrong newspapers came from?

'May I borrow one of your cookies, Mr. Jones?' Ann asked. Ann showed Skippy the cookie. 'Get the paper, Skippy!' Skippy jumped through a hole in the fence and ran to his owner's house just next door. They watched Skippy take a rolled-up paper from a stack of old papers on the White's porch and run back to the Jones's house. The right newspapers were lying at the bottom of Mr. Jones's long driveway. Ann had solved the mystery of the wrong newspapers!

10. Why was the Whites' dog with Mr. Jones?
11. Why was it quicker for Skippy to get an old newspaper than the right one?
12. Why did the mystery of the wrong newspapers happen?

27 Building Content-Area Comprehension and Literacy through an Integrative Curriculum Strategy Using Reading, Writing, and Concept Mapping Strategies

Nancy R. Romance, Michael R. Vitale,
Patricia Widergren, and Janette Hameister, USA

Content-area comprehension (literacy) and writing are critical for success in today's technological society, including the areas of business, the medical sciences, and engineering. Mirroring these dynamics, the use of content-rich passages (e.g., science content) to assess students' comprehension skills has become more prominent in high stakes national and international reading tests. Reflecting this emphasis, this paper develops awareness of key elements of a general research-based model, Knowledge-Based Comprehension (KBC), for enhancing student content-area comprehension, which has been validated in a variety of classroom settings. A summary of past research findings and present research initiatives relating to the use of the KBC model are presented along with systemic implications for the curricular development of student proficiency in content-area reading and writing.

The most fundamental responsibility of education is the preparation of students who are literate to the degree that they are proficient readers and can clearly communicate to a variety of audiences. Complementing this challenge is the awareness that we now have a research base and associated tools to understand how proficiency in literacy develops, why some learners experience difficulty, and how to effectively promote literacy among all students. However, despite our advanced knowledge about literacy, we are faced with a high percentage of students and adults who are functionally illiterate (AFT, 1999). More specifically, such illiteracy translates into students experiencing difficulty with learning how to read, with a lack of decoding fluency, and with a lack of comprehension when reading complex materials in order to gain an increased content understanding.

The Knowledge-Based Comprehension Model

Imagine, for just a moment, a thirteen-year-old student who is experiencing difficulty comprehending a chapter in an eighth-grade science text dealing with biological organisms. Terms such as Eukaryota, Prokaryote, endoplasmic reticulum and golgi bodies and how they are related to each other and to core concepts in biology would certainly transform an already painful task of reading into an impossible situation. It is precisely this scenario that served to prompt the development of the Knowledge-Based Comprehension Model (KBC) described here.

The underlying design of the KBC model (e.g., Romance & Vitale, 2001) uses the *organisational structure of the content discipline* (e.g., history, biology, elementary science) as the basis for constructing content-rich units in which reading/writing serve as critical components for student learning and effective teaching (Bruner, 1977; Chi, et al., 1988; Novak, 1998; Vitale & Romance, 1999). For *teachers,* the KBC model focuses on the teacher-generation of propositional concept maps as a meaningful context for organizing content-area material into integrated curriculum units, for planning conceptually-relevant learning activities for instruction, and for serving as a framework for assessment tasks.

For *students,* the KBC Model incorporates the use of modeling techniques to promote *student* construction of concept maps as a basis for organising the content-area material they read. In turn, these student-generated concept maps facilitate comprehension because they help students represent and access the knowledge to be learned in the form of visual displays (Mintzes, et al., 1998). In this way, the construction of concept maps serves as a learning tool for students in that key concepts and concept relationships represented in the form of vocabulary are meaningfully organised and much easier to remember. Finally, the concept maps created by the students also serve as a well-organised blueprint to promote the development of writing skills.

The KBC Model has been effectively implemented in a variety of classrooms at the upper elementary level. A major multi-year implementation called Science IDEAS (Romance & Vitale, 1992; Romance & Vitale, 2001) consistently resulted in significant and educationally-meaningful achievement gains in reading for both regular and low-performing students. Further, the Science IDEAS model improved the writing performance of students as measured by the *Florida Comprehensive Assessment Test* (FCAT Writes!), administered to every fourth-grade student in the state. A related application of the KBC Model is currently underway at the college level to enhance the reading comprehension and achievement of first-semester chemistry students (see Romance, Vitale, & Haky, 2000). In general, the wide-range of applicability of the KBC model is indicative of its instructional potential to use 'learned knowledge' to scaffold and support literacy goals for a broad range of learners in a variety of contexts.

Building Prior Knowledge

Inherent in the KBC Model are selected literacy strategies which promote reading comprehension and writing development. Primarily, the model requires a highly content-rich environment. That is, use of the KBC Model emphasises conceptually-oriented content-area material as the primary basis for reading and writing. Romance and Vitale (2001) have shown this approach to be effective with all levels of learners. The emphasis on content-rich material promotes in-depth understanding of concept relationships. This provides a framework for the organisation of what students have learned and its subsequent accessibility in the form of prior knowledge. Constructing such meaningful relationships among concepts as ideas is also recognised as the basis for deep-level understanding and comprehension. In this regard, examination of the expert-novice literature (Chi et al., 1988) has clearly shown that the major difference between these two levels of cognition (i.e., experts vs. novices) is the degree to which individuals have constructed and can readily access conceptually-organised knowledge frameworks. Thus, in emphasising a strong knowledge-based perspective, the expert-novice literature clarifies how prior knowledge must be considered as the key element for all forms of comprehension.

Developing Comprehension and Writing

In addition to building prior knowledge, the literature suggests that a content-rich environment is a logical requirement for developing common student comprehension strategies such as summarising, clarifying, questioning and visualising. Because the KBC model explicitly integrates reading and writing within the teaching of content-rich subjects, student comprehension skills are repeatedly practiced and extended through applications in related and unrelated contexts. In fact, it would be difficult to imagine teaching content-rich subjects without integrating the skill areas of reading and writing. As a bonus, at the elementary school level, an integrated approach enables classroom teachers to find time to provide literacy instruction within science and social studies, a practice which is slowly beginning to gain strength in the United States.

The use of concept maps for teaching and learning, an integral part of the KBC Model, has been shown to be a powerful strategy for enhancing student learning (Novak, 1998). As students learn to construct maps built around important concepts in content-rich subject areas, they become able to organise knowledge to be learned into visual displays. So powerful is the process that many students automatically apply the strategy to all subjects they study. Further, concept maps emphasising core concept relationships promote the development of clear, organised writing in that they assist the learner in focusing on the key concepts and big ideas and identifying meaningful supporting information while guiding learners to see how ideas are connected from one paragraph to the next. Thus, the KBC Model involves numerous opportunities for the development of student proficiency in reading comprehension and writing.

Conclusion

Within the framework above, the KBC Model (or any strong knowledge-based model) and the associated research findings raise a number of paradigmatic questions regarding curriculum in the field of reading (as represented by elementary-level basal texts) and the credibility of the dominant perspectives of the field of reading itself regarding what reading should and *should not* be (e.g., NAEP, 2000), particularly at the upper elementary levels and beyond. Included among these questions are: (a) How is the prevailing view of reading relevant to preparing students for comprehension in grade 9-12 setting and beyond? (b) Do schools need a reading curriculum beyond grade 2 and if so, what for? (c) If the reading curriculum beyond grade 2 were eliminated, would it be missed? (d) If reading were eliminated as a curriculum, how could a knowledge-based curricular strategy replace it? And, (e) What is the long-term future of the field of reading as presently defined, given the development of knowledge-based instructional models?

REFERENCES

Bruner, J. (1977). *The process of education.* Cambridge: Harvard University Press.

Chi, M. T. H., Glaser, R. & Farr, M. J. (1988). *The nature of expertise,* Hillsdale, NJ: Lawrence Erlbaum Associates.

Mintzes, J. J., Wandersee, J. H. & Novak, J. D. (1998). *Teaching for science understanding: A human constructivist approach.* San Diego: Academic Press.

Novak, J. D. (1998). *Learning, creating and using knowledge.* Mahwah, NJ: Lawrence Erlbaum Publishers.

National Assessment of Educational Progress. [NAEP]. (2000). *Reading framework for the National Assessment of Educational Progress: 1992–2000.* Washington, DC: National Assessment Governing Board.

Romance, N. R. & Vitale, M. R. (1992). A curriculum strategy that expands time for in-depth elementary science instruction by using science-based reading strategies: Effects of a year-long study in grade four. *Journal of Research in Science Teaching, 29*(6), 545-554.

Romance, N. R. & Vitale, M. R. (2001). Implementing an in-depth expanded science model in elementary schools: Multi-year findings, research issues and implications. *International Journal of Science Education, 23,* 373-404.

Romance, N. R., Vitale, M. R., & Haky, J. (2000). Concept mapping as a knowledge-based strategy for enhancing student understanding. *The Workshop Progress Newsletter, 2,* 5-8.

Teaching reading is rocket science: What expert teachers of reading should know and be able to do. Monograph No. 372. (1999). Washington, DC: American Federation of Teachers (AFT).

Vitale, M. R. & Romance, N. R. (1999). Portfolios in science assessment: A knowledge-based model for classroom practice. In Mintzes, J.J., Wandersee, J. H. & Novak, J. D. (Eds.) pp. 167-196). *Assessing science understanding.* San Diego: Academic Press.

Nancy Romance may be contacted at romance@fau.edu

28 Flexible Grouping: Grouping Students for Direct and Indirect Reading Instruction?

Jeri K. Gustafson and Mary W. Strong, U.S.A.

The principle behind flexible grouping is that children are placed in temporary groups based on their level of independence as learners and groups are periodically created, modified, and disbanded to meet the needs of students (Harp, 1989; Unsworth, 1984; Young, 1990). An important element of flexible grouping is that there are no permanent groups as groups are created, modified, and disbanded to meet the needs of the students (Barbour, 1990; Unsworth, 1984). During flexible grouping, it is likely that children will belong to more than one group at a time (Flood et al., 1992; Jongsma, 1990; Wiggins, 1994). According to research, some of the grouping arrangements that are categorised as flexible grouping options include: whole class instruction, small group instruction, pairs or peer-tutoring, cooperative learning groups and research groups

A recent position statement issued by the International Reading Association (2000) provides a researched-based description of six qualities of excellent reading teachers. One of the six qualities is that excellent teachers use flexible grouping. Evers (1999) contends that master teachers employ flexible grouping and create a comfortable learning environment. Educational change however is not easy. Bridge (1995) examined whether Kentucky primary teachers were adopting changes in literacy instructional practices after the Kentucky Reform Act was mandated. Bridge conducted classroom observations and teacher interviews with 98 teachers and concluded that half of the teachers were having difficulty implementing flexible grouping practices and varying their instruction to meet individual needs. A study conducted by Roberts and Goedeken (1996) randomly surveyed 300 elementary reading and language arts teachers in the state of Iowa and revealed that 29.4% of them still utilised ability grouping all or some of the time. The survey indicated that various other grouping arrangements, including independent or individualised reading and/or cooperative learning groups, may be filling the gap left by the declining use of small homogeneous groups.

A Study of Grouping

In 1989, a large urban school district in the United States, serving approximately 33,000 students, adopted a new basal reading series for K-5

(Kindergarten to Grade 5) reading instruction and purchased $800 worth of trade books for each classroom's use. At that time, it was recommended by school administrators that all K-5 teachers in the district utilise flexible grouping arrangements related to students' needs and interests in reading and writing. Currently, the district is in the process of selecting new reading curriculum materials and is interested in obtaining information pertaining to how K-5 students are being grouped for reading instruction. The purpose of the present study is to examine how K-5 teachers in a large urban school district currently group students for reading instruction. The primary question guiding the study is, 'With a recommendation to use flexible grouping arrangements, how are K-5 teachers grouping their students for reading instruction?' Another objective was to compare the grouping arrangements used by lower primary (Grades K-2) and upper primary (Grades 3-5) teachers.

Method

A survey was developed to gather information on current grouping practices. The first part of the survey dealt with grouping arrangements used for direct reading instruction. Direct reading instruction was defined on the survey as 'teacher-led reading instruction where the teacher is directly involved with the student(s) as they engage with print materials. Direct reading instruction includes teacher-led instructional activities such as guided reading, shared reading, large or small group discussions, skills presentations, etc.'. Five grouping arrangements were listed (1) whole class heterogeneous instruction, (2) whole class homogeneous instruction, (3) small group heterogeneous instruction, (4) small group homogeneous instruction, and (5) individualised instruction.

The second part of the survey gathered information on grouping arrangements used for indirect reading instruction. Indirect reading instruction was defined on the survey as 'reading instruction where the teacher is less directly involved with the students as they engage with print materials. During indirect reading instruction, the teacher serves as a facilitator or monitor to focus learning and guide students' work. Indirect reading instruction includes independent reading or seatwork time, reader's and writer's workshops, group literacy projects, etc.'. There were eight grouping arrangements listed under indirect reading instruction: (1) cooperative learning groups, (2) peer tutoring, (3) reading centers, (4) independent reading, (5) reader's workshop, (6) writing process groups, (7) independent seatwork, and (8) research groups. These eight grouping arrangements were not defined on the survey. Therefore, teachers were allowed to formulate their own definitions of each grouping arrangement with the assumption that they would have similar understandings of what was meant by each one.

The target audience for the survey consisted of all kindergarten through fifth grade regular classroom teachers in the district. The final sample consisted of 608 teachers: 66 kindergarten, 111 first grade, 103 second grade, 94 third grade, 92 fourth grade, 81 fifth grade, 33 kindergarten through second grade multi-age combinations, and 28 third through fifth grade multi-age combinations. Of the 608 teachers surveyed, 268 or 44.1% returned the survey.

Results

Looking specifically at direct reading instruction, Grade 1 teachers in this study devote the largest amount of time per week to direct reading instruction with 557 minutes per week (MPW) or 9.3 hours on average. After Grade 1, the average number of minutes per week during which teachers engage in direct reading instruction declines at each grade level, with Grade 5 teachers devoting only 345 MPW or 5.7 hours per week to direct reading instruction, approximately 3.5 hours per week less than Grade 1 teachers.

Similarly, Grade 1 teachers also devote the largest amount of time per week to indirect reading instruction (481 MPW). As with direct reading instruction, there is a significant decline in the use of indirect reading instruction as students move from Grade 1 to Grade 5. Grade 5 teachers in this study engage their students in indirect reading instruction for 359 MPW, approximately 2 hours less per week than Grade 1 teachers. Overall, there is a decrease of approximately 5.5 hours per week devoted to total reading instruction as students progress from Grade 1 to Grade 5.

For the sample as a whole, the elementary teachers in this study spend slightly over seven hours per week engaging their students in direct reading instruction and just under seven hours per week engaging their students in indirect reading instruction. Taking into consideration that the teachers in this district interact with their students a total of 6.5 hours a day or 32.5 hours per week, these teachers are spending approximately 43 percent of their time engaging students in either direct or indirect reading instruction.

Grouping for Direct Reading Instruction

Kindergarten teachers in this study use primarily whole-class heterogeneous instruction followed by small-group heterogeneous instruction and then individualised instruction. The use of heterogeneous instruction in kindergarten, both whole class and small group, is likely a product of the wide range of abilities of children as they enter school. Between Grades 1 and 4, teachers responded that the primary grouping arrangement they used for direct reading instruction was small homogeneous groups, followed by whole class heterogeneous instruction and individualised instruction. Teachers in Grade 5 reported using whole class heterogeneous grouping followed by small homogeneous groups.

Although small homogeneous group instruction is the most used grouping arrangement through Grade 4 and the second most used grouping arrangement in Grade 5, the amount of time devoted to small homogeneous group instruction consistently decreases from Grade 1 through Grade 5. Grade 1 teachers in this study spend approximately 5 hours per week instructing students in small homogeneous groups whereas Grade 5 teachers spend less than 2.5 hours per week.

Grouping for Indirect Reading Instruction

Teachers in Grades 1-5 responded that the three primary grouping arrangements they used for indirect reading instruction were: independent reading, independent seatwork, and writing process groups. Kindergarten teachers indicated the most commonly used grouping arrangements used in their classrooms were independent seatwork, reading centres, and writing process groups. Kindergarten was the only grade level where the use of reading centres was one of the top three grouping arrangements for indirect reading instruction.

Primary and Intermediate Teachers

To compare the time spent by primary teachers (K-2) in the various grouping arrangements for direct and indirect reading instruction to the time spent by upper primary teachers (Grades 3-5), two one-way multivariate analyses of variance (MANOVAs) were conducted. Subsequent univariate analyses of variance (ANOVAs) were run to determine more specifically where significant group differences could be found.

The results of the MANOVA for direct reading instruction revealed significant differences in the ways primary and intermediate teachers group students for direct reading instruction, F (1,266) = 31.38, p .001. In subsequent univariate analyses of variance (ANOVAs), lower-primary teachers were found to use whole class-heterogeneous instruction, small-group homogeneous instruction, and individualised instruction significantly more often than upper-primary teachers.

The results of the MANOVA for indirect reading instruction revealed non-significant differences in the ways lower- and upper-primary teachers group students for indirect reading instruction (F (1,266) = .77, p = .38). Subsequent univariate analyses of variance (ANOVAs) revealed significant between-group differences in the amount of time per week that the two groups of teachers allocate to the use of centers, independent reading, literature study groups, writing process groups, and research groups. However, since the overall MANOVA F was non-significant, caution needs to be exercised when interpreting these univariate analyses of variance because of the possibility that these between-group differences were caused by chance or Type I error.

Conclusion

This study has helped the school district involved to better understand how K-5 students are being grouped for direct and indirect reading instruction. Currently, teaching practices and grouping arrangements in lower- and upper-primary classrooms are in a state of change and fluctuation (Allington, 1992). Some teachers are still holding on to the practice of ability grouping while others have eliminated ability groups completely and have replaced them with various other grouping arrangements (see Hiebert & Colt, 1989). Results of this study indicate that small homogeneous grouping is still being used at all grade levels, primarily at the early primary grades. However, a variety of other flexible grouping arrangements are also being used.

REFERENCES

Allington, R. L. (1992). Reconsidering instructional groupings. *Reading Horizons, 32*, 349-355.

Barbour, N. H. (1990). Flexible grouping: It works! *Childhood Education, 67*, 66-67.

Bridge, C. (1995, December.) Implementing large scale change in literacy instruction: A second look. Paper presented at the Annual Meeting of the National Reading Conference. New Orleans, LA.

Evers, B.J. (1999) Teaching children to read and write. *Principal (4), 78*, p. 32, 34, 36, 38.

International Reading Association (2000). Excellent reading teachers: A position statement. Newark, DE: Author.

Flood, J., Lapp, D., Flood, S. & Nagel, G. (1992). Am I allowed to group? Using flexible patterns for effective instruction. *The Reading Teacher, 45,* 608-16.

Harp, B. (1989). What do we put in the place of ability grouping? *The Reading Teacher, 42,* 534-535.

Hiebert, E. H. & Colt, J. (1989). Patterns of literature-based reading instruction. The *Reading Teacher, 43,* 14-20.

Jongsma, K. S. (1990). Making decisions about grouping with basals. *The Reading Teacher, 44,* 80-82.

Roberts, S. K. & Goedeken, K. (1996). Survey of Iowa elementary teachers. *Iowa Reading Journal, 9,* 30-37.

Unsworth, L. (1984). Meeting individual needs through flexible within-class grouping of pupils. *The Reading Teacher, 38,* 298-304.

Wiggins, R. A. (1994). Large group lesson/small group follow-up: Flexible grouping in a basal reading program. *The Reading Teacher, 47,* 450-460.

Young, T. A. (1990). Alternatives to ability grouping in reading. *Reading Horizons, 30,* 169-183.

SECTION 8

Secondary Reading

29 Reading in Secondary Schools: A Case for Situated Reading

Edward H. Behrman, U.S.A.

Situated cognition theory suggests that an ideal learning system should promote individual conceptual development as learners participate in social settings across different contexts. Because situated theory holds that cognition and activity are intertwined, it must acknowledge that different contexts (classroom versus real-world) produce different kinds of learning. A resolution could be to provide students with multiple learning contexts both in school and beyond. Therefore, in order to promote advanced content literacy in secondary schools, the locus of learning may need to be widened to include workplace communities, affording opportunities for students to progress from 'reading to learn' to 'reading to do.'

This paper proposes an alternative view that may change the way we envision reading instruction for secondary-level pupils: through the lens of reading as situated activity. Underlying this proposal is the belief that a fundamental purpose of reading instruction in the upper grades should be to expand pupils' range of reading experiences, with particular attention to extending content literacy in authentic contexts. In order to provide rich and meaningful contexts that promote advanced content literacy, the locus of learning must be widened. Advanced literacy development in the upper grades requires participation not only in school, home, and peer communities, but also in workplace communities that provide authentically-situated learning opportunities. Moving toward advanced literacy should be an educational goal for all students, not just the academically talented.

Situated Cognition and Reading

In contrast to a cognitive position that views cognition as an internalized, individual phenomenon (Reynolds, Sinatra, & Jetton, 1996), situated cognition theory has attempted to define cognition in terms of both internal and external processes (Kirshner & Whitson, 1998). Situated cognition theory is based on the union of cognition and context. Amount and quality of learning depend upon physical setting, tools or resources available to the learner, and interpersonal transactions engaged between learner and community (Brown, Collins, & Duguid, 1989; Cobb &

Bowers, 1999; Greeno, 1997; Greeno, Collins, & Resnick, 1996; Putnam & Borko, 2000). The learner constructs mental models that incorporate objects from the environmental situation (Greeno, 1991). Alexander (2000) underscores that 'learning is held to be both individual *and* social; that is, the learner and the community are inherently related in formal learning. For this reason, it is essential to consider the social dynamics, even as we consider the variability within and across individuals as they progress from one learning environment or situation to another' (p. 31).

Situated cognition emphasises contextualised learning from active participation in a community of practice (Lave, 1996). The novice becomes enculturated in the accepted knowledge and habits of the community (Lave & Wenger, 1991), with knowledgeable others in the community serving as mentors by providing scaffolds to support the novice's learning (Gee, 2000). The community is also transformed by its interactions with the novice. Individual knowledge influences the common knowledge of a group, and common knowledge of a group influences individual knowledge (Bloome & Egan-Robertson, 1993). Therefore, an ideal learning system should promote individual conceptual development as learners participate in social settings across different contexts (Anderson, Greeno, Reder, & Simon, 2000).

It is likely that the role of context becomes even more pronounced as learning moves past the introductory stage. Whereas the goal of introductory learning is content exposure and general orientation to a domain, during advanced learning, the goal is deeper understanding, reasoning, and application in a variety of contexts. Learning domains become ill-structured as more complex conceptual elements interact in patterns that are inconsistent from case to case (Spiro, Coulson, Feltovich, & Anderson, 1994). Educational methods used during introductory learning – that emphasise compartmentalisation of knowledge and presentation of clear examples – lead students to numerous misconceptions, including overgeneralisation and oversimplification, and present conceptual knowledge too abstractly to be effective in context-bound applications (Spiro, Coulson, Feltovich, & Anderson, 1994).

For many years, much secondary-level reading instruction has been shaped by a non-situated view that defined reading behavior as generic activity transferring readily across contexts. For example, developmental reading classes in middle schools, study skills classes in high schools, and reading labs for underperforming students at all levels are based on the presumption that once a student learns particular reading strategies, these strategies will be utilised in a wide variety of reading situations across many content domains. Even the prevailing model of reading in the content areas (e.g., Alvermann & Phelps, 1998; McKenna & Robinson, 1997; Roe, Stoodt, & Burns, 2001; Vacca & Vacca, 1996), which recognises that literacy activities are shaped by demands of the content domain, nonetheless depends on a social process of teacher-directed reading activities that may not be present in all reading situations. However, a situative perspective recognises that learning in one situation may have generalisability to another situation only to the extent that the situations share patterns of activity (Greeno, 1997).

Each reading situation is bound by the interrelated dimensions of the *individual reader*, who brings a unique array of knowledge, skills, strategies, interests, and motivation; the social and physical features of the *discourse community*; the *conceptual domain*, at the broad, narrow, and topical levels; and the *task* itself, which includes both goal and genre (e.g., 'analyse Lincoln's position on slavery by reading political speeches made before, during, and after the election of 1860'). The individual's knowledge, interests, etc. are of course largely socially determined by participation in multiple communities. Similarly, the placement of a body of learning within a particular conceptual domain is itself determined by social practice, as are the accepted modes of inquiry within that domain, which in turn affect the way a task is developed.

A Re-Vision of Secondary Reading

Because of the important role of social participation in learning, situated cognition theory suggests that students be provided with opportunities to problem solve in group settings, so that individuals can create and share mental models (Reynolds, Sinatra, & Jetton, 1996), while also receiving overt instruction from a master or more advanced peer (Gee, 2000). In addition, the learner should be immersed in 'ordinary practices of a culture' (Brown, Collins, & Duguid, 1989) that afford learners a transition from peripheral to more central participation in a community of practitioners (Lave & Wenger, 1991). A measure of the 'ordinariness' or authenticity of school-based literacy practices is the extent to which they relate to literacy practices outside school (Gee, 2000). Tierney and Pearson (1994) have therefore cited 'the need to situate content area learning in real classes and problems that exist outside the classroom and the school' (p. 516).

Unfortunately, situated cognition theory has yet to refine a distinctive educational approach to provide these situated contexts (Kirshner & Whitson, 1998). For example, both literal apprenticeships and cognitive apprenticeships have been offered as educational approaches to support situated cognition theory (Kirshner & Whitson, 1998). A critical pedagogical issue facing situated theorists is whether authentic contexts can be experienced in school alone (e.g., through role playing, simulations, and cooperative projects), or whether students should also engage in 'lived' contexts outside of school. Brown, Collins, and Duguid (1989) have asserted, 'When authentic activities are transferred to the classroom, their context is inevitably transmuted; they become classroom tasks and part of the school culture' (p. 34). School is a particular learning situation with its own sets of practices, affordances, and constraints, which may not be replicated in non-school settings (Greeno, 1997). Because situated theory holds that cognition and activity are intertwined, it must acknowledge that different contexts (classroom versus real-world) produce different kinds of learning. A resolution could be to provide students with multiple learning contexts both in school and beyond.

One important 'lived' context beyond the classroom walls is the workplace. Both cognitive and situated perspectives agree that 'Part of what children must prepare for is to participate effectively in social practices in their communities and work situations' (Anderson, Greeno, Reder, & Simon, 2000, p. 12). Workplace literacy demands are pervasive and challenging. Adults spend more time reading on the job than at leisure (Guthrie & Greaney, 1991), as more than 90 percent of all occupations require reading and writing (Mikulecky & Drew, 1991). Professionals read on average over two-and-a-half hours per day at work (Mikulecky, 1982), including reading for knowledge gain, extracting information to solve problems, and reading documents to guide activities (Guthrie, Siefert, & Kirsch, 1986). Workplace reading situations are usually quite different from classroom reading situations:

> …many high school students are unprepared for how literacy skills are used in the workplace. Most workplace reading, writing, and computation is done to accomplish tasks and make assessments. Rather than reading from a single text, workers must gather information from several sources to solve problems, provide services, and perform tasks. (Mikulecky & Drew, 1991, p. 671)

Underlying this disconnect between classroom reading and workplace reading is the issue of transfer. Work-based literacy processes may be more distinct from school-based processes than educators acknowledge (Resnick, 1987). Although much schooling is based on an assumption of fluid transferability of skills from classroom to workplace situations, research does not support this assumption (Mikulecky & Drew, 1991). Effective workplace literacy programs include tasks and materials linked directly to the workplace context (Sticht & Mikulecky, 1984), validating Gee's (2000) assertion that there is no 'reading in general,' but only contextually situated literacy.

Therefore, another model of secondary reading may be useful in helping students develop advanced, contextualized content literacy. It is not proposed here that secondary reading programs be redesigned to provide occupational training. However, it appears that secondary pupils might need more exposure to various 'lived' contexts, including workplace communities, to allow them opportunities to contextualize content learning and to progress from 'reading to learn' to 'reading to do.'

Adapting the Secondary Curriculum

Many secondary students, especially those from economically-disadvantaged backgrounds, have a diminished opportunity to experience the necessary integration of literacy learning and workplace context. Students may have limited exposure to professionals who utilise advanced literacy skills in their occupations. Thus, students may have little opportunity to visit professional job sites on an informal basis (going to see a parent, relative, or family friend). Instead, students are presented with distorted images by television and movies, where the glamour and excitement of a profession are portrayed, not the preparation, training, and literacy skills needed for success. Consequently, a student's representation of a profession may not include the relationship between school-based learning and the literacy demands of the job. Further, the misimpression that academic learning is unrelated to 'real life' is reinforced among many students who work after school in non-professional occupations (e.g., fast food, retail).

To place students in contexts that provide opportunities for advanced content literacy development, secondary schools would need to consider several departures from current practice, including

- Restructured time patterns in and out of school to promote authentic reading and writing situations.

- Project-based learning.
- Traditional apprenticeships providing exposure to 'lived' contexts or internships combining exposure to 'lived' contexts with participation in simulated or 'contrived' contexts that provide diminishing levels of support.
- Extensive site visits to local businesses and other agencies where professionals are engaged in situated literacy activities.
- Use of mentors from local businesses and other agencies.
- Use of a variety of social configurations (individual, partners, small groups, large groups) to promote literacy.
- Access to a wide range of resources (including print media and electronic tools), rather than reliance on a single text, as a regular part of the learning activity.

For example, a literacy curriculum based on situative principles is currently under development at National University in Los Angeles. Community Partners in Literacy (CPL) will enhance content literacy by combining school-based instructional activities with site visits to community business partners. For each Learning Module, students will first meet in a classroom setting to discuss what they know about a particular industry and to prepare for their site visit. Next, students will visit a community business, where they will interact with professionals using literacy skills on the job. Then, students will return to the classroom setting to engage in an academic project based on literacy skills that are used in that business. Classroom activities will utilise cooperative learning, with students organised into learning groups to complete short-term or intermediate-term projects. Representatives from community businesses will serve as mentors to the cooperative learning groups. Site visits are anticipated to domain-related industries in biology (pharmaceuticals, biotechnology, hazardous waste disposal, human medicine, and veterinary medicine); economics (banking/lending, financial management, accounting, insurance, and real estate); and government (legislative, public administration, law, criminal justice, and public service).

Conclusion

A literacy curriculum including these features may be threatening to those who wish to restrict literacy learning to the narrow context of the classroom and limit students' exposure to mentors besides the content teacher. In Ivey's (2001) recent review of secondary reading research, however, she concludes that 'we need more documentation of motivating contexts that also lead to greater literacy achievement, particularly for students who are still experiencing difficulty' (p. 2). The proposed situated view of secondary reading expands communities of practice to include workplace contexts, with workplace mentors serving as knowledgeable others bridging students from school literacy to workplace literacy. Ongoing curricular development and evaluation are needed to study innovative programs for secondary students that situate reading in authentic workplace contexts.

REFERENCES

Alexander, P. A. (1998). The nature of disciplinary and domain learning: The knowledge, interest, and strategic dimensions of learning from subject matter text. In C. R. Hynd (Ed.), *Learning from text across conceptual domains* (pp. 263-287). Mahwah, NJ: Erlbaum.

Alexander, P. A. (2000). Toward a model of academic development: Schooling and the acquisition of knowledge. *Educational Researcher, 29*(2), 28-34.

Alvermann, D. E., & Phelps, S. F. (1998). *Content reading and literacy* (2nd ed.). Needham Heights, MA: Allyn & Bacon.

Anderson, J. R., Greeno, J. G., Reder, L. M., & Simon, H. A. (2000). Perspectives on learning, thinking, and activity. *Educational Researcher, 29*(4), 11-13.

Bloome, D. (2001). Boundaries on construction of literacy in secondary classrooms: Envisioning reading and writing in a democratic and just society. In E. B. Moje, & D. G. O'Brien, *Constructions of literacy: Studies of teaching and learning in and out of secondary schools* (pp. 287-304). Mahwah, NJ: Erlbaum.

Bloome, D. & Egan-Robertson, A. (1993). The social construction of intertextuality in classroom reading and writing lessons. *Reading Research Quarterly, 28*, 305-333.

Brown, J. S. Collins, A., & Duguid, P. (1989). Situated cognition and the culture of learning. *Educational Researcher, 18*(1), 32-42.

Cobb, P. & Bowers, J. (1999). Cognitive and situated learning perspectives in theory and practice. *Educational Researcher, 28*(2), 4-15.

Damon, W. (1991). Problems of direction in socially shared cognition. In L.B. Resnick, J. M. Levine, & S. D. Teasley (Eds.), *Perspectives on socially shared cognition* (pp. 384-397). Washington, DC: American Psychological Association.

Gee, J. P. (2000). Discourse and sociocultural studies in reading. In M. L. Kamil, P. B. Mosenthal, P. D. Pearson, & R. Barr (Eds.), *Handbook of reading research, vol. 3* (pp. 195-207). Mahwah, NJ: Erlbaum.

Greeno, J. G. (1991). Number sense as situated knowing in a conceptual domain. *Journal for Research in Mathematics Education, 22*, 170-218.

Greeno, J. G. (1997). On claims that answer the wrong questions. *Educational Researcher, 26*(1), 5-17.

Greeno, J. G., Collins, A. M., & Resnick, L. B. (1996). Cognition and learning. In D. C. Berliner & R. C. Calfee (Eds.), *Handbook of educational psychology* (pp. 15-46). New York: Macmillan.

Guthrie, J. T. & Greaney, V. (1991). Literacy acts. In R. Barr, M. L. Kamil, P. Mosenthal, & P. D. Pearson (Eds.), *Handbook of reading research, vol. 2* (pp. 68-96). Mahwah, NJ: Erlbaum.

Guthrie, J. T., Siefert, M. & Kirsch, I. W. (1986). Effects of education, occupation, and setting on reading practices. *American Educational Research Journal, 23,* 151-160.

Ivey, G. (2001). *Literacy learning and teaching for adolescents: Where has a decade of research taken us?* Paper presented at the annual meeting of the American Educational Research Association, Seattle, WA.

Kirshner, D., & Whitson, J. A. (1998). Obstacles to understanding cognition as situated. *Educational Researcher, 27*(8), 22-28.

Lave, J. (1996). Teaching, as learning in practice. *Mind, Culture, and Activity, 3,* 149-164.

Lave, J. & Wenger, E. (1991). *Situated learning: Legitimate peripheral participation.* Cambridge: Cambridge University Press.

Lorch, R. F., Klusewitz, M. A., & Lorch, E. P. (1995). Distinctions among reading situations. In R. F. Lorch & E. J. O'Brien (Eds.), *Sources of coherence in reading* (pp. 375-398). Hillsdale, NJ: Erlbaum.

McKenna, M. C., & Robinson, R. D. (1997). *Teaching through text: A content literacy approach to content area reading instruction* (2nd ed.). White Plains, NY: Longman.

Mikulecky, L. (1982). Job literacy: The relationship between school preparation and workplace actuality. *Reading Research Quarterly, 17,* 400-419.

Mikulecky, L. & Drew, R. (1991). Basic literacy skills in the workplace. In R. Barr, M. L. Kamil, P. Mosenthal, & P. D. Pearson (Eds.), *Handbook of reading research, vol. 2* (pp. 669-689). Mahwah, NJ: Erlbaum.

Putnam, R. T. & Borko, H. (2000). What do new views of knowledge have to say about research on teacher learning? *Educational Researcher, 29*(1), 4-15.

Reynolds, R. E., Sinatra, G. M., & Jetton, T. L. (1996). Views of knowledge acquisition and representation: A continuum from experience centered to mind centered. *Educational Psychologist, 31,* 93-104.

Resnick, L. B. (1987). Learning in school and out. *Educational Researcher, 16*(9), 13-20.

Roe, B. D., Stoodt, B. D., & Burns, P. C. ((2001). *Secondary school reading instruction: The content areas* (7th ed.). Boston: Houghton Mifflin.

Spiro, R. J., Coulson, R. L., Feltovich, P. J., & Anderson, D. K. (1994). Cognitive flexibility theory: Advanced knowledge acquisition in ill-structured domains. In R. B. Ruddell, M. R. Ruddell, & H. Singer (Eds.), *Theoretical models and processes of reading* (4th ed.) (pp. 602-615). Newark, DE: International Reading Association.

Sticht, T. G. & Mikulecky, L. J. (1984). *Job-related basic skills: Cases and conclusions* (Information Series No. 285). Columbus: Ohio State University, National Center for Research in Vocational Education.

Tierney, R. J., & Pearson, P. D. (1994). A revisionist perspective on 'Learning to learn from text: A framework for improving classroom practice.' In R. B. Ruddell, M. R. Ruddell, & H. Singer (Eds.), *Theoretical models and processes of reading* (4th ed.) (pp. 514-519). Newark, DE: International Reading Association.

Vacca, R. T., & Vacca, J. A. (1996). *Content area reading* (5th ed.). New York: HarperCollins.

30 Reading Literature in Slovenian Vocational Schools

Boža Krakar Vogel, Slovenia

Vocational schools in Slovenia offer 3-year programme in which students aged 14-17 years are trained for different professions such as bakers, car mechanics, tailors and sales assistants. Most of the students attending vocational schools were poor academic achievers in primary school and have little interest in reading.

Slovenia educators believe that encounters with literature are an important educational opportunity for all students, including those in vocational education. For this reason, our recent educational reform involves the introduction of mother tongue syllabi at vocational schools, with 40% of class time in language and literacy being devoted to reading literature.

Before the latest reform, which began in 1996, the literature curriculum for vocational schools was basically a shortened version of that for grammar schools. The new selection of recommended readings is better suited to the reading interests and abilities of vocational school students. The same goes for the reading strategies and reader response stimuli in the new textbooks.

Recent Reforms

In the Slovenian school system, primary schools are currently being re-shaped on a national basis from eight-year programmes into nine-year programmes. Secondary schools offer various types of programmes. Four-year grammar schools prepare students for university studies (they could be described as having combining features of British grammar, preparatory and comprehensive schools). Four-year vocational school programmes train students for certain professions in areas such as business, tourism and engineering, and qualify students for admission to lower-level tertiary programmes in their field. Three- and two-year vocational programmes aim solely at training students for various professions, mainly in the service sector, while *shortened vocational programmes* merely equip trainees with the skills needed to perform certain types of manual labor. In all these programmes, Slovenian Language and Literature is a core general education subject featuring 30%-50% literature.

The fact that Slovenian vocational schools teach literature is one of the main features which distinguishes their curriculum from the curricula of vocational schools in some other countries such as Denmark The reason for including literature in vocational school curricula lies in the fact that in Slovenia, literature has played a central role in the preservation of our language, culture and nationhood through centuries of foreign rule. Since independence (1991), the reasons have expanded to include the importance of reading literature for personal growth and the socialisation of an individual and the development of imagination, creative thinking and empathy.

However, because of a lack of awareness that different target populations require different educational approaches[1], the aims and content of teaching literature in vocational schools have traditionally been essentially the same as those for grammar schools. Like in the latter, students of vocational schools were familiarised with representatives of the canon from the point of view of literary history, beginning with ancient civilisations in their first year, then moving to the Middle Ages, then to Realism and finally, at the end of their schooling, 20th century literature. The syllabus was based on that of grammar schools; the difference was that for vocational schools some more demanding works were left out and thus the quantity of material to be covered was smaller. Readers for vocational schools[2] also had shortened versions of the general literary history sections, less demanding both in terms of content and terminology, and included additional exercises for grammatical analysis, speaking and writing, which were not contained in the grammar school readers. This was the entire scope of differentiation on the level of curriculum which is in Slovenia traditionally firmly centralised[3] and defines not only the aims but also the content of instruction.

Further adaptation of demanding literary works (e.g., Sophocles' *Oedipus*, Dante's *The Divine Comedy*, Shakespeare's *Romeo and Juliet*, and some of the Slovenian classics such as *Prešeren* and *Cankar*) has been left to individual teachers. As observations of classroom practice have shown, some of them, using personal approaches and interesting motivational techniques, have been very successful with their vocational school students. However, some of the teachers 'reformed' their teaching in inappropriate ways, by teaching to their students the findings of modern literary sciences and expecting them to understand and interpret literary texts far removed from their personal experience, even when the teachers themselves noticed that their students often had trouble even reading simple newspaper articles.

The new curricula took all these facts into account as well as some findings of empirical research done on this purpose.

Leading Research Findings

Let us look at some findings of the research on reading and literary competence of students in three-year vocational schools, which has contributed to an awareness of their needs, clearer goal-setting, better teacher-training and, consequently, more successful teaching of literature.

What does a future car mechanic, cook, tailor etc. like to read? Mostly newspapers and magazines with little text. Under 'books', students listed titles such as *Robinson Crusoe, Robin Hood, Five Friends, Asterix,* and works of Slovenian youth fiction authors such as Desa Muck, Vitan Mal and Nejka Omahen. Many, however, read books only because they were required to do so. Most of them never even come into contact with books outside of school; their families don't purchase them and they do not go to libraries in their spare time.

As far as genre is concerned, prose definitely prevails over poetry and drama, and even with prose more voluminous texts are avoided. Interestingly, the students find it important to read Slovenian classics, even though they do not enjoy it, as they feel that 'we need to know something about Slovenian writers because they are a part of our culture and history.' (Lampiè 1996, Piškur 1999: 25).

When reading a book, they mostly pay attention to the plot and the protagonists, with whom they identify on an emotional level. If they come across shorter textual elements that they did not understand (individual words or names), they simply ignored them. They also skipped boring long descriptions. If there were too many such elements, they put the book away.

This reader profile is a realistic point of departure for successful teaching of literature which will provide students with positive experiences and make them keener to read. This does not, of course, imply that we should merely adapt to their existing horizon of expectations and have them read only comics, adventure books and trivial romances. It does, however, mean that we need to start the journey towards some higher aims (various types of communicative reading, classics and modern genres) at this realistic point, rather than with Sophocles or Dante.

A New Reading Syllabus

Changing the reading syllabus was therefore one of the most important steps of the reform in this field. Since then, works to be discussed are no longer chronologically ordered from old to modern, and the repertoire is no longer limited to a selection of canonical works. Students are now familiarised with literary works in thematic groups, according to the different ways these are linked with real life. For example, they compare visual and textual communication in an advertisement and a comic, an ordinary and a literary letter (with an extract from *The Lady with the Camelias*), a personal and a literary diary (e.g., with Charriere's *The Butterfly*). They read recipes, instructions, memos and invitations written in a literary style, and learn to distinguish between a newspaper and a literary report (e.g., with *The Good Soldier Švejk*), and between a CV and a biography etc. Most of the texts are taken from Slovenian literature, and many have a humourous component. Topics range from adventure, romance and history to modern living, family problems and science fiction. From a literary point of view, the texts are not the most demanding, and are characterised by vivid plots and communicative language, whether the authors are representatives of the canon or of modern genres.

In the final year, a chronological overview is made of the development of Slovenian literature since 16th century, and the main features of each period are outlined. We believe that this represents a minimum level of general knowledge for every citizen of Slovenia, since for centuries literature has been one of the main factors of our nationhood. The consciousness of this role of literature is a means of forming the Slovenian social identity. Of course, rather than requiring vocational school students to read the most demanding classics, the less demanding works of the greatest Slovenian authors have been selected, and the descriptions of literary periods are not overly packed with facts. This 'traditional' way of rounding off the teaching of literature in vocational programmes might appear somewhat more conservative than the teaching of literature in comparable programmes in other countries. However, it must be pointed out that some countries with similar historical backgrounds to Slovenia still have a fair share of national literary histories in their curricula.

The selection of appropriate texts is not the only factor which contributes to successful literature instruction. We also need to systematically introduce activities which open up the texts and make the students feel that reading is something they are mastering.

Before the reform, i.e., before the new views of teaching literature found their way into practice, the main student activity in literature classes was writing. Students hurriedly wrote down the teacher's explanations about authors, their works and other facts of literary history. Then they reproduced those facts in tests.

All this has now changed. In accordance with the new curriculum, the basic activities in a literature class are reading and guided discussion, which ensures that the students understand the readings and can talk about their experiences and express their opinions. There is also a lot of reading aloud, listening and viewing of filmed versions of works of literature. Students are encouraged to express their perceptions of the texts read both in speech and in writing. When students are required to respond in writing to a reading text, they mainly produce short, not too demanding text types such as summaries or descriptions of characters. Other tasks range from developing a story to dramatisation to 'translating' a poem into a prose passage. The possibilities of using electronic mail are not widely exploited as yet (e.g., writing to authors or other 'literature people', writing to peers about reading literature). Vocational school students are encouraged to evaluate texts on the basis of their own experience rather than from a literary point of view, which would be expected of grammar school students. Fluent reading aloud and an oral presentation of what they have read is a part of the final exam. Knowing literary theory is not primarily a matter of being able to define terms, but being able to recognise and name things students encounter in a text (e.g., whether the text is a short story or a lyrical poem, whether it has stanzas or chapters, is stylistically simple or complex, whether the language is literary or colloquial etc.). By the end of their schooling, students have learned about the most important representatives of Slovenian literature through the ages, and read their works. The final exam tests their familiarity with the authors, their lives and the times in which they lived, and their works that have been read. The curriculum includes ten authors from the 16th to the 20th century, presented through one text each; the texts include several poems and prose passages, one short story and one comedy.

The reform of teaching literature in vocational schools that has been introduced with the new curriculum of 1998 has been supported by the publication of a series of textbooks called *Potovanje besed* (A Journey of Words) by Jana Kvas. Her textbooks have a clear didactic outline with a progression from the familiar to the new. They include literary texts, explanations, questions, pictures and charts, and are complemented by a series of workbooks.

The significance of the new curriculum and textbook is that they draw on the student's everyday experience and that they guide him/her towards reflective observation gradually, with easy-to-master steps and in simple language. In cases of texts which are really close to the readers' experience, such as with comics, this can even lead to dealing with complex questions of aesthetic evaluation.

Reading Habits and Attitudes

How were all the novelties accepted by teachers and students? In a survey done by M. Piškur in 1999, 100 first-year students and 100 third-year students of vocational schools (in programmes for car mechanics) were asked about their reading habits, abilities and interests. Around 60 % of students from both groups stated that they liked the new textbooks. The author of the study considers this to be satisfactory result, especially compared to the unpopularity of literature classes before the reform, when similar questionnaires revealed a very low interest in texts read in school.

Some surveys about the reform process have also been carried out among teachers (Tekavec, 1999). The main questions asked concerned how the teachers evaluated the changes and at what pace individual changes were being applied in practice. Forty-two teachers from different vocational schools around the country evaluated the curriculum reform of 3-year vocational programmes as something positive (3 judged it to be 'excellent', 20 'good', 16 'acceptable' and 3 'poor'). A similar evaluation applied to the new textbooks, which the teachers considered well-supported, motivating and 'really the only textbooks we've got'. It is true, however, that some teachers resent the absence of a chronological overview of world literature and the explicitness of the more traditional textbooks.

Conclusion

The surveys quoted, as well as other types of research (observation and personal communication), show that the reform of the teaching of literature in vocational schools has so far successfully introduced more student-centredness at the levels of curriculum development and the preparation of development. Of course, there is some room for further improvement at this level, but improvement is even more necessary in classroom practice. Teachers in vocational schools deal with students coming from environments which do not encourage them to read, so they often need to compensate for this lack of encouragement in the family and broader social environment. To teach them effectively, teachers will have to continually upgrade their own professional skills in programmes of continuing education, as well as adapting their expectations to the reality of their students, who need instruction quite different from that which would suit more academic audiences of which the teachers themselves were members of during their own schooling.

The changes that have been introduced into teaching literature in Slovenian vocational schools due to the recent reform may not seem striking to many of the readers of this article, since the principles of reading and the reader-text relationship they are based on are not revolutionary. Surely, in larger countries there are more materials and professional development experts available to make reforms more efficient, while Slovenia with a population of two million has but one team of experts for each area of educational reform. In view of this, the mother tongue and literature committee has certainly done a commendable job. It has managed to bring literature closer to students and at the same time uphold those elements of educational tradition that are essential to Slovenian culture.

NOTES

1   As we can gather from some articles written by teachers and counsellors (Krakar Vogel, 1992), teachers, indeed, saw a need for more thorough differentiation, but this did not have an impact on the curriculum. Curriculum designers have traditionally been academics with little or no practical experience of teaching in schools, and so, despite their obvious expertise in the field of literature, have not had a proper awareness of how their ideas of teaching literature relate to students' practical needs.

2   Some important authors of textbooks for vocational schools were: Kopriva, Remic Jager, Gregoraè… Teachers in some of the programmes also prepared their own material packs, some of which evolved into quality textbooks (e.g., J. J. Beg).

3   The new national curricula are still centralised to a certain extent, but teachers can now choose among several alternatives in terms of content/ literary works to be taught. This has some disadvantages, but also an important advantage. It rules out the possibility of an individual teacher selecting what to teach solely on the basis of his or her personal preferences. Slovenian teachers seem to find the range of options offered in the new curriculum an appropriate solution, as they do not oppose the principle of curricular design involved, but they have reservations about the literary works offered to them to choose from.

REFERENCES

Appleyard, J. A. (1991). *Becoming a reader.* Cambridge University Press.
Krakar Vogel, B. (2000/01). *Obravnavanje literarne klasike v sodobni šoli – na primeru Prešerna.* (Reading literary classics in modern schools – the example of Preserna). Jezik in slovstvo, št.4-5.
Kvas, J. (1996). *Potovanje besed* (A journey of words) 1. Knji evnost 1.Uèbenik za prvi letnik triletnih srednjih šol. Ljubljana.
Lampiè, A. (1996). *Bralne sposobnosti in navade uèencev triletnih programov* (Reading competences and habits in three-years vocational schools). Diplomska naloga. FF Ljubljana.
Piškur, M. (1999). *Bralne navade in interesi uèencev triletne poklicne šole* (Reading habits and interests in vocational schools). Diplomska naloga. FF Ljubljana
Tekavec, B. (1999). *Poskus prenove pouka knji evnosti v triletnih srednjih šolah* (The literature teaching reform in three-year vocational schools). Diplomska naloga. FF Ljubljana
Uèni naèrt za pouk slovenšèine v triletnih poklicnih šolah. (1998). (Curriculum for Slovene language and literature in three-year vocational schools) Predmetna kurikularna komisija za slovenšèino. Ljubljana.

31 Vocabulary Instruction for Struggling Adolescent Readers

Michele L. Simpson, Michelle Francis Anderson, Carol Strickland Hall and Tom A. Simpson, U.S.A.

Although a mastery of the basic phonological and structural processes is extremely important to literacy development, many adolescents have learned these processes and still have significant reading difficulties. These difficulties manifest themselves when students are assigned by their teachers to read challenging expository materials (Simpson & Randall, 2000). These textbook assignments are often crammed with difficult content area concepts, multiple-meaning words, and technical jargon. We know from the extant literature that there is a close relationship between students' vocabulary knowledge and their subsequent reading comprehension (Francis, 1999; Stahl, 1999). We also know that struggling readers have qualitatively and quantitatively different vocabularies from their more successful counterparts (Blachowicz & Fisher, 2000). Given what the research suggests, it seems logical to assume that many at-risk adolescent learners could enhance their reading comprehension if they were to increase their word knowledge.

Researchers have suggested that many struggling students lack a sufficient vocabulary because they are not fluent readers who choose to read (e.g., Nagy & Scott, 2000). Hence, one solution to the problem would be to increase the amount of reading expected of students with the hope that they would learn more words, in an incidental manner, from context. Although this perspective appears on the surface to have merit, it does not completely address the problems of at-risk adolescents who struggle with challenging text. Struggling adolescent readers need more. That is, they need to alter their beliefs about word knowledge and they need some form of explicit vocabulary instruction (Blachowicz & Fisher, 2000; Francis, 1999). In this article the authors will offer some suggestions for nudging at-risk adolescents' beliefs about knowing a word and then outline four guidelines to enhance word knowledge.

Nudging Adolescents' Beliefs About Vocabulary Knowledge

The authors have found from focus groups and their classroom interactions with at-risk adolescents that these students have naïve conceptions of what is involved in knowing a word (Francis, 1999). That is, adolescents typically believe that vocabulary learning is simple and quick, involving no more than the memorisation of a concise one-word definition. Moreover, they rarely see the necessity of knowing how to pronounce the targeted vocabulary word or being able to use the new word in a meaningful sentence they have generated. Given that instructional materials and tests typically reinforce these misconceptions, it is not surprising that students believe vocabulary knowledge to be so simplistic (Simpson & Randall, 2000).

Researchers interested in changing students' beliefs have suggested that the best way to do so is by directly examining and discussing their misconceptions (e.g., Guzzetti, Snyder, Glass, & Gamas, 1993). In terms of vocabulary instruction, we have found it useful to explain what is involved in knowing a word. We discuss with our students that full vocabulary knowledge is not an 'all or none' proposition, but instead will involve them in knowing a word in stages. These stages involve knowing the synonyms, antonyms, and examples of a word, sensing the relationships that might exist between the targeted word and other words, and understanding the characteristics and nuances of the word (Nist & Simpson, 1997; Stahl, 1999). Such full and flexible word knowledge, we explain, occurs over time from multiple exposures and from their active involvement (Blachowicz & Fisher, 2000; Stahl, 1999). These explanations, however, mean little until we provide the students with concrete activities that operationalise our notions of word knowledge.

In order to help our students understand that complete word knowledge occurs in degrees or stages and to enhance their word awareness, we have devised a self-evaluation checklist (Nist & Simpson, 1997). The students fill out the checklist before beginning a unit that includes a group of targeted words. Using the checklist, they circle one of three choices:

1. *No understanding. I have never seen or heard this word before.*
2. *Partial understanding.* I recognise this word, but I could not provide the exact meaning nor could I use it in a sentence.
3. *Full understanding.* I know this word because I can define it accurately and precisely and use it in a meaningful sentence.

Once they finish the checklist, we then discuss their ratings and the implications of those ratings.

Another way in which we help nudge students' beliefs about what is involved in knowing a word is through the use of word maps (Schwartz &

Raphael, 1985). A word map visually represents three important processes involved in understanding a word. To build a map, students write a word (e.g., *conifer*) they are studying in a box placed in the centre of their paper. In another box placed at the top of their paper, they write a brief answer to the first question 'What is it?' This question seeks a name for the class or category that includes the word or concept. For example, in defining *conifer*, the category is 'tree.' Then the students focus on a box on the right hand side of their paper that poses this question: 'What is it like?' This second question asks students to identify properties and characteristics for their targeted word. For the word *conifer*, students might fill in the boxes with information such as: 'cone-bearing'; 'always green'; or 'needles instead of leaves.' Finally, the students address the third word map question in a box at the bottom of their paper: 'What are some examples?' Students might fill in examples such as the 'Douglas fir' or 'Norfolk pine' for the word *conifer*.

With college students, we have discovered it useful to incorporate these same three processes into what we call a concept card (Nist & Simpson, 1997). Concept cards are just more elaborate flashcards, but have the advantage of portability and built-in opportunities for self-testing. The discussions, the self-evaluation checklists, and the word maps/concept cards have enhanced our students' metacognition and metalinguistic understanding of words, and provided them with a concrete format for modifying their beliefs about word knowledge.

Vocabulary Guidelines Tailored for Struggling Adolescent Readers

When teachers provide students with words in a list to be studied, assign them to look up the words in a dictionary, and then test them shortly after without any feedback or discussion, it is a miracle that any learning occurs. Yet, college students have described such a pattern of instruction (Francis, 1999). These traditional methods are counterproductive and probably 'fuel' students' misconceptions about word knowledge (Simpson & Randall, 2000). Our first guideline emphasises that struggling adolescent readers require an intensive cycle of vocabulary instruction that focuses on a limited amount of words (Blachowicz & Fisher, 2000). Beck, Perfetti, and McKeown (1982), for example, found that at-risk readers needed up to 12 instructional encounters with a word to improve their comprehension. Obviously, with such an approach, fewer words are targeted, but they are taught in depth.

A second guideline focuses on the importance of oral language and discussions in the early stages of word-learning. Long before students are asked to generate sentences or complete written activities, our instruction begins with a discussion of definitions, synonyms, and antonyms for a word. This discussion allows us to hear and clarify our students' misunderstandings and to shape their definitions. Students then 'try out' sentences using the new word with their partners and share their sentences orally with the entire class. Hence, after 20 minutes, students hear countless examples of how to use a word correctly and how not to use the word. These oral language activities also help at-risk readers to understand the connotative nuances and syntactic rules that govern word knowledge and actively engage them in learning (Stahl, 1999).

A third guideline stresses the importance of using the dictionary and contextual analysis as a back-up strategy rather than a beginning point in learning a word. Most commercial materials tout the usefulness of these two traditional vocabulary strategies; however, the research studies have not concurred. In terms of the dictionary, researchers have determined that interpreting a dictionary entry and identifying an appropriate definition are extremely difficult tasks (McKeown, 1990; Scott & Nagy, 1997). McKeown suggested that dictionaries give 'multiple pieces of information but offer no guidance in how they should be integrated' (p. 6). For example, one of our students looked up the word *vacuous* in the dictionary. The entry for *vacuous* is: 'devoid of matter, empty, stupid, lacking serious purpose.' Unable to synthesise the vague parts of this definition, he wrote this sentence: 'The glass was *vacuous* because I was thirsty and drank all the juice.'

With regard to contextual analysis, researchers have suggested that this strategy is not as powerful as believed (Beck & McKeown, 1991; Nagy & Scott, 2000). Published materials like to demonstrate the usefulness of context clues, but the passages for those activities have been created rather than borrowed from naturally occurring texts (Schatz & Baldwin, 1986). Natural contexts are just not that rich and revealing, especially for struggling adolescent readers. We are not suggesting that students not be taught how to use the dictionary or context clues. Instead, we have found it more productive to use these traditional strategies after class discussions of a word and after students have completed their word maps or concept cards. At this point, students are ready to use the information provided by dictionaries and context in a more productive manner.

A fourth guideline focuses on the importance of providing reinforcement and evaluation activities that mirror the level of thinking necessary for full word-knowledge. When teachers use activities that require recognition, such as matching and multiple choice, students are passively guessing and therefore camouflaging their lack of understanding. However, there are creative activities and alternative test formats that measure students' full word-knowledge.

Beck and her colleagues (1981) employed, with considerable success, a question-asking activity that paired two targeted words. To answer these paired-word questions, students must determine if any relationships exist between the words, an essential process in understanding words. For example, when we taught the words *stay* and *exonerated* to college students, we used this paired question: 'If a governor issued a *stay* on a convicted killer's execution, would that individual be *exonerated*? Why or why not?' Paired-word questions are easy to develop and can be used in oral or written formats.

Another creative activity capitalises upon the important process of exclusion. When students practice *exclusion*, they discriminate between, negate, and recognise examples and non-examples. After studying a group of words, we used this example with our students as a reinforcement activity:

Directions: Choose the word that does not relate to the other two words. Write it in the blank 'Exclude.' In the blank labelled 'General Concept', write a concept or idea that describes the remaining two words.

progressive   innovative   feudalistic

A. Exclude _____

B. General concept _____

To answer this question, students had to determine that the word *feudalistic* was different and that the other two words were similar in that they described new or revolutionary ideas or beliefs. Obviously, teachers will first need to model the thinking processes involved in these two activities because they are unique. However, at-risk readers, with initial scaffolding and feedback, can learn to complete these activities independently and successfully (Nist & Simpson, 1997).

Conclusion

In conclusion, it appears that the traditional methods of vocabulary instruction have not always benefited struggling adolescent readers who grapple with difficult expository text. Rather than teach more words superficially, we are recommending attempted modification of students' beliefs about vocabulary knowledge and implementation of a programme that builds their awareness and metalinguistic understanding of words and provides them with the relevant activities to use those words in their own communicative tasks.

REFERENCES

Beck, I., & McKeown, M. (1991). Conditions of vocabulary acquisition. In R. Barr, M. Kamil, P. Mosenthal, & P. D. Pearson (Eds.). *Handbook of reading research* (Vol. 2, pp. 789-814). White Plains, NY: Longman.

Beck, I, Perfetti, C. A., & McKeown, M. (1982). The effects of long-term vocabulary instruction on lexical access and reading comprehension. *Journal of Educational Psychology, 74,* 506-521.

Blachowicz, C., & Fisher, P. (2000). Vocabulary instruction. In M. Kamil, P. Mosenthal, P. D. Pearson, & R. Barr (Eds.), *Handbook of reading research* (Vol. 3, pp. 503-523). Mahwah, NJ: Erlbaum Associates.

Francis, M. C. (1999). *Students' beliefs about vocabulary in relation to their performance on vocabulary and reading comprehension tasks.* Unpublished master's thesis, University of Georgia, Athens, Georgia.

Guzzetti, B., Snyder, T., Glass, G., & Gamas, W. (1993). Promoting conceptual change in science. A comparative meta-analysis of instructional interventions from reading education and science education. *Reading Research Quarterly, 28,* 116-159.

McKeown, M. (1990, April). *Making dictionary definitions more effective. Paper presented at the annual meeting of the American Educational Research Association, Boston, MA.*

Nagy, W., & Scott, J. (2000). Vocabulary processes. In M. Kamil, P. Mosenthal, P. D. Pearson, & R. Barr (Eds.), *Handbook of reading research* (Vol. 3, pp. 269-284). Mahwah, NJ: Erlbaum Associates.

Nist, S., & Simpson, M. (1997). *Developing vocabulary concepts for college thinking. Boston: Houghton Mifflin.*

Schatz, E., & Baldwin, R. (1986). Context clues are unreliable predictors of word meanings. *Reading Research Quarterly, 21,* 439-453.

Schwartz, R., & Raphael, T. (1985). Concept of definition: A key to improving students' vocabulary. *The Reading Teacher, 39,* 198-205.

Scott, J. & Nagy, W. (1997). Understanding the definitions of unfamiliar verbs. *Reading Research Quarterly, 32,* 184-200.

Simpson, M., & Randall, S. (2000). Vocabulary development at the college level. In R. Flippo & D. Caverly (Eds.), *Handbook of college reading and study strategy research* (pp. 43-73). Mahwah, NJ: Erlbaum Associates.

Stahl, S. (1999). *Vocabulary development. Cambridge, MA: Brookline Books.*

32   Reading Literature through Textbooks: Adolescents' Knowledge and Literacy Practices

Angelina Ferreira Rodrigues, Portugal

Reading practices don't depend merely on the reader's characteristics or on the type of text, but are also framed by the social contexts in which reading occurs. One of these contexts is the school. Here, the pedagogical materials used for promoting reading practices are very important. Textbooks, in particular, are important because of their roles and functions and because of the reading practices they promote.

Textbooks are important cultural and pedagogical devices (Johnsen, 1993), irrespective of their formal and discursive presentation or the status and functions given to them. As cultural devices, they are very often sources of controversy (Choppin, 1992), because of their ideological functions and the values they transmit which can vary according to time and place. As pedagogical instruments, their role is to provide written support for teaching and learning. They provide information about goals, syllabuses and teaching and learning strategies; they outline the knowledge, values and attitudes underpinning any subject, including literature.

Whatever view we take about the nature of literature, there are clearly some phenomena which are recognised by educational administrators and by the general public as appropriate for study in schools and universities (Brumfit & Carter, 1991). In other words, literature has always been associated with school education through the reading of literary texts and the acquisition of knowledge.

In Portugal today, the official syllabi, the school textbooks and other regulative texts reveal Portuguese literature as the central content of the school subject known as Portuguese. So, if knowledge about literature and the reading of literary texts are important for literary education, the role that textbooks play is particularly important.

School practices concerning reading are strongly regulated by school textbooks and their constituent elements – texts, activities and evaluation devices – can be seen as defining not only knowledge, but also pedagogy and evaluation.

In this sense, analyses of school textbooks (see Castro, 1995; Dionísio, 2000; Rodrigues, 2000), can be seen as a most relevant way of accessing knowledge, attitudes and values concerning the reading of literature and, in some respects, how literary education is defined and understood. School textbooks also give us important information about the purposes of reading literary texts and the abilities that are implied in students' practices, including cognitive strategies. It is also possible to infer how meanings are constructed and if the focus of presentation is on comprehension (Goodman, 1994). We can infer students' knowledge about literary texts and genre conventions, and whether or not students are likely to be able to establish links among different kinds of texts. We can also gain insights into how they might link reading of literary texts with other literacy practices including speaking and writing.

In this paper, we consider some secondary school Portuguese textbooks in order to identify and to analyse aspects of reading literature – what, how and why students read literature in upper secondary school (10th, 11th and 12th grades; 15-18 years old). The analysis focuses on the textual information in Portuguese textbooks – in the literary selections themselves and in the exercises (sets of questions, guidelines and instructions) that follow them. This provides insights into the literacy culture that is promoted in schools (see Harris & Hodges, 1995).

Description of the Corpus

In Portugal, a broad range of textbooks for teaching the Portuguese language to students at upper-secondary school are now available. It was necessary to select a few for the current study. Three textbooks were selected. They were judged to be representative of the contents of Portuguese language study, and of the different course options that are available, such as humanities and science.

All secondary-school Portuguese textbooks are organised in teaching-units; such units include several of the following elements:

- informative texts about authors and their historical, social or literary context
- literary texts
- activities to guide the development, understanding and interpretation of text, such as sets of questions, guidelines or other instructions
- critical texts that refer to the main text.

Our initial purpose is to present the textual information in our *corpus* in order to identify and organise the content. Then we attempt to characterise practices in literature instruction, including the instructions for reading different literary texts.

Analysis and Discussion

As we can see in Table 1, the contents of the textbooks for the different grades are not immediately related to literature. Instead, they refer to some of the dimensions of literature – literary movements, authors and literary texts of different genres. The informative texts that introduce the teaching-units in the textbooks are also related to literature (Table 2).

TABLE 1: CONTENTS OF PORTUGUESE TEXTBOOKS FOR UPPER SECONDARY SCHOOLS

Textbooks/ Teaching Units	10th Grade	11th Grade	12th Grade
Textual Information	1. Portuguese traditional novels	1. To (re)find Baroque poems; Argumentative texts (Sermons) of António Vieira	1. *Signs and Symbols* - poetry, from poets of the (Middle Ages) to Herberto Helder
	2. First medieval phase (from XII to middle of the XIV century) Poetry	2. From Neo-classicism to Pre-Romanticism New classicism/ Portuguese Arcade Poems (Correia Garção and Bocage)	2. *Voices and Masks* - Almeida Garrett and António Patrício's Theatre
	3. Second medieval (XV century) Poetry	3. Romanticism in Almeida Garrett Poems (*Folhas Caídas*) [Fallen Folds] Dramatic Text (*Frei Luís de Sousa*) Narrative Text (*Viagens na Minha Terra*)	3. *Fictions and Realities* - four novels of XX century
	4. First classical phase (XVI century) Dramatic texts (2 integral texts of Gil Vincente) Lyric texts (poems of Luís de Camões) Epic narrative (*Lusíadas* of Camões) [extracts] Poems of XX century	4. From Romanticism to Realism/Naturalism Narative Text (*Os Maias*) Eçde Queirós 5. To Learn Alone (Journalistic texts) 6. To Organise Ideas (synthesis about literary genres)	4. *Contexts and Convictions* - the argumentative discourse

They refer mainly to Portuguese classical literature, presented according to a diachronic principle. Their function is to contextualise the literary texts in the historical, social, cultural and literary frame. This perspective (the same in all textbooks) allows the reader to acquire some knowledge about linguistic, historical and literary issues and about the different genres – narrative, lyric and dramatic – always represented in the different school grades, in several forms. When poetry or short narratives are being introduced, the introductions are integral to the texts themselves; otherwise, they come across as fragments or 'brief mentions'. It is unclear whether students view these introductions as pieces of literature in and of themselves.

TABLE 2: TOPICS OF INFORMATIVE TEXTS IN PORTUGUESE TEXTBOOKS FOR UPPER-SECONDARY SCHOOL

Texts Topics	10th Grade	11th Grade	12th Grade
Information Texts	Introduction The narrative is as old as human Kind. 1. The popular novel Main characteristics of popular novel The existence of the popular novels in Portugal 2. Medieval society (social structure; medieval culture/ religion) Origin/evolution of Portuguese language. The study of a literary text (Phonic component; Morphology and Syntax; Semantic component) Poems (definition; context; poets; verses; parallelism) . 'cultural horizon'	Epoch: dates and facts Baroque: cultural context Baroque in history of Portuguese literature (cultist and 'conceptism') About Baroque poetry Themes of Baroque poetry Father António Vieriera (the man and his time; the missionaary ideal of A. Vieira; St António's sermon) (New classicism/ Portuguese Arcade Correia Garção: Texts (themes) Bocage and his time (the man; the books ...	Poetry of the Middle Ages The Painting, The Architetecture, The music of the epoch Palace's Poetry Berandim Ribeiro Sá de Miranda The Paint, The Architecture of the time of palace poets The lyric texts of Camões Luís de Camões - (impossible) biography Camões and the tall towers Camões and the Rebaussabce Movement Camões, mannerist poet The Two styles in Camões Neoplatonic Camões and Petrarca Camões - poet of tensions and contradictions. Painting of Camões, time. BaroquePoetry

Usually, in the textbooks, the literary texts are followed by instructions for reading. This implies a central position for reading as an instructional activity in Portuguese schools (Castro, 2000). Other practices, such as speaking and writing, do not stand alone; they are included in the guidelines under such headings as 'Pedagogical Suggestions' and 'Guidelines for Reading'. They depend on reading, since they arise after students have read literary texts.

If we look at the examples in Table 3, we can verify that many of the instructions are about structural, formal or linguistic issues, like 'Action, Characters, Time, Space, Narrator', the narrative sequences ('The flashbacks' or 'The multiple moments of description'); phonic, morphologic

TABLE 3: EXAMPLES OF SETS OF QUESTIONS – 10th GRADE

Narrative Text	Lyrical Text	Dramatic Text
[integral text] [popular novel] A. Narrative categories 1. Action [...] 2. Characters [...] 3. Space [...] 4. Time [...] 5. Narrator. Ways of representation and expression [...] B. Language [...] C. Interpretation 1. Read the novel 'noticing' the proverbs that [we] present you. These, as you know, are the result of popular knowledge. [...] (pp. 34-35)	'1. As a model to practice on other occasions, we present the identification of the elements and values of the three levels of analysis that structure text meaning.' Phonic level (verses, rhyme, rhythm, ...) Morphologic and syntactic levels (nouns, pronouns, adjectives, verbs, adverbs, phrases) Semantic level (stylistic forms) (pp. 118-119) [All lyric texts have a thematic suggestion that introduces the literary text] like this: Mother doesn't believe the lies of her daughter: she was late because of her date at the 'font' [place where people go and bring water; place where young people can meet] with her boyfriend (lover).	The Auto da Feira [XVI] is structured in three parts or three frames that we 'll analyse. First Frame (vv. 1-181)- 1. Introduction 'Mercúrio is the only character in this introduction. ' [...] Second Frame (vv. 182-510) 2. Act II (vv. 182-217) ' The main character of this act is Time. ' [...] 3. Act III (vv. 218-351) ' Serafim is Time's assistant' [...] 4. Act IV (vv. 236- 351) ' The Devil comes on the scene...' 5. Scene V (vv. 352-510) 'The principal character Auto arrives in Rome' [...] (p. 255)

and semantic levels, etc.... Such activities are much more about the textual construction and about the linguistic issues than about the construction of meaning. These are sometimes presented beforehand through the 'discursive frames' (Sousa, 2000) that introduce the questions, as we can see in the following examples:

- The discourse of Restelo's Old Man is a persuasive text, well structured.
- The narrator tries to attribute a deeper and more serious meaning to this narrative.
- Telmo announces the tragedy without trying to change the pattern of the action.

Alternatively, students may be directed to engage in 'reading' activities such as the following:

- Relate country/town through these oppositions: man/society; authenticity/ hypocrisy; heaven/hell; freedom/slavery [...].

The predominance of these kinds of 'ready-made interpretations', through 'the discourse *about* and *around* the text' (Sousa, 2000), have deep implications for the processes in which students engage as they read various texts. It seems that these interpretations lead the reader to adopt a passive role. The possibility that the reader might engage in comprehension – that is, in trying to make sense of the text (Goodman, 1994) – is removed because the reader is not guided in such a direction. The reader is already provided with the end product of reading through the discursive frames found in the texts (see Table 4). Instructions can be viewed as limiting interpretative operations – that is, their role is to regulate the meaning that the reader ascribes to the text, rather than to guide the reader towards a personal interpretation.

TABLE 4: SAMPLE EXTENSION ACTIVITIES – 10th GRADE

Narrative Text	Lyrical Text	Dramatic Text
We suggest you see the movies *Francisca* or *Vale Abraão* of Manuel de Oliveira	Make a global commentary on the poem, in which you talk about neo-classical character, in what concerns the structure, the language and the selected theme.	Compose a text to describe each one of these characters [Frei Luís de Sousa - Almeida Garrett- XIX century]
If you have an opportunity , you must see *Manhã Submersa*, based on the book with the same name by Vergílio Ferreira [writer of XX century]	From your study of Antero de Quental's poetry [XIX-XX centuries], compose a dissertation on the theme: Antero - The pilgrim looking for the light. From the reading of poems and extracts presented above, compose a personal commentary entitled The fugitive poet of others and himself.	In a clear dissertation supported by the text, develop the theme 'A possible message of Frei Luís de Sousa' After reading alternatively these reflections, work on a dissertation which develops and clarifies the question - 'Who is D. João de António Patrício? [XIX-XX centuries]?'
Write, alone or in a group, a journalistic report of this event [traveller in XVIII century]		

In this sense, the reader engages in efferent reading, because 'attention is centred more on what is to be extracted and retained after the reading event [...] than on what is being lived through during the reading event' (Rosenblatt, 1994: 1066-1067). In other words, readers can say little about their perceptions or about their cognitive strategies and, in this case, about their readings.

From an analysis of textbooks, we can say that the reading of literary texts is regulated in many ways, not only by the guidelines or sets of questions, but also by the texts that introduce, explain or present a critical opinion about them. Although this discourse around literacy texts limits the ways in which the reader might process texts, it can, of course, be a source of knowledge (sometimes the only one) about literary history, literary conventions, or literary criticism.

From this point of view, the role of the readers/students is more active if we consider that some of the guidelines are centred on literary knowledge as we can see in the following examples:

- Identify traits of the romantic writer at the ideological level, in relation to the purpose of writing, and at the level of multiple discourses and hybrids of literary genres.
- From the analysis of the last five poems, comment on and critique the work of Maria Lucília Pires. Justify the obsessive poetic treatment of Death, in terms of historical and cultural context.

Such examples illustrate that the textbook can be a means of acquiring specific knowledge in what concerns the *textual* and the *field stances* (Beach, 1994) – that is, knowledge about text structure conventions, literary or genre conventions and, in this case, knowledge about Portuguese literature. When this happens, the aim is much more to know about literature than to read literature.

Conclusion

From the analysis of these textbooks, we can verify that literature is the most important value in the Portuguese curriculum. This means that the textbook is a powerful means of promoting a certain culture, in this case, a certain literary culture: to know about literature (mainly about classical Portuguese literature). Thus, in the school context, the knowledge is more important than the ability to read literature sensitively.

As can be inferred from Table 4, students enjoy few opportunities to read different texts for different purposes in different contexts. The instructions concerning writing and speaking practices are centred on literary issues. The way in which reading of literary texts is promoted in textbooks doesn't allow readers to develop links between text events and their own prior experience; moreover, opportunities to establish inter-textual links are few and far between.

The assumption is that this kind of culture, conveyed through textbooks, is the most important one to develop in the Portuguese curriculum in secondary schools. However, some questions must be raised: are the ways in which literary texts are read in schools promoting the practice of reading literature? And do the instructions in textbooks promote the abilities one needs to be truly literate? Because 'being literate in a culture requires the ability to use [and not only to know] a range of different text types or models [...]' (Beach, 1994: 1206) and their social functions.

REFERENCES

Beach, R. (1994). Adopting multiple stances in conducting literacy research. In R.B. Ruddell, and M.R. Ruddell (Eds.), *Theoretical models and processes of reading* (4th ed). Newark, DE: International Reading Association.

Brumfit, C.J., & Carter, R.A. (1991). *Literature and language teaching*. Oxford: Oxford University Press.

Castro, R. V. de (1995). *Para a Análise do Discurso Pedagógico. Constituição e Transmissão da Gramática Escolar*. Braga:Universidade do Minho.

Castro, R. V. de (2000). Ways and factors of adolescent reading: discourses about reading. In I. Austad and E.T. Lyssand (Eds.), *Literacy - Challenges for the New Millennium, Selected Papers of the 11th European Conference on Reading*. Stavanger: Center for Reading Research, Stavanger University College/Norwegian Reading Association.

Choppin, A. (1992). *Les manuels scolaires. Histoire et actualité*. Paris: Hachette.

Dionisio, M. de Lourdes (2000). A construção escolar de comunidades de leitores. Leituras do manual de Português. Coimbra: Almedina.

Goodman, K. S. (1994). Reading, Writing, and Written Texts: A transactional Sociopsycholinguistic view. In R. B. Ruddell and M. R. Ruddell (Eds.), *Theoretical models and processes of reading* (4th ed). Newark, DE: International Reading Association.

Harris, T., & Hodges, R.E. (Eds.). (1995). *The literacy dictionary. The vocabulary of reading and writing*. Newark, DE: International Reading Association.

Johnsen, E. (1993). *Textbooks in the kaleidoscope. A critical survey of literature and research on educational texts*. Oslo: Scandinavian University Press.

Rodrigues, A. (2000). *O ensino da literatura no ensino secundário. Uma análise de manuais para-escolares*. Lisboa: Instituto de Inovação Educacional.

Rosenblatt, L.M. (1994). The transactional theory of reading and writing. In R.B. Ruddell and M. R. Ruddell (Eds.), *Theoretical models and processes of reading* (4th ed.). Newark, DE: International Reading Association.

Sousa, Mª de Lourdes Dionísio de (2000). Reading pedagogic discourse. Social linguistic features of school teaching practices of reading. In I. Austad and E.T. Lyssand (Eds.), *Literacy -Challenges for the new millennium, Selected Papers of the 11th European on Reading*, Stavenger: Center for Reading Research, Stavenger University College/Norwegian Reading Association.

This text has been developed in the context of a research project – Literacies. Contexts. Practices. Discourses (FCT-POCTI 33888/99), funded by Fundação para a Ciência e Tecnologia.

33   Reading Motivation in the First Year of Secondary School

Tanja Jalenko, Slovenia

In this report, I would like to represent pupils' engagement in reading belles-lettres (literature) in the first year of the four-year technical schools, describe what they read, and examine their motivation for reading. An improved understanding of first-year students' reading may lead to didactic interventions designed to improve interest in reading and reading ability.

The aim of our research was to explore motivation for reading, not only in relation to the reading in literature classes at school, but also in the home context. Hence I also set out to examine motivation for reading books recommended in students' programmes of study as well as books recommended by teachers. I drew on society's current cultural and sociological viewpoints in order to interpret adolescents' orientation towards reading.

In order to develop students' interest in reading, it is important to give them opportunities to choose reading materials for themselves. Lack of freedom may lead to a situation in which students do not read enough, or do not read at all, during their free time. Then there may be conflict between the student and his/her environment – between adolescents who are led by their own desires, and adults who want to lead adolescents.

Libraries and schools tend to use prizes to create interest; but this is unnatural stimulation that does not lead to inner motivation. For example, when children receive a prize for reading a prescribed number of books, many will choose works that are below their current ability, in order to read more. Inner motivation can be defined as a desire to learn, the consequence of which is a 'reader for life'. The development of positive attitudes depends on the satisfaction one has got from previous reading experiences.

Developing Interest in Reading

Discussing texts at school during literature lessons enables students to develop a framework for understanding texts, and alerts them to other points of view besides their own. They must confront the viewpoints of other students. This is how they learn to assimilate other points of view, and to express their own. In this way, early secondary-school reading is one of the rare opportunities – and for many students the last – to engage in a search of texts' eternal truths. That is why teachers should direct discussion in such a way that it is as pleasant as possible and leads not only to reading but also to meeting readers who would like to exchange reading experiences. Students can stimulate their fellow students. They can seek to achieve their reading goals. They can benefit from the positive experiences that are a prerequisite for further reading.

In my country, we have recently begun to become aware of the meaning of reading, and of possibilities for exchanging adults' reading experiences. This, in turn, can benefit younger readers. While reading clubs can encourage reading, teachers of Slovene literature can promote reading with suitable motivational methods. Reading can be accorded importance and presented in a stimulating way.

The Reading Habits Questionnaire

A questionnaire on reading habits was administered to students in the first year of technical four-year programmes. It covered 5% of all registered first-year students in 1998/99 – 275 male and 174 female students. The students resided in Ljubljana, Celje, Novo Mest and Kranj. They were enrolled in programmes for electricians, chemical technicians, building technicians, horticultural technicians, economy technicians and management technicians.

Literature lessons are provided in the second or third years of the four-year programme, and are adapted to students' capabilities. Didactic guidelines outline what should be covered in four-year schools and tested in the final examination. Books and workbooks are designed to address various ability levels.

The questionnaire asked for information about students' engagement in and motivation for leisure reading, and sought to ascertain what students read and why. We wanted to explore reasons underlying the students' responses – what influences came from their family, their peer group, and their primary school. We also wanted to explore students' views on what was good and bad about their school programmes. Some questions also asked for suggestions for promoting leisure reading at home.

Results

Reading Preferences

First, students were asked about how they spent their leisure time. Television viewing, participation in sport, and playing computer games were the most popular activities. Just one quarter of students mentioned reading as a leisure activity; most of these mentioned reading magazines and newspapers. Students reported reading, on average, for 25 minutes per day.

Reading was reported to represent a burden by 80% of students; many of these reported that they found reading hard to understand, and that texts were too wide-ranging. They reported that they had encountered many uninteresting themes, and that their reading materials did not answer their questions about life or about the world. On the other hand, 60% of pupils agreed that human beings cannot live properly without literature (belles-lettres).

What attracts some students to literary works is the story – the characters and their dealings with different situations and motivations. They were least attracted by factual information. A few reported being attracted by poetry.

Half of the students reported a preference for prose over other text forms. They referred to the interesting content in prose, stating that it sometimes addressed the problems that are of greatest interest to them as adolescents.

Literature Lessons

One quarter of students indicated that the greatest influence on their reading practices was their peer group; one third indicated the school as having the greatest influence, while 11% mentioned parents and other family members.

One-third of students reported having bought a book (other than a prescribed one) at least once in their lives. One third reported receiving a book as a present. The influence of parents is this regard is important. The purchase of a book by parents can serve to foster interest in reading.

Just one quarter of students reported enjoying literature lessons at school. Those who responded positively referred to reading stories and excerpts from larger works. Aspects of literature that the students found to be interesting included discussions about literature, writers' biographies, and discussions during lessons. Students who responded negatively referred to the difficulty of texts and the sets of question related to those texts, as well as lessons that lacked stimulation. Some perceived literature lessons to be unrelated to their future education and work; others objected to reading literature at home.

Pupils made several suggestions for improving literature lessons, including the following:

- A stronger focus on reading the works of contemporary authors
- More reading of books that address adolescents' life experiences
- Individual choice of texts
- Discussing particular works over a longer period of time
- More relaxed atmosphere during the literature lessons
- Reading of works that had been made into films
- More interesting and useful information
- More possibilities for student involvement during discussions
- More reading of the whole works at school
- Less questioning and more discussion
- Less literary history and theory
- Teacher to read some literary works aloud, without discussion

Motivation for Reading

Based on the literature on reading, we have attempted to define motivation for reading. I distinguish between motivating students to read during the preliminary phase of a literature lesson and the process of developing motivation over time.

Boza Krakar Vogel distinguishes between two types of literary text interpretation at school: total interpretation which includes all the phases of receiving and comprehending the text; and partial interpretation, which usually occurs as fragments of the text are read, and does not address meaning in the broader context of the complete text. However, my primary interest is in motivation as a process that aims not only to engage students in discussions about texts, but also to influence students' more general attitudes towards reading literary texts.

Motivation in this sense can be defined as a process of promoting reading, which can be stimulated with outer and inner motivators. When inner motivation is established, the reader can experience satisfaction while reading a text and value what is read. Such feelings transfer to the reading of new texts.

The process of supporting motivation has to be planned. It should lead to students reading less pretentious texts in the first year of secondary school; it has to consider students' developmental stages to a greater extent than the current curriculum does; at the same time, it should derive from students' reading interests and their expectations about reading. Reading experiences are sensations – positive reading experiences influence students' attitudes towards unread texts.

Advancing motivation to read begins with teachers learning about their students. Teachers must be aware of students' reading interests and attitudes – what they do in their free time; whether they engage in reading as a hobby; what they like to read; which literary topics they are interested in. The absence of positive role models and lack of choice in selecting artistic texts can contribute to poor motivation. Particularly important here are the interests of the social group of which the student is a member. Discussions about students' reading preferences can play a motivating role. We have to enable students to set their own purposes for reading, in the context of the class-group to which they belong. The reading process thus becomes a balance between adolescents' choices and preferences, and what we, as adults, want them to learn. Motivation to read is progressed when we help students to locate suitable texts based on their interests. On the other hand, texts that are too difficult may lead to negative motivation, and indeed frustration, as students progress at a slower rate and develop negative expectations about reading.

34 PONDARRS: An Integrated Procedure for Content-Area Reading

Nancy Marshall, U.S.A.

Good reading instruction helps students use the processes and strategies that good readers use. These include:

- activating prior knowledge relevant to the topic and structure of the text (Anderson & Pearson, 1984)
- using graphic organisers to help understand information (Alvermann & Boothby, 1986)
- developing a purpose for reading the text (Anderson, 1982)
- anticipating content in the text (Alvermann & Swafford, 1989)
- directing attention to the important information in the text (Neisser, 1976)
- constructing meaning based on a synthesis of prior knowledge and new information (Bartlett, 1932), and
- using this meaning to modify existing knowledge (Neisser, 1976).

The Reading Cycle

These strategies form an ongoing cycle of learning that has been identified as the Reading Cycle (Marshall, 1989, 1992). In the Reading Cycle, a reader uses relevant prior knowledge, attitudes and beliefs about the topic of a text, and knowledge of how to generate a purpose for reading. Purpose, in turn, helps direct attention to selecting the relevant information from the text. This information is then combined with prior knowledge to create meaning. Then, to close the cycle, new meaning is tied back into prior knowledge through the processes of assimilation and accommodation. The reader's newly-enhanced knowledge is then used to refine the purpose for reading as the cycle begins again.

Teacher-Guided Reading Comprehension

Ideally, a teacher-directed reading lesson should help students move around the Reading Cycle. However, the Cycle describes what the reader should do to process text efficiently but does not help the teacher decide how or when to provide instruction. We know that teaching can occur before students encounter new information (pre-reading instruction), while students are reading (guided reading), and after reading (follow-up). If we link the reading strategies to these different phases of instruction, we arrive at some valuable insights into what should be taught at each point in a teacher-guided comprehension lesson:

1. Pre-reading
   a. Elicit/build student prior knowledge
   b. Help students organise this prior knowledge
   c. Help students create a purpose for reading
2. Guided Reading
   a. Help students direct attention to the important information in the text
3. Follow-up
   a. Help students construct meaning based on text and organised prior knowledge
   b. Help students apply the meaning they have constructed to their lives.

PONDARRS

A teacher who uses this outline to guide instruction now knows when and what to teach, but there is still one piece of the equation missing: how to teach the lesson that follows the Reading Cycle. This is the purpose of PONDARRS. PONDARRS is a process that is somewhat similar to such known procedures for teaching content-area reading as SQ3R (Robinson, 1946) and KWL (Ogle, 1986). Both of these techniques are useful when working with individual reading assignments such as chapters or parts of chapters from textbooks, but they fail to help students to integrate information across chapters, or from multiple sources, or to enable students to rethink initial understandings. Furthermore, they fail to make use of graphic organisers and other visual means of representing complex information.

PONDARRS overcomes all of these limitations. It is intended to be used when students are studying broad topics that are incorporated into units of instruction and make use of multiple texts so that a variety of views of a topic can be explored. It is also designed to make continuous use of graphic representations of the meaning, so that newly-learned information can be added to existing graphic representations and so that changes can be made to the initial representation when the new information causes students to reconsider the organisation, or even to question the validity of initial understanding. In this way, PONDARRS permits the teacher to use the graphic organiser to model the processes of assimilation and accommodation.

The specific steps in the PONDARRS process include:

Prereading:

1. Introduce the topic.

2. **P:** Elicit the students' Prior knowledge of the topic. This usually requires the teacher to develop questions that lead the students to probe their existing knowledge from several angles, so that the full range of knowledge, including any partial knowledge or misconceptions, can be exposed.

3. **O:** Organise the random list of prior knowledge. This is a simple step in which the teacher helps the students recognise the various ways the listed prior knowledge can be linked together.

4. **N:** Turn the clustered list into a Network (graphic representation showing concepts and relationships).

5. **D:** Use empty nodes, conflicting information, etc. to help students Develop questions that may be answered in the various texts. Initially, the teacher will have to develop the questions since students are not used to asking questions when they have no concept of how to answer them. This also helps the teacher make sure that questions will direct attention to all of the important information. Given time and repeated exposure to PONDARRS, the teacher's role in this step can be faded out.

Guided Reading:

6. **A:** Have students read a variety of texts in order to Answer the questions. When first using PONDARRS, it is a good idea to assign student or a group of students to one or two questions. Then have the students share their answers with the whole class, so that all students have all the information.

Follow-up:

7. **R:** Revise the network previously created by adding in newly-learned information. This will produce a lot of information in the network and may even lead to changes in the initial network. When adding information that fits into the existing network, students are visually

engaging in the process of assimilation. When modifying the network in light of new information, the students are engaging in the process of accommodation. Thus, the kinds of thinking associated with new learning are made concrete in the PONDARRS lesson.

8. Repeat the DAR steps until the unit is covered.

9. *R:* Resimplify the network. This requires students to cluster information into higher-order categories. Such synthesis is an essential component of efficient learning (Brown, Campione, & Day, 1980).

10. Turn the network, which is not linear, into an outline by making the central topic into the title of the outline, the concepts directly connected to the central topic into the Roman numerals, etc. (This is an optional step. However, personal observation has shown that students in grades 5 through 8 produce better written summaries if they first create an outline. The outline forms a template for organising the written summary: this helps younger students.)

11. *S:* Finally, students produce a written Summary of the information related to the topic. If the outline is produced, the writing of a summary is relatively easy. There should be a paragraph for each Roman numeral, in which all the information behind the capital letters, but none of the details from the Arabic numerals, are included. A sentence per capital letter is optimal.

This is a complex process, and it takes considerable time to use. For a typical unit of instruction, a week can be spent on the prereading part of the process alone. Likewise, it can take a week to do the final three steps of the process. As a result, a unit that usually takes three weeks to teach can take five weeks. However, the amount of learning that occurs is so much greater that the additional time spent is well worth the effort.

Informal data collected by graduate students engaged in individual action research studies have shown that there is an increase in the scores on unit exams of from ten to 20 percent for students who received content-area instruction within the context of PONDARRS. These data held true regardless of the topic, subject-area or grade-level of the students. Action research data also showed that the extra time required for using PONDARRS decreased with repeated use of the method. After approximately five repetitions of the process, the amount of time needed for unit instruction was the same as when PONDARRS was not used, and the increased performance on the unit tests remained just as high. Another benefit of using the PONDARRS process was also documented in the action studies. Students were able to do better papers based on library research. It is assumed that this occurred because the students had been taught how to ask and answer questions, how to organise the information, and how to turn the organised information into a summary. Thus PONDARRS not only improves learning in content-areas, but also provides students with guidance in the use of important study skills.

REFERENCES

Alvermann, D. E., & Boothby, P. R. (1986). Children's transfer of graphic organizer instruction. *Reading Psychology, 7,* 87-100.

Alvermann, D. E., & Swafford, J. (1989). Do content-area strategies have a research base? *Journal of Reading, 32,* 388-390.

Anderson, R. C. (1982). Allocation of attention during reading. In A. Flammer & W. Kintsch (Eds.), *Discourse processing* (pp. 292-305). Amsterdam, Netherlands: North Holland Press.

Anderson, R. C., & Pearson, P. D. (1984). A schema-theoretic view of basic processes in reading. In P. D. Pearson (Ed.), *Handbook of reading research* (pp. 255-292). New York: Longman.

Bartlett, F. C. (1932). *Remembering: A study in experimental and social psychology.* Cambridge, England: Cambridge University Press.

Brown, A. L., Campione, J. C., & Day, J. D. (1980). Learning to learn: On training students to learn from text. *Educational Researcher, 6,* 14-21.

Marshall, N. (1989). The students: Who are they and how do I read them? In D. Lapp, J. Flood, & N. Farnan (Eds.), *Content-area reading and learning: Instructional strategies* (pp. 59-69). Englewood Cliffs, N.J.: Prentice Hall.

Marshall, N. (July 1992). The unit approach to teaching reading comprehension. Paper presented at the Meeting of American and Russian Reading Educators, Moscow, Russia.

Neisser, U. (1976). *Cognition and reality: Principles and implications of cognitive psychology.* San Francisco, California: W. H. Freeman.

Ogle, D. (1986). K-W-L: A teaching model that develops active reading of expository text. *The Reading Teacher, 39,* 564-570.

Robinson, F. P. (1946). *Effective studying.* New York: Harper and Brothers.

35 From Repetition to Reader Response: Using Children's Trade Books to Teach Subject Matter

Barbara Kane Schneider and Mary W. Spor, U.S.A.

A growing trend in publishing is the creation of wonderful informational non-fiction children's literature that can be used in classrooms to encourage students to engage with subject matter. These informational trade books are different from more traditional textbooks which may over-generalise information or make it impersonal. The increased use of visuals including photographs, the unconventional formats of 'discovery' books and 'engineered' books, highly specialised and age-appropriate topics, and the emphasis on accuracy and authenticity as well as clarity and directness make it possible for students to translate subject matter from the abstract to the real in informational trade books. These books can be used to develop scientific inquiry, transform content from lists of unrelated facts into knowledge, and provide diverse viewpoints.

In addition to being aesthetically pleasing, informational trade books encourage children to become real readers of literature across the curriculum. Huck (1977) states, 'Literature can help the child to begin to develop a sense of wonder, the excitement, the tragedy of man's discoveries and mistakes, … Not to use them is to deny children their right to participate in the drama of the making of our civilization' (p. 368).

Reader Response

Reader response is one way to move students beyond the who, what, when, and where of non-fiction and to promote engagement with text. Beginning with the Anglo-American Seminar on the Teaching of English at Dartmouth College, New Hampshire, USA, in 1966, 'response' became a key word in relation to the study of literature. Research in responding to literature refers directly to two major aspects: the examination of the student's role as a responder and the examination of the teacher's role as the one who helps to elicit student response (Spor, 1986). Both are interrelated and according to Purves (1968), 'Literature teachers often discuss but seldom define response to literature. It encompasses the cognitive, affective, perceptual, and psychomotor activities that the reader of a poem, a story, or a novel performs as he reads or after he has read' (p. 23). The activities described by Purves move students beyond repetition to higher levels of thinking.

In relation to the **teacher,** the research on response tells us that

- Teachers need to use techniques to develop students' interpretation skills (Squire, 1964).
- A child's response will become undisciplined if s/he does not learn a way of ordering it (Purves & Rippere, 1968).
- Striving to awaken new modes of response within the reader is the responsibility of the teacher in the role of facilitator and response guide (Hancock, 1993).

In relation to the **student,** the research on response tells us that

- Rich cultural experiences correlate highly with rich poetic experiences and understanding is increased (Vergara, 1946).
- Individual response patterns are caused by the reader's own unique experiences (Squire, 1964).
- Comprehension of text involves both the author's text and what the reader brings to it (Kelly, 1990).

Stoodt (1981) points out that what we already have in our heads is our only basis for both making sense of the world and learning more about it. The way in which a person perceives the world is in a large part determined by what he knows and expects. This is the basis of the response process.

Strategies that Facilitate Reader-Text Interactions

The combination of the reader's prior knowledge with what the author writes can develop into increased comprehension through strategy-based instruction. According to the *Standards for the English Language Arts* (International Reading Association, 1996), '...students need to learn an array of processes and strategies for comprehending and producing texts' (p. 16). Many strategies can be used by students before, during and after reading, to facilitate reader-text interactions with informational trade books. Below are descriptions and examples of three such strategies.

The K-W-L Strategy

The K-W-L Strategy (What I Know-What I Want to Know-What I Learned) (Ogle, 1986) helps to activate prior knowledge and experiences, set appropriate goals or questions to be examined and provides a mechanism for developing metacognition relative to comprehension of content. This strategy can be used individually, with small groups, or with the entire class. Prior to reading, the teacher asks students to list or tell what they already know about the topic and what they would like to know. While reading, students answer their own questions, culminating in written responses to and/or a discussion of what they have learned. This can be extended to include discussions and/or notations about where to locate supporting information for the 'What I Learned' column and questions about additional concepts to explore.

For example, a teacher might introduce a book such as Russell Freedman's *Lincoln: A Photobiography* by asking students to share information that they already know (or think that they know) about Abraham Lincoln. Responses might be: 'He was very tall and had a beard. He wore a big, black hat. He was president. He freed the slaves.' This discussion serves several purposes. It clues the teacher regarding the amount of information that the students already have. It also activates prior knowledge or schema and focuses students' attention on the subject at hand.

During the evolving discussion, the teacher would help students decide what they wanted to know and help them formulate appropriate lines of inquiry. Questions such as: 'When did he become president? How did he free the slaves? Why did he free the slaves?' and 'Where was he born?' might logically evolve. These questions would then guide students' reading and give them a sense of ownership of the material.

KWL

K What I Know	W What I Want to Know	L What I Learned*
He was very tall and had a beard. He wore a big, black hat. He was president. He freed the slaves.	When did he become president? How did he free the slaves? Why did he free the slaves? Where was he born?	Lincoln is known as a great leader and became president in 1861. He was called 'Honest Abe' and was born in Kentucky. He was loyal to the Union and believed that the country could not last if it were half slave and half free. He issued the Emancipation Proclamation.

*Ask students to support their responses with information from the text.

After reading, students share what they learned by filling in the "L" column. This requires reflection, provides an opportunity to correct inaccurate information, and helps students to focus on the content. This is also a good time for the teacher to raise the issue of further inquiry for those who are particularly interested in this subject. Each step of this strategy is designed to engage the students with the material by providing opportunities for response to the content.

The Double-Entry Journal

The Double-Entry Journal provides an opportunity for students to write their reactions to a prompt (a statement or quotation) provided by the teacher or by fellow students. Prompts can be used by students before, during, or after reading, to help them focus on specific aspects of text. A vertical line is drawn to divide a paper in half. On the left side, the teacher provides a prompt from the text. On the right side, the student develops his/her reaction to that prompt. Prompts might be: What is the most surprising/ confusing/ significant/ disturbing fact that you read? What adjective, noun, verb, or mark of punctuation would you change? How would the information about _____ directly affect your life if you were _____?

Double-Entry Journal

Teacher Prompt	Response
What is the most surprising information that you read about Abraham Lincoln's early life? Explain why this was surprising to you.	Student specifies the information and explains why this information was surprising.
'Lincoln never forgot the names of his first teachers—Zachariah Riney followed by Caleb Hazel – who ran a windowless log schoolhouse two miles away. It was called a 'blab school.' Pupils of all ages sat on rough wooden benches and bawled out their lessons aloud' (page 8).	Student explains why the quotation was chosen and/or writes a personal response to it.

These responses can be further developed and/or shared. For example, using the book Lincoln: A Photobiography, the teacher would assign the material to be read. The teacher would then give a prompt such as 'What is the most surprising information that you read about Abraham Lincoln's early life?' or 'What is the most important thing that Lincoln did?' and

'Explain why.' Or the teacher or student could choose what (s)he considers a striking quotation from the book, to which the student would respond by explaining why (s)he chose this particular quotation, or by writing a personal response to it. Such prompts are designed to guide and engage the student with the material, but still promote a sense of ownership. A lively discussion should ensue when the students share their responses.

Readers' Theatre

Readers' Theatre provides a venue for students to identify significant aspects of the material read by writing dialogue that they read orally to an audience. This is typically done at the conclusion of a unit of study and can be as elaborate or as simple as the teacher wishes to make it. It can also become a form of assessment, a writing/performing/art extension of the material, and an opportunity to include students who learn differently. The premises for this strategy might include:

- How would characters A, B, C, D, and E respond to a quotation from the text?
- How would figures from different time periods or different texts respond to each other if they had dinner together?
- What would proponents of different viewpoints (e.g., environmentalists and manufacturers) argue if they met?
- What actions or events would individual characters change about their own lives? How would our lives be different if they had changed?

This strategy works best with small groups of students when they work together to develop dialogue in written form on the same topic. Responses must be based upon informed reading. Typically, students present their dialogue orally at a long table to their peers, who then have an opportunity to pose questions regarding the efficacy of the presenter's comments.

Conclusion

Probst (1988) identifies the components of a response-based curriculum and classroom as (1) a teacher who is receptive to student responses, (2) students who are willing to remain tentative about their initial reactions/responses to reading, (3) students who are willing to think with rigor, (4) a sense of community or cooperation in the classroom, (5) use of suitable literature. Along similar lines, Galda and Beach (2001) point out that the reader-text transaction is influenced by what teachers say and do, the texts they choose and how they choose them, and tasks they set for their students. Informational trade books combined with strategy-based reader response to supplement and/or teach subject matter will help to move students from repetition to reader response, developing readers as well as thinkers.

REFERENCES

Freedman, R. (1987). *Lincoln: A photobiography.* Boston, MA: Houghton Mifflin.

Galda, L. & Beach, R. (2001). Response to literature as a cultural activity. *Reading Research Quarterly, 36* (1), 64-74.

Hancock, M.R. (1993). Exploring and extending personal response through literature journals. *The Reading Teacher, 46,* 466-474.

Huck, C. (1977). Literature as the content of reading. Theory into practice, 16, 363-71.

Huck, C. (1982). I give you the end of a golden string. *Theory into practice, 21,* 315-21.

International Reading Association. (1996). *Standards for the English language arts.* Newark, DE: International Reading Association.

Kelly, P. R. (1990). Guiding young students' response to literature. *The Reading Teacher, 43,* 464-470.

Ogle, D. M. (1986). K-W-L: A teaching model that develops active reading of expository text. *The Reading Teacher, 29, 564-570.*

Probst, R. E. (1988). *Response and analysis: Teaching literature in junior and senior high school.* Portsmouth, NH: Heinemann.

Purves, A. C. (1973). Literature education in ten countries: An empirical study. New York: John Wiley.

Purves, A. C. & Rippere V. (1968). *Elements of writing about a literary work: A study of response to literature* (Research Report No. 9). Urbana, IL: National Council of Teachers of English.

Spor, M. W. (1986). The effect of four methods of response to literature on reading comprehension. Ann Arbor, MI: University Microfilms International.

Squire, J. R. (1964). *The response of adolescents while reading four short stories.* Urbana, IL: National Council of Teachers of English.

Stoodt, B. D. (1981). *Reading instruction.* Boston, MA: Houghton Mifflin Co.

Vergara, A.D. (1946). *A critical study of a group of college women's responses to poetry.* New York: Bureau of Publications, Teachers' College, Columbia University.